The Theory and Interpretation of Narrative Series

Contents

Acknowledgements   vii

Preface   ix

Introduction   xiii

1. Mosaic, Dialogue, Discourse, Theft, and Mimicry:
   Charlotte Brontë Rereads William Makepeace Thackeray   1

2. Dialogue and Narrative Transgressions in
   Ann Brontë's *Tenant of Wildfell Hall*   30

3. Becoming a Man in Thomas Hardy's *Jude the Obscure*   47

4. Gender Geographies: The Lady and the Country House in
   Wilkie Collins's *Woman in White* and Mary Elizabeth
   Braddon's *Lady Audley's Secret*   64

5. Private Space and Public Woman: Victorian
   Working-Class Narratives   77

6. Cultural Capital and the Gendering of Values: Victorian
   Women Writers   91

7. Nation and Nationality: Queen Victoria in the Developing
   Narrative of Englishness   111

Notes   131

Works Cited   145

Index   157

Acknowledgments

It gives me great pleasure to acknowledge the encouragement and assistance I have enjoyed in the process of writing this manuscript. First, I warmly thank the Theory and Interpretation of Narrative Series editors James Phelan and Peter Rabinowitz for providing continuing support for this manuscript. As I shifted from a professorial position to a full-time administrative job as dean, they insisted I should not let this project lapse. In addition, their attentive and smart comments—as well as those of an anonymous reader—to an early draft have made this a much better book than it would otherwise have been.

I am also indebted to the indefatigable efforts of three talented research assistants. Melanie Almeder at the University of Florida began working on the project with me, and Emily Blair at the University of California at Davis helped me see it to completion. Both enabled me to discover new possibilities in the arguments I was developing. Finally, I owe a debt of gratitude to Dominick Tracy, also of UC, Davis, for his efficient and expert assistance in preparing the book's index.

I also wish to thank the capable staff of the British Library, who helped me to unearth some long-buried narratives of working-class writers that inform my discussion in chapter 5. Parts of chapters 1, 2, 3, 4, and 7 have been published in earlier forms in other volumes, and I thank the editors and presses for allowing me to reshape those materials and arguments for this book.

Finally, I thank Jerald Jahn for reading and, yes, rereading chapters and for continuing to express enthusiasm for the project. They are rare companions who are willing to take virtually the same journey with us once again and who yet express fresh delight at every prospect.

Preface

This is not the book I initially conceived when I first spoke with editors James Phelan and Peter Rabinowitz about providing a volume for their series on narrative. Increasingly I became interested in the close interplay between gender as manifest in specific literary works and gender as manifest in Victorian culture. The latter does not reflect a shift away from form toward culture but rather a steady concern for form-in-culture. The process has entailed explication, exploration, and discovery. Reading and analyzing Victorian novels provided me with an education for reading and interpreting the broader culture.

I began by exploring ways of reading gender in some key novels, novels that allowed me also to introduce ideas I would develop and examine for their theoretical implications in later chapters. For example, what has been a longstanding interest I've had in how women writers respond to themes and narrative structures of precursor male writers is introduced explicitly in my first chapter, devoted to a close analysis of Charlotte Brontë's *Shirley*. But that same preoccupation, threaded like a leitmotif through the manuscript, is picked up again in Chapter 4, when I look at Wilkie Collins's *Woman in White* and Mary Elizabeth Braddon's *Lady Audley's Secret*. Unsurprisingly, then, I have ultimately found it necessary and important to theorize aspects of that relationship and their possible implications for canon formation, the subject of Chapter 6. Now the intertextual pairing is between Anthony Trollope's *Warden* and Margaret Oliphant's *Phoebe Junior*.

My interest in thinking about intertextual relationships between male-female pairs of writers has pushed me to think as well, in Chapter 2, about women writers responding to each other. Such considerations enhance our appreciation of the very real differences that structured a newly emerging tradition of female authorship. Novels of the Brontë sisters readily invite such an analysis, especially because those of the youngest sister, Anne, have repeatedly been judged and found wanting when compared to those of Charlotte and Emily. A similar assessment of greater and lesser works has been accorded to two later Victorian women writers: George Eliot and Margaret Oliphant. Hence, when I turn to questions of aesthetic value and canons in Chapter 6, questions implicitly raised in my discussion of Anne and Charlotte Brontë are revisited in a more sustained and explicit way in a discussion of Eliot and Oliphant. As always, more remains to be said because Charlotte's reputation has only recently risen in response to the advent of feminist criticism, whereas George Eliot's work has garnered more sustained interest. The analyses in Chapter 6 seek to illuminate that difference as well.

If intertextual pairings make one thread through this book, then another is the relationship of literary form to form-in-culture. For example, the chapter on Collins and Braddon also sets in motion for me another train of thought, one focusing on the larger cultural narrative of space to which both are responding. This examination leads to further questions of how gender intersects with class in Victorian England. Long interested in class, I have felt the limitation of having few readily available literary texts through which to explore its effects on working-class women. In the analysis of working-class women's access to private and public space that is the subject of Chapter 5, I hear echoes and elaborations of my argument in Chapter 3, which concentrates on the construction of masculinity in *Jude the Obscure*. There I have kept my analysis tightly focused on Jude Fawley's difficulty in achieving an adequate gender identity, but that discussion gestures toward both class and the social production of space that Chapter 5 emphasizes. Hardy's novel delineates beautifully how gender definitions are inflected by class, even as its structure reveals space as contested and political. Always an advance on one front has led to another path opening up elsewhere. To reiterate what I said earlier, I have chosen here to be suggestive rather than exhaustive.

Hardy's novels lie in the background of Chapter 6 as well, a path I suggest but leave unexplored. Here the focus on canons and aesthetic value explicitly addresses issues implicit in the analyses of chapters 1, 2, and 4, of Brontë and Thackeray, Braddon and Collins, and Anne and Charlotte Brontë. But it leaves unexamined questions dramatically highlighted by a novelist such as Hardy, some of whose novels are revered, others of which are reviled.

The final chapter on Queen Victoria comprehends both space and gender as it analyzes the relationship of a national imaginary—the idea of Englishness—to the reigning female monarch. Although grounded in a specific place, England, and rooted in its soil, the idea of Englishness makes transparent the geopolitical, contested nature of space. Nation, like nationality, is a representation through which gender and class values circulate.

The discovery that writing this book has entailed for me will continue. The kinds of questions I have been asking about Victorian culture and the narratives I've explored keep opening themselves up to new considerations, new complexities. This is perhaps the keenest pleasure of the enterprise, learning, as Henry James remarked about achieving closure in novels, that "Really, universally, relations stop nowhere. The key is to draw the circle wherein they appear to do so."

Introduction

During the past decade I have repeatedly returned to questioning how gender enters into and influences narratives. That it does so has long been established by distinguished scholars, at least since the very beginnings of feminist criticism. Inevitably, my grasp of gender and narrative form has broadened and deepened as my understanding of both concepts has gained in complexity. Whereas I began by examining the effect of a woman's signature on a particular work, looking at individual novels for traces of a gendered consciousness, increasingly I have focused my critical gaze on the larger narratives by which Victorian culture defined itself: narratives of nationality, aesthetic value, and, most recently, space. Unlike the story contained in an individual novel , such as Charlotte Brontë's *Shirley* or Anne Brontë's *Tenant of Wildfell Hall,* these narratives are more inchoate and difficult to encapsulate. However, it is important to begin exploring them because the function of narration fundamentally defines and constitutes a concept even as it names it. And to read all of these different kinds of "texts" through the lens of gender yields fascinating insights into the Victorian age.

Gender has thus served as my Ariadne's threat—not to lead me out of a critical maze but into a rich and rewarding labyrinth of textual meaning that could not finally be limited to engagements only with literary texts. It led me, in short, to cultural studies. And the priority I continue to give gender stems from its ability to limn both the complex resources of narrative and the subtle dimensions of a nineteenth-century world that shapes ours even today.

I hope to demonstrate here my conviction that we continue to have much to gain from looking both narrowly and broadly at texts. In short, although the trajectory here is from analyses of specific literary works to considerations of broad cultural narratives, it is not meant to endorse a move away from literature but to acknowledge a diastolic moment that has as its systolic reflex a continual return to literary texts, which are extraordinarily expressive and complex representative vehicles.

I attribute great importance to literary narratives precisely because of their representative concision and complexity. Their language operates more connotatively and suggestively than does the language of historical, political, economic, or sociological tracts, which often strive for denotative transparency. Readings of fictive texts are necessarily varied and multiple, a fact that lends a delightful friability to the interpretive enterprise. In contrast, interpretive interest in fact-based texts often derives from their very failure to be as self-evident in their conclusions as they would wish.[1]

Differences between literary and nonliterary texts point to larger questions of value. I first came seriously to such questions through the pervasive absence (if I may use an oxymoron that I find tellingly expressive) of women writers from the British canon of literature in which I was educated. In seeking to understand why one text had priority over another, I was led to think about how literature both reflects and shapes our culture. And if sometimes I seem to want to deplore the values that have determined the exclusion of women and writers of color and lower classes from the canon, that impassioned advocacy springs from an underlying conviction that narratives matter profoundly for their shaping and transformative potential. They work on a visceral level. My own analyses foreground what values are at stake and, particularly, how aesthetic values are caught up in social and political positions in often troubling ways.

I suspect it is not surprising, therefore, that I focus first on Victorian novels. Alluding to Mikhail Bakhtin's *Dialogic Imagination,* Catherine Stimpson summarizes nicely one source of our continuing fascination with novels: "As a genre . . . the novel resists rigidities. It refuses to pull a reader into the pit of orthodoxy. Instead, the novel is like a stadium in which several beliefs and aesthetic ideologies collide. 'Dialogic,' transcribing many voices, the novel is radical and conservative, canonical and noncanonical. It writes up the conflicts that ideology papers over."[2] Although critics such as D. A. Miller and Lennard Davis have challenged this dialogic vision of the novel and its power to resist orthodoxies, arguing, in fact, that the novel genre participates centrally of the embourgeoisement of the reader, nonetheless, recent theorists have found unconvincing the postulation of that kind of totalizing power for narrative.[3] Narratives in general and novels in particular are especially rich contexts in which discursive conflicts manifest themselves. And rather than view them as either subversive instruments or disciplinary mechanisms, I locate their aesthetic complexity in their capacity to perform both subversive and disciplinary functions.

It is not only narrative form that interests me here. What more broadly informs my discussion is a conviction that novels, which represent worlds in formation, engage us because of the relationship they purport to establish with what I will call, for want of a better term, material reality. Their poetics is deeply involved with their politics, by which I mean simply their values and investments. *How* something is represented relates intimately to *what* is represented and *why*. And the complexity of the poetics, or the how, informs our perception of what is represented.

Using narrative theory broadly defined as a tool for exploration, my perspectives throughout are shaped by my feminism and my ongoing interest in the representation of women and their experiences. In my examination of Victorian narratives, however, I give priority to gender as a category of analysis, as opposed to a primary or exclusive focus on women or "woman." This attention to gender has yielded many of the fruits Elaine Showalter foresaw in 1989, when she claimed that defining the analysis of gender as the objective of feminist criticism in literary studies completely opens up the textual field, "problematizes the dominant," and "moves feminist criticism from the margin to the center."[4] At the same time, it has been threatened by the dangers she anticipated, particularly the temptation to depoliticize feminist criticism and to declare both the arrival of postfeminism and the obsolescence of the study of women and women's writing (185).

The turn to gender studies has been fueled from a number of sources. Judith Butler's influential *Gender Trouble* set forth a genealogy of gender as a performative construction and provocatively questioned whether constituting the category of "women as a coherent and stable subject" resulted in "unwitting regulation and reification of gender relations . . . a reification precisely contrary to feminist aims" (1990, 5). The tension introduced for many feminists by Butler's argument was succinctly captured in Tania Modleski's ironic title *Feminism without Women: Culture and Criticism in a "Postfeminist" Age* (1991). Arguing for the centrality of the concept "women" to feminist analysis, Modleski protests that "In the final analysis it seems more important to struggle over what it *means* to be a woman than over whether or not to be one" (20). The deliberately tendentious choice of language in "whether or not to be one" intends to impugn any suggestion that one can simply adopt the gender of choice every morning, just as one dons one's clothing, a position Butler, of course, has disavowed in *Bodies That Matter* as an utter misunderstanding of her earlier work.

But the persistent belief informing critiques such as Modleski's is that there must be ways to invoke women as a category without making essentialist claims. To that end Gayatri Spivak's formulation of essentialism as a *strategy* "one cannot not use" has been helpful.[5] Spivak adds that "The body, like all other things, cannot be thought, as such" and continues: "As a text, the inside of the body (imbricated with the outside) is mysterious and unreadable except by way of thinking of the systematicity of the body, value coding of the body. It is through the *significance* of my body and others' bodies that cultures become gendered, economicopolitic, selved, substantive" (1993, 20). Spivak systematically reads the body, not as inviolate essence, but as complex coded text that itself bodies forth and is embodied in culture. She postulates women, then, as simultaneous result and cause of culture.[6]

Although Victorians would not have framed these issues as they have been posed by late-twentieth-century theorists, nineteenth-century novelists certainly demonstrate in their literary practice an awareness that these *are* significant issues to engage, and we can enlarge our own understanding of their narrative complexity by using a number of different frameworks for reading Victorian texts. That is, those novelists knew that women were products of their culture and acknowledged, too, that the precise interactions of nature and nurture were important to consider. In short, I argue that the questions asked and insights enabled by contemporary theories are present in these Victorian texts and often await theoretical formulations for their full articulation. Particular contemporary theories on which I focus allow us to elucidate a process by which gender is culturally constructed while simultaneously acknowledging that men and women also shape the culture that has produced them. In addition, such theoretical perspectives let us focus on what it meant that gender in Victorian England was a defining term to a Brontë, a George Eliot, a Thomas Hardy, or a Queen Victoria and her populace. And they allow us to think about such questions in a rich variety of ways.

Spivak's insight that cultures become gendered through the significance of bodies has resonance for both historical figures, such as Queen Victoria or Margaret Oliphant, and fictional characters, such as Brontë's Caroline Helstone or Hardy's Jude Fawley. Something like this recognition, which she arrives at through the inadequacy of "abstraction" as a dominant category to capture the complexity of Victorian life, informs Mary Poovey's adoption of a revised woman's "way of knowing," a "kind of knowledge that is based not on generalizations abstracted from disinterested observa-

eyall experience forms
moral stance = bad woman in society
Introduction   xvii

tion but on personal experience, preferably gained by one body's immediate contact with another.[22] Poovey's postulation of experience that is not
essentialist but nonetheless bodily is one profound effect of the turn to
gender as an analytic category.

I've focused on gender in this volume precisely because it does not confer an immutable identity; it is instead, like the narratives in which it is sit-
uated and articulated, another site of mutability and challenge. Close
attention to gender as a category of analysis opens up the complex manifestations and contradictions that inhabit not only this identity marker but
others in relation with it, such as class, sexuality, race, ethnicity, and
nationality, which are also sites for contestation and disruption. And a
wide-ranging group of essays has proven to be a compelling way to address
a concept like gender in its complexity and mutability during the Victorian
age. Even here readers will find that there is much more that I could have
analyzed. I have hoped to be suggestive rather than exhaustive. Thus, it is
perhaps more accurate to say that this is a book whose construction I could
not have imagined until I had participated in formulating the kinds of
questions enabled by the turn to gender as analytic category. It is also a
book that works synergistically rather than synthetically. Its essays, that is,
do not contribute to an overarching and coherent thematic or formal argument. Rather, in their interactions and conjunctions, they produce insights
and effects that each is incapable of achieving individually.

I have benefited not only from feminists theorizing woman and gender
but also from feminist critics who read narratives. The first two essays in
this volume—on Charlotte and Anne Brontë, respectively—sketch out a
narrative poetics of women's writing in the mid-nineteenth century by
bringing postmodern theory to my narrative analyses. I have long been
interested in questions of novelistic form; my feminist perspective has
determined my focus on the possibilities of narrative form for disrupting
the status quo and creating alternative visions of possibility. These are
questions that a number of feminist narratologists have profitably
addressed—Susan Lanser and Robyn Warhol prominent among them.
Susan Lanser helped to pave the way for feminists interested in formal
questions in her foundational essay "Toward a Feminist Narratology"
(1986).

Furthermore, it is not exclusively those feminist critics who think of
themselves as narratologists that have made brilliant contributions to our
understanding of narrative innovation. Sandra Gilbert and Susan Gubar's
theory of palimpsests set forth in *The Madwoman in the Attic* (1979)

provides a model for understanding the destabilizing effect of juxtaposing conventional and subversive voices. In a related vein, Nancy Miller's essay "Emphasis Added: Plots and Plausibilities in Women's Fiction" (1981) elucidates how women's literature chafes against the unsatisfactory reality contained in literary maxims that pass for the truth but are in fact masculine desiderata and not universal constructs. Two recent books, Alison Case's *Plotting Women: Gender and Narration in the Eighteenth- and Nineteenth-Century British Novel* (1999) and Eileen Gillooly's *Smile of Discontent: Humor, Gender, and Nineteenth-Century British Fiction* (1999), brilliantly demonstrate that we still have much to understand about how gender influences and shapes narrative. Whereas Case examines challenges to a convention of "feminine narration" that precludes the female narrator's power to shape her own story, Gillooly looks at humor, not simply as style or tone, but as a definitive narrative element that became a subtle but effective stratagem for critiquing a culture that denied or restricted female agency. These varied approaches to gender and narration have been highly suggestive for my own thinking on this subject, enabling me to theorize gender not simply as an aspect of character or tone but as a fundamental textual trope that reorients familiar or traditional plots toward innovative formal ends.

Looking first at Charlotte Brontë as she responds to the perspectives of a male writer, William Makepeace Thackeray, whom she deeply admired, I ask questions about how Brontë's gendered perspective shapes her narrative differently from his. Chapter 1, "Mosaic, Dialogue, Discourse, Theft, and Mimicry: Charlotte Brontë Rereads William Makepeace Thackeray," takes up theories from the hands of Julia Kristeva, Mikhail Bakhtin, Michel Foucault, Roland Barthes, and Luce Irigaray to illuminate the complex intertextual relationship between Charlotte Brontë and the man she called the "legitimate high priest of Truth." Reading *Shirley* in light of *Vanity Fair,* I explore the sophisticated gender politics that Brontë drew from her predecessor and developed further in her own novel. In this long first analytical chapter, which establishes a broad context in which to understand narrative poetics, I have three important goals: first, demonstrating intertexuality's complexity, not as mere influence or transmission, but as a dynamic encounter between cultural values; second, illustrating a rich variety of ways in which to interpret interrelationships between two texts; and third, opening up to renewed appreciation a novel often read as Charlotte Brontë's most conservative.

I follow this analysis with a consideration of Anne Brontë's *Tenant of*

Wildfell Hall to demonstrate in part how two women writing in proximity to one another out of similar traditions might develop a different gendered poetic. In "Dialogue and Narrative Transgression in Anne Brontë's *Tenant of Wildfell Hall*," I first consider the dialogic relationship between Anne's final novel and her sister's *Jane Eyre,* a conversation that may have influenced the fate of Anne's work in dramatic ways. Then I examine Anne Brontë's narrative solution in *The Tenant of Wildfell Hall* to the problem of expressing what was culturally inadmissible: female desire. This second chapter draws from Roland Barthes's *S/Z* to illustrate modes of narrative transgression that help to illuminate Anne Brontë's strategies. Particularly, it examines how the apparent propriety of the narrative technique—a woman's story enclosed within a man's—functions as part of an exchange economy that facilitates what Barthes terms "paradoxisms," transgressive weldings of antithetical terms.

From the Brontës, I turn in Chapter 3 to Thomas Hardy, in whose *Jude the Obscure* questions of masculinity have become as fraught as those of femininity in the wake of a century's preoccupation with the Woman Question. The advent of gender studies has opened the field of masculinity to critical analysis, not only in its literary representations but also in its sociological and psychological manifestations. The Victorian era has proved to be a rich period for literary exploration because its distance offers some detachment while its relative proximity facilitates identification of connections and the discovery of antecedents. Eve Kosofsky Sedgwick's groundbreaking *Between Men: English Literature and Male Homosocial Desire* (1985), which analyzes male homosocial bonds as represented primarily in Victorian novels, provided the impetus for a new area of study, queer theory, and the work of a new generation of scholars. If these first analyses, influenced by Sedgwick, tend to concentrate on relationships between men, later studies turn more insistently to questions of masculinity's construction, in part a response to the development of gender studies. The excellent work being done has had the benefit of being firmly grounded in a conviction that thinking about women always involves thinking about men and vice versa. Previously the postulate that the meaning of one always invokes and depends upon the meaning of the other often remained at a hypothetical level. Thus, at its best, the study of men and masculinity has not only brought men into the field as subjects, theorists, and critics, it has also made it easier to talk about gender assumptions presumed to be neutral or normative and has encouraged ever-increasing subtlety and sophistication in analyses of women and femininity.[8]

So it is fair to say that the seeds for such analyses of masculinity were sown within feminist criticism, and it is gratifying to see the way in which they have been cultivated and developed in recent work.[9] It is equally fascinating to discover the ways in which a new narrative of Victorian masculinity is emerging in these early book-length studies, a narrative of oppression, even victimization, and so traces the opposite trajectory of work in feminist criticism, which began by uncovering manifestations of women's victimization and has evolved to paint a picture in which differences of race, class, or ethnicity have led certain women to become themselves oppressors of other women. In all, gender as an analytic category has continually forced us to provide more subtle and complex analyses. By keeping masculinity continually before our eyes as itself a variable, not as normative or hegemonic, gender studies have forced more discriminating feminist engagements with texts.

My own work has benefited from this impetus to think through the term *masculinity* as the same kind of cultural construct that femininity is, and this analysis bears fruit in Chapter 3, "Becoming a Man in Thomas Hardy's *Jude the Obscure*," which addresses the conflicting discourses of masculinity that structure Hardy's novel. Unable to become the man his rural and working-class culture expects him to be, Hardy's eponymous hero turns to other constructions of manliness. These, however, prove equally constricting, mocking the idea of his fulfillment within the terms his culture provides. This chapter also engages the concept of Bakhtinian dialogue, now as an individual character's internal struggle between authoritatively persuasive and internally persuasive voices. Thus, it opens its own conversation with the two previous chapters in exploring differences when the dialogism complicates and frustrates a character's self-understanding rather than sets into counterpoint contrasting voices that can beautifully limn each other's limitations. Hardy's novel reaches a less affirming resolution than Anne or Charlotte Brontë's. However, in exploring the constrictions of gender and sexual constructions as they complicate and impede people's ability to know themselves and their place in society, Hardy has helped to forge a place for himself as the most modern of the Victorians.

Chapters four, five, six, and seven broaden the discussion, advancing from considering gender in literary narratives to ranging widely over both fictional and nonfictional texts, from autobiographies to essays to letters, diaries, and papers. These final chapters examine how cultural abstractions are constructed through gendered terms.[10]

The fourth chapter, on Wilkie Collins and Mary Elizabeth Braddon, provides a pivot between those analyses that focus fairly exclusively on particular literary texts and those that examine broad cultural phenomena. At the same time, this chapter shares with the one on Brontë's *Shirley* an interest in how a woman writer responded to one influential precursor text by a man. Moreover, it uses the particular text to begin exploring the gendered nature of private space in Victorian England. It is no longer a matter simply of recognizing that experiences will have a different cast and weight depending on one's gender. It is perceiving that the abstract, seemingly neutral context for that individual sociocultural experience is always already gendered, whether the space one inhabits, or the values one imbibes, or the nationality one shares—all of these abstract concepts come to us refracted through the prism of gender. Feminist geographers Gillian Rose and Alison Blunt have noted that "Feminist analyses of the power relations embedded in such geographies for a long while focused almost exclusively on the distinction between public and private space," with the assumption that private space belonged to and was often controlled by middle-class women.[11]

In this fourth chapter I wed the questions feminists are asking about what is private and what is public with the perspectives articulated by sociologist Henri Lefebvre in *The Production of Space* (1991), particularly his idea that space is socially produced. The problem, to my mind, with discussions of private and public spheres as they generally exist today is that they tend to proceed as if space were properly treated as an abstract entity waiting to be filled. Instead, Lefebvre calls for an approach "which would analyse not things in space but space itself, with a view to uncovering the social relationships embedded in it" (89). Once we focus on social relationships, a very different picture emerges of power and control over space in Victorian England. And as readers recall my earlier chapter on Charlotte Brontë, they will recognize that the reflections in *Shirley* on "reality" and "romance" early anticipate my interest in the gendering of abstract concepts like space.

I expand my analysis of gender and space in Chapter 5 by turning from representations of middle-class women to those focusing on the working classes. Bringing class to bear on the argument helps to illuminate the fundamental point about space, well articulated by Alison Blunt and Gillian Rose: "[G]endered spaces should be understood less as a geography imposed by patriarchal structures, and more as a social process of symbolic encoding and decoding that produces 'a series of homologies between the spatial, symbolic and social orders'" (1994, 3).

Examining both intertextual relations and the gendering of space in Victorian England leads me to a consideration of value and canon formation in Chapter 6. If Mary Elizabeth Braddon is as astute and subtle in her representations as I argue she is, why have her novels not endured like Collins's? "Cultural Capital and the Gendering of Values: Victorian Women Writers" employs Pierre Bourdieu's concept of cultural capital to take up the question of literary value and the emergence of a Victorian canon. Recent substantive work on these topics makes illuminating yet another approach to the somewhat tired question of the canon. Bourdieu's focus on culture as a form of capital shifts the ground for analysis from *what* is represented to the terms by which certain aesthetic objects become identified as High Culture. His is more properly a sociology of judgment than an aesthetics. I then look at three novelists—Anthony Trollope, Margaret Oliphant, and George Eliot—through the lens Bourdieu provides. Echoing my earlier analyses of Thackeray and Brontë and of Collins and Braddon, I explore not only the relationship between a male and a female novelist, Trollope and Oliphant, but also the way in which gendered expectations shape the novels and self-representations of two distinctive women writers, one peripheral and one central to the literary tradition, who tellingly identified their literary personae as Mrs. Oliphant and George Eliot. This pairing evokes my previous discussion of Charlotte and Anne Brontë.

Cultural distinction, of course, takes many different forms, and the cultural currency vouchsafed England's queen, Victoria, was in one sense an "accident" of birth. But even that accident has behind it the historical intention of an Edward, Duke of Kent, determined to subject his wife to the hardships of traveling late in her pregnancy so that his child might first receive "material nutriment" on English soil. Thus, Victoria, who was to rule England for sixty-three years, became herself a contested ground for the embodiment of nationality from the moment of drawing her first breath. Chapter 7, "Nation and Nationality: Queen Victoria in the Developing Narrative of Englishness," takes up the vexed and vexing image of England's female monarch who gave her name to this long period: Victoria Regina. A central paradox of the Victorian Age, this woman is a locus classicus for gender representations and cultural values broadly considered in Victorian England and a site for disturbance over concepts of Englishness and nationality. Unable fully to grapple with the oxymoron of maternal monarch, Victoria's subjects invested her with often contradictory values so that the queen herself becomes a preeminent focus for representation. And through these representations we discover just how fraught a concept Englishness is, the realm of national politics as fully imbricated in gender expectations as that of literary aesthetics.

Although there is a substantial corpus of work emerging on nation-ness and nationalism as "cultural artifacts of a particular kind" and on Englishness in nineteenth-century England, discussions of it have only recently begun to be theorized through gender.[12] It has been more immediately obvious to take up the question through ethnicity or race or even class, partly because Victorians themselves tended to concentrate on race or ethnicity.[13] So Sir Charles Dilke, in *Greater Britain* (1868), pronounced: "Love of race, among the English, rests upon a firmer base than either love of mankind or love of Britain, for it reposes upon a subsoil of things known: the ascertained virtues and powers of the English people" (II:403). And Dilke's invocation of subsoil as a metaphor resonates tellingly with the Duke of Kent's intentions regarding his child-to-be. Illuminating as recent studies on nationality have been, however, the relative absence of gender as an analytic category has made it possible for critics to overlook key dimensions of the concept's internal fragmentation.

Fragmentation, dialogism, intertext, paradox, transgression, power, subversion: These are terms that percolate through the narrative of this book. They all gesture toward those narrative elements of texts (and the age has no greater text than Queen Victoria herself) that contain potential for ideological subversion. We confront again and again the challenge of rereading gender in a period when certain figures, whether fictional, such as the Angel in the House, or historical, such as Queen Victoria, have been frozen into a quintessential stability. The perspectives of recent narrative and gender theory help us both to destabilize assumptions that underwrote that stability and to open up questions that undermine it.

Mosaic, Dialogue, Discourse, Theft, and Mimicry: Charlotte Brontë Rereads William Makepeace Thackeray

In enthusiastic praise of *Vanity Fair,* Charlotte Brontë wrote, "I regard Mr. Thackeray . . . as the legitimate high priest of Truth" (*Correspondence* 243). Perhaps this reverence has confused critics who see in Brontë's subsequent novel *Shirley* an unsuccessful adaptation of Thackeray's techniques. But to revere is not necessarily to imitate slavishly. And to speak, as have critics in the past, of women's texts as adaptations of men's texts corroborates notions of women's texts as belated, derivative, or secondary to the male tradition. Further, it forecloses some of the most important questions these intertextual relationships generate. I wish to engage here with a range of concepts under the rubric of intertextuality, all of which are related through their focus on language and its operations and all of which are informed by the conviction that meaning is a process of differentiation and that every text, therefore, borrows from, echoes, imitates, mimics, and parodies precursor texts.[1]

In its extreme form, the idea of intertextuality postulates an antimimetic contagion of writing and so puts paid to the notion of one text specifically imitating another and raises the question of how I will legitimately engage *Vanity Fair* in relationship to *Shirley.* My goal is broader than what a straightforward study of Thackeray's influence on Brontë would comprehend. It is more generally to attend to the effects of gendered subjectivity when two authors—one male and one female—engage with a related set of well-established literary conventions. And I take as my warrant for this consideration Brontë's admiration of Thackeray, her evident close knowledge of his work, a similarity of technique and subject, and previous critical comments that have faulted Brontë for "imitating" Thackeray's use of omniscient narration. Finally, I am not interested in reading *Shirley* as a rewriting of *Vanity Fair* but rather as a study of the

1

particular discursive intersections of these two literary texts as they interact with other discursive formulations of their culture and circulate within a broad network of political and social values. And if I seem to slight
Thackeray's achievements in *Vanity Fair,* that is a consequence of my decision to use his novel to enrich our understanding of Brontë's rather than
to give it consideration in its own right.

Key feminist critics have led the way toward my analysis by engaging
the broader field of language relations implied by intertextuality and at
the same time stipulating a gendered subjectivity as the origin of text.
Nancy K. Miller has proposed a method of reading as "arachnology": "a
critical positioning which reads *against* the weave of indifferentiation to
discover the embodiment in writing of a gendered subjectivity" (1988,
80). This method, she argues, "may allow us to refuse and refigure the
very opposition of subject and text, spider and web" (97). And Susan
Stanford Friedman has helpfully developed the concept of "political intertextuality," insisting that "we must separate the concept of intertextuality
from the death of the author" and adding that such a separation has been
common among American critics, who "have resisted the inevitability of
this connection" (159). Friedman grounds her own argument in the work
of Julia Kristeva, who coined the neologism "intertextuality" in 1966.

The concept of intertextuality as I engage it here surveys the broad field
of language relations and stipulates textual revision as a strategy for destabilizing the status quo, employing tactics that, as some have noted, have
particular power for unsettling gender arrangements. The theories of
Mikhail Bakhtin, Julia Kristeva, Michel Foucault, Roland Barthes, and
Luce Irigaray promise to produce a sophisticated gendered reading of
Brontë's *Shirley,* both in its relationship to Thackeray's *Vanity Fair* and in
itself, as well as a more suggestive poetics of women's fiction in general.

Mikhail Bakhtin develops ideas of intertextuality within his theory of
dialogism, or "double-voiced discourse," which has significant implications
for notions of artistic creativity and which suggests a liberating relationship
between "influence" and aesthetic production. In his fourth essay in *The
Dialogic Imagination,* Bakhtin speaks of the "importance of struggling with
another's discourse, its influence in the history of an individual's coming to
ideological consciousness." He adds that "One's own discourse and one's
own voice, though born of another or dynamically stimulated by another,
will sooner or later begin to liberate themselves from the authority of the
other's discourse" (1981, 348). This process of liberation receives further
impetus from the constant competition of a variety of alien voices within

any individual consciousness, any individual text. For Bakhtin all language is dialogized; that is, it bears within itself the history of its use, a "constant interaction of meanings, all of which have the potential of conditioning others" (426). His addendum—"the internal dialogism of double-voiced prose discourse can never be exhausted thematically" (324)—emphasizes the effect of dialogic language in unsettling established meanings.

Julia Kristeva develops a concept of text as mosaic that borrows from Bakhtin's formulation of text as "double-voiced discourse," and in the process of drawing from a powerful precursor to authorize her own voice, she enacts the very pattern that I identify in Brontë's response to Thackeray. Kristeva's theory conceives of intertextuality as a "mixture of textual signs, citations, and echoes." Writing in the context of Derrida and Lacan, as well as Bakhtin, Kristeva transforms Bakhtin's emphasis on the *word* to a focus on texts: "Any text is constructed as a mosaic of quotations; any text is the absorption and transformation of another" (66). Bakhtin's dialogized word and Kristeva's intertext both pinpoint the inevitable incorporation of one work by another and the effects that textual appropriations may have for liberating one's own voice. Quite literally, Kristeva has incorporated Bakhtin's voice to liberate her own, a "self-authorizing strategy [that] she uses often" (Friedman 147). Friedman adds, "This 'misreading' does not eliminate the other, but rather borrows his authority from the position of disciple. Intertextuality was paradoxically born under the guise of influence" (147). Just so, in her imitation of Thackeray's narrative omniscience, Brontë discovered a new capacity to speak authoritatively. Furthermore, having exploited the intertextual relationship with her powerful precursor as an authorizing strategy, Brontë was further enabled to explore the dialogic/heteroglossic possibilities of her own central concepts to destabilize conventional meanings and values.

Michel Foucault's concept of discourse lies aslant the Bakhtinian/ Kristevan emphasis on the transformative liberatory effects of dialogism and mosaic. Foucault defines discourse as "the group of statements that belong to a single system of formation" (*Archaeology of Knowledge* 107). He continues, "[T]hus I shall be able to speak of clinical discourse, economic discourse, the discourse of natural history, psychiatric discourse" (107–8). Foucault is less interested in the way one text revises another—all part of a literary discourse—than in the way different discursive formations operate and cooperate as a technique or "form of power which makes individuals subjects . . . subject to someone else by control and dependence, and tied to his own identity by a conscience or self-knowledge" ("The Subject and

Power" 212). Thus, although Foucault's "discourse" is not specifically about literary intertextuality, it bespeaks the fundamental intertextuality of different discursive formations. Applying Foucault, we conceive of intertextual relations between works not as transformative and liberatory but as conservative, tending to a consolidation of certain powers. Foucault's concepts give us access to the way different discursive formations interrelate to create a certain kind of gendered subject. However, by working to uncover the mechanisms by which we are subjected, an intertextual approach helps to destabilize a traditional humanistic perspective and so frees us from its normalizing tendencies.

Roland Barthes conjoins the death of the author with the birth of the text and so postulates a radical intertextuality where every text is potentially an intertext for every other. Jay Clayton and Eric Rothstein have argued that, in fact, Barthes's radical theory is constrained by his reading practice in *S/Z,* where the "interpretive results do not take one further than a highly skilled, subtle formalist might go" (23). Although this observation has merit, it is also true that Barthes's flexible interpretive tools and the interpretive framework he invents in *S/Z* open up his readerly texts to the intertextual and allusive networks supposedly more characteristic of his writerly texts. Barthes's practice, then, provides one model for my practice in this essay; his highly suggestive theories indicate a way of beginning to conceptualize the revolutionary potential in the woman's signature. That potential is encoded in Barthes's work as theft: "[T]he only possible rejoinder . . . [is] neither confrontation, nor destruction, but only theft: fragment the old text of culture, science, literature, and change its features according to a formula of disguise, as one disguises . . . stolen goods" (10). Barthes's analogy of borrowing to theft emphasizes the transgressive quality of intertextuality when one deliberately appropriates another's goods and disguises them for one's own uses. Barthes's meaning remains playful and oblique, as is his style, which thus becomes an exemplification of his meaning. I exploit his concept by focusing on theft as a technique to disrupt seemingly stable cultural encodings. Such an approach helps explain the way Brontë plays with the trope of tears in the Victorian novel. Tears serve as a primary Victorian encoding of femininity. Tears both define and undermine the woman, signifying both sensitivity and enfeeblement. That old cultural text must be appropriated—that is, stolen-fragmented and disguised, or re-presented. This process effects a transformation.

Like Barthes, Luce Irigaray investigates deliberate, even staged, responses to another's prose for the purpose of disrupting established meanings. In *The Sex Which Is Not One,* Irigaray identifies "mimicry" as an "interim strategy" for "destroying the discursive mechanism" that has oppressed woman. "It means to resubmit herself . . . to 'ideas,' in particular to ideas about herself, that are elaborated in/by a masculine logic, but so as to make 'visible,' by an effect of 'playful repetition,' what was supposed to remain invisible" (76). This formulation addresses explicitly gender issues, as the other theories do not. Parody and mimicry are strategies in which "the woman deliberately assumes the feminine style and posture assigned to her within . . . discourse in order to uncover the mechanisms by which it exploits her" (220). Applying Irigaray's concepts, I argue that Brontë stages, or exaggerates, the stylization of woman as mermaid and the posture of woman as wife.

Although these concepts of mosaic, dialogue, discourse, theft, and mimicry are related, they should not be conflated with each other, as each offers a unique angle of vision on intertextuality, particularly in *Shirley,* where I study Charlotte Brontë in relation to one key precursor text, *Vanity Fair.* Emphasizing as I do the liberatory effects of such intertextual relations, I wish to modify Nancy Miller's phrase "political intertextuality," which stresses a process of "overreading" to discern the woman's signature. I adopt instead the phrase "strategic intertextuality" to suggest both the politics of signature and its transformative potential.

The concept of strategic intertextuality opens the way for an enlarged poetics of fiction, one that shows more clearly how *Shirley* cites, absorbs, and transforms Thackeray's *Vanity Fair.* Brontë accomplishes these ends by adopting a third-person narrator who echoes key passages of narrative commentary on the ideology of womanhood, by linking domestic and carceral discourses, by revising the Victorian trope of tears, and by parodying feminine paradigms and traditional plots.

Text as Mosaic

Thackeray is astute about the realities of that Victorian icon, "the Angel in the House." He conflates her fate in the home with that of other institutionalized beings such as idiots and madmen confined to insane asylums. And he apparently caught Brontë's attention with his profound glimpse into women's lives, his perception of the discipline, the imprisonment, and the punishment. Thackeray writes,

O you poor women! O you poor secret martyrs and victims, whose life is a
torture, who are stretched on racks in your bedrooms, and who lay your
heads down on the block daily at the drawing-room table; every man who
watches your pains, or peers into those dark places where the torture is
administered, must pity you. (552)

Brontë rewrites,

You held out your hand for an egg, and fate put into it a scorpion. Show no
consternation: close your fingers firmly upon the gift; let it sting through
your palm. Never mind: in time, after your hand and arm have swelled and
quivered long with torture, the squeezed scorpion will die, and you will
have learned the great lesson how to endure without a sob. . . . Bitterness is
strength—it is tonic. Sweet mild force following acute suffering, you find
nowhere: to talk of it is delusion. There may be apathetic exhaustion after
the rack. (128)

Each passage represents a scene of torture. In Thackeray's text "poor
women . . . poor secret martyrs and victims . . . are stretched on racks."
The passive voice—"where the torture is administered"—has the effect of
disguising agency, with the result that it's not clear who is administering
the torture, especially because men are positioned as watchers and pitiers
of suffering women. Thackeray's address to "you," followed by "poor
women," communicates at once both sympathy, born of the second-person address, and distance, born of the third person. The reader is not
uncomfortably involved in the scene of torture, which is "told" rather
than "shown." Brontë begins with a second-person address and moves
immediately into the imperative voice—"show no consternation . . . close
your fingers," and so on—diminishing the distance between the narrator
and scene rather than increasing it. The torture and its effects are directly represented *as torture:* "[Y]our hand and arm have swelled and quivered
long with torture." This torture by scorpion sting is, of course, different
from the rack Thackeray has invoked, but then, quite suddenly, Brontë
introduces the "apathetic exhaustion after the rack" and so sets up a
stronger dialogic echo of Thackeray.

Despite the two narrators' shared sympathy with tortured women, formal differences abound. Thackeray represents the feminine from a greater
distance, often from the perspective of an explicitly male narrator and
narratee (e.g., "We are Turks with the affections of our women" [169],

and "Oh, be humble, my brother, in your prosperity!" [552]). And his tone reveals the irony in his own compromised position as one who benefits when women "consent to remain at home as our slaves" (169). Thackeray thus notably indicts the patriarchs who put increasing their own comfort ahead of alleviating a woman's torture.

Brontë stays focused on the woman's experience. Most important, of course, she represents the feminine experience from a woman's perspective ("let [the scorpion] sting you through your palm," and "after your hand and arms have swelled and quivered long with torture"). The choice of the second-person "you" is significant because it alludes to both the reader and, as a colloquial usage, the writer. As a result, the narrator's tone is full of anger, and any irony derives from a sense of women's folly in falling prey to "delusions" like the possibility that "sweet mild force" will well up "following acute suffering." Narrator and narratee at this moment share the female position, together in the torture chamber of Victorian ideology, which dictates that "[a] lover masculine so disappointed can speak and urge explanation; a lover feminine can say nothing: if she did, the result would be shame and anguish" (128).

A simple illustration of the difference emerges when we compare the following two narrative generalizations, which echo each other. Thackeray's narrator writes: "The best of women (I have heard my grandmother say) are hypocrites" (165). Brontë's narrator responds: "All men taken singly, are more or less selfish" (183). Virginia Woolf called this capacity for generalization about the other sex "one of the good offices that sex can discharge for sex—to describe the spot the size of a shilling at the back of the head" (*A Room of One's Own* 94), which neither sex can see for itself.

Although Sandra Gilbert and Susan Gubar are right to say that Brontë adopts a third-person narrator like Thackeray's, that claim is still too imprecise to tell us anything about *how* the text is actually working (373). In Gérard Genette's more precise terms, both narrators are heterodiegetic (outside the story they narrate). But Brontë's narrator often resembles the homodiegetic (or first-person) narrator of *Jane Eyre* more closely than she does the narrator of *Vanity Fair.* The difference lies in focalization. Genette reminds us of the crucial distinction between who sees and who *speaks,* that is, between mood and voice, and thus invites us to consider carefully how heterodiegetic narrators are dramatized. Who sees in Brontë's *Shirley* is often an impassioned and angry woman who exhorts "Men of England," "Men of Manchester," "Men of Yorkshire," and

"Fathers" to release their daughters from crippling custom. This narrator usually stands at a great remove from the narratee she most frequently postulates, a comfortable and complacent patriarch. Consider this exhortation: "Men of England! look at your poor girls, many of them fading around you, dropping off in consumption or decline; or, what is worse, degenerating to sour old maids, —envious backbiting, wretched, because life is a desert to them" (378). Sometimes parodic, sometimes complacent, sometimes self-righteous—the narrator shifts and so testifies, as does her tendentious tone, to the uneasiness of the narrator/narratee-as-patriarch relationship.

The narrator of Thackeray's novel, in contrast, often adopts a comfortable, genial, and kindly perspective on the world, and this position comprehends women's lives within the general tale of vanities unfolded. Although it is not uncommon for Thackeray's narrator to take on different, and harsher, personas at other points in the narrative, overall Thackeray's novel charts a movement toward an all-encompassing, tolerant, and humane perspective, that is, toward the concluding tableau of a London fair that includes both Becky and Amelia and that exposes the vanity of all human life. The final vision is produced from a consonance of values between the narrator and narratee: "Which of us is happy in the world? Which of us has his desire? Or, having it, is satisfied?" The first-person plural bespeaks an amiable companionship that is unavailable to Brontë's more tendentious narrator.

By shifting from Thackeray's companionable friendship between narrator and narratee, Brontë also dramatically shifts the effects of her narrative, and it no longer seems adequate to conclude (as Gilbert and Gubar do in an otherwise insightful discussion) that Brontë was trying to create the calm objectivity and magisterial omniscience of a Thackeray and thereby "becomes enmeshed in essentially the same male-dominated structures that imprison her characters" (373). Indeed, the case appears quite otherwise: Brontë wishes to expose "calm objectivity" as a by-product, if not of ideological conservatism then of fortunate distance. Rather than enmeshing her in male-dominated structures and ideologies, her revision becomes a wedge for exposing further the ideological gap that Thackeray's irony has already opened between the idealization and the reality of women's lives. Thackeray's voice, which Brontë echoes, authorizes her own more urgent tones, but her urgency, which cannot assume congruence with another, in turn lends authority to very different narrative ends.

Just as Brontë authorizes her own further exploration of the gaps between womanly ideals and realities through intertextual references to Thackeray, she also continues to draw from her powerful precursor—that "legitimate high priest of Truth"—to structure a dialogic relationship within the novel itself. Thackeray's "novel without a hero" plays on the tensions that realistic representation sets up with generic conventions for romance. So Thackeray memorably represents the Battle of Waterloo from the perspective of Brussels' panicked citizens, notably Jos Sedley. And the "heroic" soldier, George Osborne, about to betray his wife, is only briefly reported upon: "lying on his face, dead, with a bullet through his heart." Thackeray sustains this dialogic tension throughout his novel, so that the morally suspect Becky Sharp concludes the novel's history at the London fair, once again jostling elbows with the virtuous Amelia Sedley.

Thackeray's dialogic insight bore fruit for Brontë and is mirrored in *Shirley's* formal dialogism, which is powerfully embodied in the novel's explicit tension between "realism" and "romance." The seemingly inconsistent presentation of reality has been a source of critical complaints of disunity.[2] But those complaints result from attempting to impose monological readings on the text. Brontë has, in fact, created alternative visions of romance and reality that remain in dialectical tension with one another. This dialectical tension between reality and romance creates a space for artistic play: the "both/and" of the novel rather than the "either/or" of monological interpretation. In that space for play, Brontë has first presented the terms *romance* and *reality* as they exist in patriarchy, then deconstructed them in order to suggest alternative feminist readings, and finally represented the patriarchal and feminist realities in tension, refusing assimilation, each interrogating the ultimate significance of the other.

The novel's opening immediately establishes the realism/romance dialogue. The narrator tells us that realism is the fare. In contrast to *Tom Jones,* in which Fielding promises a full board, no eleemosynary diet, Brontë's narrator suggests that parsimony is to shape our first course: "cold lentils and vinegar without oil . . . unleavened bread with bitter herbs, and no roast lamb" (39). This generic diet of realism is called "real, cool, and solid . . . unromantic as Monday morning." We are cautioned not to expect romance, "sentiment and poetry and reverie" (39).[3] That patriarchal version of realism is repeatedly enforced for the female characters, most tellingly in chapter 7, where Caroline is cherishing "a marvelous fiction . . . almost always unreal" of romance with her cousin Robert. The narrator instructs us that "the true narrative of life is yet to be commenced": "Elf-land lies behind us, the shores of Reality rise in front" (121). The narrator continues, "[T]he

school of Experience is to be entered, and her humbling, crushing, grind-
ing, but yet purifying and invigorating lessons are yet to be learnt" (122).
When Caroline suffers the inevitable disappointment of her hopes, as
Robert realizes the imprudence of such a match, the narrative voice, angry
and eloquent, protests: "You expected bread, and you have got a stone;
break your teeth on it, and don't shriek because the nerves are martyrized. . . . You held out your hand for an egg, and fate put into it a scorpion. Show no consternation: close your fingers firmly upon the gift; let it
sting you through your palm" (128). The female character must suffer, but
the female writer, enjoying a larger perspective that encompasses her characters, frames their lives and despairs. She expresses their agonies, but she
has already put in place the terms of their redemption by becoming, from
the novel's inception, something of a quick-change artist, full of sleight of
hand and playful mockery of patriarchal realities.

   This pattern of suffering, in part over the eclipse of romance, also
structures the early chapters of *Vanity Fair*. Two personable and attractive
young women from Miss Pinkerton's Chiswick Mall cannot help but
emerge "trailing clouds of glory," so to speak. The world lies all before
them. But only a scant journey lands Amelia "on the bank of her new
country," where she is "already looking anxiously back toward the sad
friendly figures waving farewell to her across the stream" (250). The narrator exposes the romance that lies behind the conventions of even realist
fiction: "As his hero and heroine pass the matrimonial barrier, the novelist generally drops the curtain, as if the drama were over then: the doubt
and struggles of life ended: as if, once landed in the marriage country, all
were green and pleasant there" (250).

   The romance of *Shirley* begins simultaneously with its realism; indeed,
the romance comes first.[4] The narrator's promise to depict the "real, cool
and solid" is meant to correct mistaken expectations already formed by
the whimsical imagery of the novel's first paragraph. The novel opens: "Of
late years, an abundant shower of curates has fallen upon the north of
England: they lie very thick on the hills" (39). The image is wonderfully
ludicrous and diminishing of male pretension. The dismantling of a patriarchal reality in favor of a larger, feminist "romance," in fact, is often
marked by the narrator's sharply edged humor. And so, ironically, despite
these clerical "showers," the novel's "present years are dusty, sun-burnt,
hot, arid." When men impose their values on the world, it becomes an
arid, dusty place. Let us "dream of dawn," the narrator requests, and it is
this dream that drops us into the "real" discussed earlier. But we should

be struck by the contradictions. If the narrator's dream is of the real, then her real is a dream. In this subtle way Brontë begins to interrogate the relationship between realism and romance through a novel that deals with "dawn" and origins, incorporating fairy tales, monsters, and ogres and taking us back to Eve, our Great Mother, to rewrite the primordial myth of our beginnings.[5]

When we speak of patriarchal and feminist realities, we are speaking of value-laden perspectives, not necessarily of individual male and female experiences. Brontë enhances her novel's dialectical tensions by including class as a relevant category with gender. So Louis Moore, the impoverished tutor, and William Farren, Robert Moore's workman, have greater affinity to Caroline Helstone, with her habit of submission, than to Robert Moore, the mill-owning master. Louis, like Caroline, vows to "look life in its iron face: stare reality out of its brassy countenance" (464). And, in similar ways, Shirley Keeldar has greater affinities to Robert, with his habit of command, than to Caroline Helstone. But just as Brontë understands and represents the ways in which class can shape individual experience, she also recognizes that gender, as a category, is nonnegotiable. Class may change; gender does not. In short, women remain entrenched in the contradictions of their worlds. We may explain the curious episode of Shirley's dog bite (something feminist critics have puzzled over) as a narrative inscription of her ultimate dependence. Facing the prospect of rabies and madness, she is forced to choose a master to tend her in her anticipated debility. As a corollary to her submission, Louis Moore must assume the position of master when he marries Shirley. Shirley remarks, "Louis . . . would never have learned to rule, if she had not ceased to govern" (592). It seems that with the erasure of class difference, he must take on all of the prerogatives of maleness in patriarchy.[6]

Brontë is consistently presenting a series of dialectics—master/servant, rich/poor, aristocrat/peasant, man/woman—to concretize the overarching dialectic of reality/romance. Only by questioning the very grounds of reality can she recontextualize our vision. We examine this process in two pivotal episodes of *Shirley,* both involving sickness: Caroline's serious fever and Robert's recuperation from the gunshot wound.

Two significant events mark Caroline's near-fatal illness: the complete absence of Shirley (her soothing bondswoman) and the discovery of her mother, Mrs. Pryor, a discovery that curiously emphasizes that mother's partial displacement by William Farren. It is surprising, in one sense, that Brontë should decide in structuring her narrative to send Shirley on a trip with relatives prior to Caroline's serious fever. But that narrative decision emphasizes the disruption Robert's proposal to Shirley has wreaked in the girls' relationship.

It is ironic, too, that Caroline falls ill at this particular juncture, for she has suffered many previous humiliations at Robert's hands from the recognition that Shirley has supplanted her in his interest. The submerged text, one that we can reconstruct only retrospectively, however, writes her illness as a response to Robert's proposal to Shirley, undisclosed to Caroline or the reader at this time. Yet Caroline seems to sense the final betrayal—in which Shirley becomes an unwitting accomplice—and collapses: "[T]he undermined structure . . . [sinks] in sudden ruin" (402).

Caroline is redeemed from that collapse and near destruction by the recovery of her mother. Again, one voice speaks out of a regenerative feminist sensibility while, at the same time, a patriarchal voice undermines the daughter's romance of the recovered mother. The reunion between Mrs. Pryor and Caroline discloses the snake in a patriarchal Eden, recalling Caroline's earlier words about the "mother Eve": "She coveted an apple and was cheated by a snake" (315). Mrs. Pryor's poignant words—"I bore you—nursed you . . . I am your true mother" (409) are contaminated by her admission that she so mistrusted her "tiny, fair infant," a mirror of her husband, that she abandoned her to the loneliness and emotional privation that have been Caroline's lot. The mother still fragments her daughter's being: "[T]he outside *he* conferred; but the heart and the brain are *mine*" (410). This tendency to separate and label—not to see things whole—is the legacy of her experience in patriarchy. She fears the father and reads him as omnipotent, able to corrupt her innocent daughter by the inheritance of his face. The dislocations between mother and daughter leave room for the flowering relationship between William Farren and Caroline, underscoring both their joint victimization by Robert and their mutual interest in gardening, perhaps in the creation of a new Eden: "They took a similar interest in animals, birds, insects, and plants; they held similar doctrines about humanity to the lower creation" (420). The concept of "lower," of course, belongs to patriarchal hierarchy.[7]

Patriarchal reality, as defined by Brontë's narrator, implies a diminished, subservient lot for women. To accept reality means to accept restriction, emptiness, futility, absence of vocation or avocation, enforced idleness or meaningless activity, starvation, wasting, madness. Brontë has an impressive power to make us feel the coffin of social custom contracting around Caroline in her enforced silence upon witnessing Robert's courtship of Shirley, spelling loss of both friend and lover, and in her restricted movement expressed in her inability to escape the scene of her torture through meaningful work. This is woman's reality within Victorian patriarchy.

The narrator, in deconstructing patriarchal reality, reveals its hypocrisies and establishes the reality and validity of what patriarchy has dismissed as romance. This becomes the feminist reality. At the same time, questioning patriarchy's reality, the narrator discovers that it conceals a pernicious romance of male power, privilege, and prerogative. She uncovers that patriarchal romance that masquerades as reality even as she discloses the feminist reality that is branded as romance in patriarchy. Often, through penetrating irony and wit, the narrator reveals herself in the process of deconstructing the hierarchical relationship between patriarchal and feminist realities.[8]

The narrator establishes immediately that a world watered by curates and clerical doctrines of a tradition steeped in patriarchy will be a dry and dusty place. At the outset Brontë is beginning to demystify patriarchal reality. The key to a new humanist or feminist reality is simple. "Nothing," the narrator tells us, "refines like affection" (113). The reality and truth of the affections elevate, ennoble, and redeem. Powerful and influential men sin most often against this reality. Blind to feeling, men act out an image of their self-importance, in fact, play the patriarchal romance of self-importance that requires that women be "inferior: toys to play with, to amuse a vacant hour and to be thrown away" (138). This is a dangerous romance. This self-deluding romance is similar to the one Mrs. Pryor condemns when she counsels Caroline that "romances are pernicious" because their false pictures "are not like reality: they show you only the green tempting surface of the marsh, and give not one faithful or truthful hint of the slough underneath" (366). Men like Helstone and Yorke thus fall into the sough of their marriages.[9]

It is, of course, Robert Moore who falls most dangerously prey to this patriarchal romance of power, prestige, and self-importance. His disdain for the workmen's suffering is of a piece with his proposal to Shirley Keeldar. His arrogance blinds him to the reality of Shirley's feelings, and he misreads her friendship as love. He is not deceived about his own feelings—he knows he does not love Shirley—but believes a violation of those feelings is no sacrilege if it is committed in the name of aggrandizing power.

His patriarchal romance is subjected to the test of a feminist reality, enacted through a fairy-tale romance. Critics have noted the expiatory nature of Robert's gunshot wound (Hook 31), but that is only a small part of his expiation. If the gun of a crazed workman avenges Robert's wrongs to his men, the sequel avenges his wrong to Caroline. In a pointedly comic sequence, replete with ogres, good fairies, and castles, Robert is transported to the top of the Yorke mansion to be imprisoned by the redoubtable Mrs. Horsfall. The episode impishly alludes to fairy tales such as Sleeping Beauty and Rapunzel: a helpless maiden in a high tower, under enchantment and confinement by an evil witch, awaiting release and rescue. Of course, since the lovely and helpless maiden is here a cocky and confident master, the situation is both laughable and morally telling. Robert Moore, who has previously claimed "my mill is my castle" (56), now imprisoned in another castle, must learn of his dependence: his need for home, hearth, and fellowship.

Robert must experience a dependence inflicted on him by women to discover the real reliance and dependence he has on others. Brontë's narrator is comic, almost Dickensian, in her relish of the young man's predicament.[10] As elsewhere, the narrator's irreverent tone signals the replacement of a narrow reality by a broader vision. Even when Moore faces a crisis, the tone remains amused: "They [the doctors] wrought and wrangled over his exhausted frame. They three were on one side of the bed, and Death on the other" (525).

Robert's isolation intensifies after the crisis; he is deprived of all human contact, affection, and activity during his recuperation so that he can experience how poorly he, too, fares under the privation that has been common to Caroline's life. His sole company is Mrs. Horsfall, who at "that moment . . . began her reign." Appropriately for the fairy tale, the narrator reveals that "she was no woman, but a dragon"; all others are "cowed by the breadth, the height, the bone, and the brawn of Mrs. Horsfall" and, thus, "as to Moore, no one now ventured to inquire about him: Mrs. Horsfall had him at dry-nurse"(526).

> Robert Moore had a pleasant time of it: in pain, in danger; too weak to move; almost too weak to speak; a sort of giantess his keeper; the three surgeons his sole society. Thus he lay through the diminishing days and lengthening nights of the whole drear month of November. (526)

The narrator's ironic "Robert . . . had a pleasant time of it" betrays a barely disguised glee that he should feel what Caroline has felt. We enjoy what becomes Caroline's innocent revenge with Mrs. Horsfall as her agent. Moore begins his captivity feebly resisting Mrs. Horsfall, but she teaches him "docility in a trice. She made no account whatever of his six feet— his manly thews and sinews . . . when he was bad, she sometimes shook him" (526).

The fairy tale plays itself out as Robert's new reality.[11] Martin Yorke promises Caroline "to see Mr. Moore, in spite of the dragon who guarded his chamber," and ultimately he facilitates Caroline's visit to Robert by putting "the whole house and all its inhabitants . . . under a spell" (532, 539).

The fairy tale ends with a magical transformation. Robert himself observes, "[S]ix weeks ago I passed out at this gate . . . a proud, angry, disappointed man; I come back sadder and wiser" (554). I term this change magical; it is, of course, the real stuff of which novels are usually made: a letting go of one's illusions, an education into the nature of the world. But here the conditions of education belong to the realm of fairy tale. This man learns, not by encountering and striving with the world as men usually do, but through the enforced privation, seclusion, isolation, and helplessness characteristic of women's experience.

The novel with two female protagonists turns out to be a novel of a man's education. What initially seemed the romance in need of correction—Caroline's—is subtly transferred to Robert. In conclusion, however, we must recall that Brontë's whole tale is a "dream of dawn." The world from which the narrator writes—these "dusty late years" with their arid "showers of curates"—remains untransformed.

The point of the conclusion is that the contradictions persist. It is tempting for readers to subordinate Robert's patriarchal reality with its male romance to the feminist reality of his fairy-tale entrapment and transformation. Our impulse is to read toward a monological meaning of the happily-ever-after disclosed by the ending.[12] Yet the ending introduces and resists the monology. That monology exists only temporarily and precariously to produce a pair of marriages. But, with those marriages, the "fairies" disappear once and for all from the countryside, the fairies who have figured as significant transforming presences throughout the novel.

Brontë may mock the patriarchal reality, show its pretensions, disclose its covert and pernicious romance; she may deconstruct its hierarchical priority to subject it to another fuller reality, but she also reconstructs it within the novel as a final indigestible and unassimilable fact. It exists in Shirley's submission to Louis, in her insistence that he needs to be master;

it is present in Robert Moore's "daydreams embodied in substantial stone and brick and ashes . . . in a mighty mill, and a chimney, ambitious as the tower of Babel" (599). It is appropriate that a novel about hunger and starvation should present an indigestible morsel of this magnitude. The feminist and patriarchal visions will not meld. The tension between them becomes the synthesizing power of the novel's plot, Bakhtin's higher unity. The novel's deconstruction of romance and reality requires a conclusion that we read as both success and failure, as realistic and romantic, a conclusion that does justice to the novel's multiple voices that, miraculously, never devolve into Babel, a conclusion that finally defies the "judicious reader putting on his spectacles" looking for a monological moral.

The pair of marriages that ties up *Shirley* gestures to the second pair of liaisons that brings *Vanity Fair* to its borne: Amelia with Dobbin and Becky with the short-lived Jos Sedley. The idea of a second love, of course, entirely undercuts the ground of unique and undying love on which romance is built. Becky, however, could never afford the luxury of romance and realistically takes whatever she is offered. Amelia has had to sacrifice the long romance she has nurtured about George Osborne, whereas faithful Dobbin, a "spooney," must face his own reality, that he "has barter[ed] away [his] all of truth and ardour against [Amelia's] little feeble remnant of love" (647). Thus, Thackeray has gestured to another pernicious consequence of romance, the way an unwitting man may be encouraged to preserve an idealized image of his beloved and so limit his own happiness.

Text as Discourse

Ideological issues focus on that idealized icon of womanhood in Victorian England, the Angel in the House. In nineteenth-century discourse, the home became an institution encoded as feminine. The celebration of home (with its presiding feminine angel) as a refuge from the harsh realities of the commercial world masked its status as a prison for women, enforcing the kind of self-discipline Foucault points to in *Discipline and Punish*. Both Thackeray and Brontë image the disciplinary controls exerted by the home (controls that actually work on the mind as would those in Bentham's proposed Panopticon) as bodily tortures. Thackeray is comfortably explicit: "[Amelia's] life, begun not unprosperously, had come down to this—to a mean prison and a long, ignoble bondage. . . . How many thousands of people are there, women for the most part, who are doomed to endure this long slavery?" (552). Brontë picks up the echo of Thackeray's idea and extends its historical implications by critiquing the institutionalization and discipline of women's lives, the way in which the normative, the ideology of womanhood, becomes a straightjacket or prison. Thus, in *Shirley,* marriage is for women a kind of tomb or cave or torture chamber (Moglen 186). Based on Mary Cave's marriage to Matthew Helstone and Mrs. Pryor's union with his brother, James, called the "man tiger," the narrator predicts that a second Mrs. Helstone, "inversing the natural order of insect existence would have fluttered through the honeymoon a bright, admired butterfly, and crawled the rest of her days a sordid, trampled worm" (139).

To demonstrate the breadth of Brontë's grasp and depiction, we may refer to *Discipline and Punish* and its discussion of the emergence of new modes of discipline in the late eighteenth and early nineteenth centuries. These new modes include (1) an unseen but all-seeing surveillance, (2) a regime of the norm, and (3) various techniques of the self and its sexuality (D. A. Miller viii). In discussing the locus and operation of discipline, Foucault notes parenthetically that it would be interesting one day to explore "how intrafamilial relations have become 'disciplined'" (215). Brontë, in fact, anticipates this provocative idea in *Shirley*. There she depicts the disciplinary action of the normative in women's lives, in both Victorian house architecture and domestic occupation. The house and its routines become spaces structured for the inculcation of a social ideology that proves particularly destructive for women.

Foucault points out that the nineteenth-century prison depended on two major principles to enact its reform. The first is strict isolation. Without insisting on a rigid homology between the operations of prisons and the ideal upper-class home, we can still be struck by Caroline Helstone's extraordinary isolation in the novel. Mark Girouard, in *Life in the English Country House,* notes that nineteenth-century architecture began to enact rigid segregations: between masters and servants and between men and women. The essential quality of the Victorian home was privacy (285), but another word for privacy is isolation. In the Victorian house, rooms became encoded as masculine or feminine. For example, the dining room was a masculine space decorated in "massive oak or mahogany" to mirror "masculine importance," whereas the drawing room became a feminine space capturing "feminine delicacy in spindly gilt or rosewood, and silk or chintz" (292).

Such historical details confirm the inscription of sexual difference and the disciplinary action of segregation and isolation in the home. They work on Caroline both to sap her energies and to preclude rebellion or dissent. The narrator tells us at one point, "Caroline was limited once more to the grey Rectory; the solitary morning walk by remote byways; the long, lonely afternoon sitting in the quiet parlour which the sun forsook at noon" (375), a routine that the narrator summarizes as the "solitude, the sadness, the nightmare of her life" (381). The preponderance of nouns, adjectives, and verbs suggesting isolation is noteworthy: "solitary," "remote," "lonely," "quiet," "forsook," "solitude." Rose Yorke describes Caroline's life as a "black trance like a toad's, buried in marble" and "a long slow death." The rectory is a "windowed grave," her life "monotony and death" (384, 385). Caroline longs for a profession or a trade "fifty times a day" because labor can give varieties of pain and prevent us from breaking our hearts with a single master-torture. "Besides," Caroline adds, "successful labour has its recompense; a vacant, weary, lonely, hopeless life has none "(235). But Caroline is already so well disciplined by her lady's life that she can take no effective action.

The second principle that Foucault articulates as necessary to the regulatory action of prisons is work: "Work is defined, with isolation, as an agent of carceral transformation" (240). Ironically, Foucault cites the women's workshop at Clairvaux as "the perfect image of prison labour." He quotes from Foucher's 1838 text *De la reforme des prisons:* "on a throne, above which is a crucifix, a sister is sitting; before her, arranged in two rows, the prisoners are carrying out the task imposed on them, and, as needlework accounts for almost all the work, the strictest silence is constantly maintained. . . . It seems that, in these halls, the very air breathes penitence and expiation" (243). I term this example ironic because anyone who has read *Shirley* will be aware of the prominence of needlework in Brontë's novel—where sewing is a disciplinary activity.

Caroline first appears in the novel subject to just such a regimen as Foucher described. She is under the instruction of her cousin, Hortense, who is teaching her "fine needlework" (103):

The afternoon was devoted to sewing . . . unnumbered hours [of] fine embroidery, sight-destroying lace-work, marvelous netting and knitting, and, above all, [of] most elaborate stocking-mending. . . . It was another of Caroline's troubles to be condemned to learn this foreign style of darning, which was done stitch by stitch so as exactly to imitate the fabric of the stocking itself; a wearifu' process, but considered by Hortense Gérard . . . as one of the first "duties of woman." . . . No time did [Hortense] lose in seeking up a hopeless pair of hose, of which the heels were entirely gone, and in setting the ignorant English girl to repair the deficiency: this task had been commenced two years ago, and Caroline had the stockings in her work-bag yet. She did a few rows every day, by way of penance for the expiation of her sins. (107–8)

Brontë, writing on domestic life, employing terms such as "condemned," "penance," "expiation," and "sins," echoes Foucher's writing on prison discipline. At one point Caroline argues, "If I sew I cannot listen; if I listen, I cannot sew" (115), pointing to the way sewing curbs and regulates activity of the mind.

When Caroline returns to her uncle at the rectory, he approves her day with the words, "Well, that will do—stick to the needle . . . and you'll be a clever woman some day" (122). At home, if she is not sewing for the Jew basket (134), she is making dresses for herself: "Some gloomy hours had she spent in the interval. Most of the time had been passed shut up in her own apartment [sewing]; only issuing from it, indeed, to join her uncle at meals" (243–44). Again, Caroline's routine echoes Foucault's discipline of work punctuated by meals. Later, Caroline asks the logical question that is focalized through the narrator's satiric eyes: "What do [fathers] expect [daughters] to do at home? If you ask, they would answer, sew and cook. They expect them to do this, and this only, contentedly, regularly, uncomplainingly all their lives long, as if they had no germs of faculties for anything else: a doctrine as reasonable to hold, as it would be that the fathers have no faculties but for eating what their daughters cook, or for wearing what they sew" (377).

As assiduously as Caroline sews, Shirley avoids the needle. With heavy irony the narrator relates: "[Shirley] takes her sewing occasionally: but, by some fatality, she is doomed never to sit steadily at it for above five minutes" (372). Or we are told, "After tea Shirley reads, and she is just about as tenacious of her book as she is lax of her needle" (373). Playing the transvestite Captain Keeldar—independent, wealthy, and parentless—Shirley can assume many male freedoms and prerogatives and so throws into relief the narrow disciplines of a woman's usual lot.

Of course, Victorian ladies did not spend all their time in isolation or at their needle. Their isolation might otherwise be enviable; one might see it as privacy, a room of one's own. The corollary discipline in their lives Caroline characterizes as "unprofitable visiting"—the routine of morning calls and afternoon teas (377). I mentioned earlier that the drawing room became a feminine space in Victorian England. Girouard adds that the "drawing room acquired two new functions in the Victorian period, as a result of the inane ceremony of morning calls and the more genial celebration of afternoon tea" (293). Morning calls "(which by the late nineteenth century took place in the afternoon) . . . involved carriage visits from one local hostess to another and a quarter of an hour's polite conversation in the drawing room" (293). Such rituals virtually held mistresses hostage in houses, morning and afternoon, giving and receiving these "inane" visits.

These rituals function in ways similar to Bentham's proposed Panopticon, a prison designed so that the inmates would be constantly under an unseen but all-seeing surveillance. Although ladies at home did not live in glass cells, there was the constant possibility that they would be visited at any moment. They had, in effect, to be always ready for the regulatory gaze of society. Morning calls and afternoon teas served as a continual check over their behavior. This control was further enhanced by a normative code of behavior set out in the etiquette books, a widely popular innovation in the Victorian age.

The first view we have of Caroline Helstone at home presents her subject to just such a disciplinary regimen. The narrator relates, "When she had dined, and found herself in the Rectory drawing-room alone, having left her uncle over his temperate glass of port, the difficulty that occurred to and embarrassed her was—How am I to get through this day?" (130). The doorbell interrupts her thoughts, and curates join her uncle in the male space, the dining room. Caroline has a new worry "lest they should stay to tea." Her fate is sealed when four ladies are announced to her in the drawing room, and Caroline wishes herself "meantime at Jericho" (131). The social rituals are an agony to Caroline—her visit with the ladies is punctuated, we are told, by silences of five minutes, and the ordeal leaves Caroline with a full sense of her "ignorance and incompetency." The narrator is both savage and funny in the following comment: "Pause third came on. During its continuance, Caroline was feeling at her heart's core what a dreaming fool she was; what an unpractical life she led; how little fitness there was in her for ordinary intercourse with the ordinary world" (133). She can revive "the flagging discourse" only "by asking them if they would all stay to tea" (133).

One form of discipline gives way to another as Caroline feels the pressure of the normative. Tea must be followed "in the natural course of events" by music. Caroline has opened the piano, we are told, "knowing how it would be" (140). For Caroline, the result of this discipline, called entertaining, is a "sort of brain-lethargy" and a "deadened spirit" (141). She escapes briefly to the dining room and "rested herself—rested at least her limbs, her senses, her hearing, her vision—weary with listening to nothing and gazing on vacancy" (142). This is a characteristically grim picture of institutional control, the power of the normative in women's lives. What began with Thackeray's metaphor for Amelia's imprisonment in "woman's lot" expands in Brontë's novel to become an exploration of the connections and links between two seemingly different discursive formations: the domestic and the carceral.

Text as Theft

To turn from Foucault to Barthes is to take up a dramatically different idea, the notion of cultural revision, and thus to think about intertextuality in a very different way. The "old text of culture" undergoes a change of features, as in Brontë's "theft" of the Victorian trope of tears, a powerful signifier of femininity. Brontë appropriates metonymic associations of tears—sobs, sighs, weepings—as attributes of a landscape, of nature, of fate. So personalized through a feminine trope, the destructive powers of nature and fate are read as woman inspired, as a consequence of rage simmering below the surface of women's acquiescence in domestic arrangements that disempower them.

Tears were the Victorian trope par excellence for femininity, ushered in with Victoria, the girl queen, and Barrett Browning's poetic paean to her:

> God save thee, weeping Queen!
> Thou shalt be well beloved!
> The tyrant's sceptre cannot move,
> As those pure tears have moved!
> The nature in thine eyes we see,
> That tyrants cannot own—
> The love that guardeth liberties!
> Strange blessing on the nation lies
> Whose Sovereign wept—
> Yea, wept, to wear its crown!

In her portrait of a weeping monarch, Barrett Browning attempts to bridge the gap in the signifier "tears" between strength of sensibility and weakness of will.

Why do "real" women cry? The multiple answers to this question

embed femininity simultaneously within cultural discourses of sensitivity
and enfeeblement. Women cry because they feel deeply. Because they
sympathize. Because they love. Because they're tender. Because they're
true. Because they're happy. Because they're sad. Because they're weak.
Because they're dependent.

Thackeray's genial irony reveals his relish for this feminine trope. In the
opening pages of *Vanity Fair*, Amelia Sedley drowns in a rhetoric of tears.
Everyone, including Amelia herself, cries at her departure from Chiswick
Mall: "[She had a pair of eyes, which sparkled with the brightest and honestest good-humour, except indeed when they filled with tears, and that
was a great deal too often; for the silly thing would cry over a dead canary
bird; or over a mouse, that the cat haply had seized upon; or over the end
of a novel, were it ever so stupid" (14–15). From introduction to farewell,
Amelia's story is awash in tears: "Emmy's head sank down, and for almost
the last time in which she shall be called upon to weep in this history, she
commenced that work" (658). Women's work.

For Becky Sharp, Amelia's dark side, "Nobody cried," and the implied
inversion also holds true: She cried for nobody (16). At her crisis, discovered by her husband with Lord Steyne, her schemes exploded, she sits "in
the midst of her miserable ruins with clasped hands and dry eyes"
(516–17). The narrative indictment implicit in her "dry eyes" anticipates
Becky's textual reentry as the bewitching, yet treacherous, "syren."
Thackeray's negative interpretation of the opposing signifier "dry eyes"
keeps women under the tyranny of the sign "tears."

In contrast, Brontë "pursues what was implicit in Thackeray's representation of Amelia, the way a woman's tears inscribe her within a cultural
economy of prescribed suffering. Brontë's narrator in *Shirley* enjoins
women to short-circuit the signifying current so that dry eyes encode
power. As the tears that image her sensibility dry up, so does her susceptibility to disappointment, disease, death: "You expected bread, and you
have got a stone, break your teeth on it, and don't shriek because the
nerves are martyrized. . . . You held out your hand for an egg, and fate put
into it a scorpion. Show no consternation: close your fingers firmly on the
gift; let it sting through your palm. . . . The squeezed scorpion will die,
and you will have learned the great lesson how to endure without a sob"
(128). In Brontë, the answer to the question "Why not cry?" is plain: "If
you survive the test—some, it is said, die under it—you will be stronger,
wiser, less sensitive" (128).

Into the narrative spaces left blank because there are no tears to fill them pour the woman's questions, effectively silenced in Thackeray's text: "How am I to get through this day?" (130). "What am I to do to fill the interval of time which spreads between me and the grave?" "What was I created for, I wonder?" "Where is my place in the world?" (190).

It remains, then, for Brontë to fragment the old text of culture, tears, to change its features through disguise: "[Caroline] returned from an enchanted region to the real world: for Nunnely wood in June, she saw her narrow chamber; for the songs of birds in alleys, she heard the rain on her casement; for the sigh of the south wind, came the sob of the mournful east" (189). Women may be dry eyed, but the world weeps. Rain and winds, disguised sobs and sighs, imbue the world with a feminine sensibility that threatens to rend the fabric of existence. The sobs of the future sound an apocalyptic note: "The future sometimes seems to sob a low warning of the events it is bringing us. . . . At other times this Future bursts suddenly, as if a rock had rent, and in it a grave had opened, whence issues the body of one that slept. Ere you are aware, you stand face to face with a shrouded and unthought-of Calamity—a new Lazarus" (399). What rough beast slouches toward Bethlehem to be (re)born? Is it woman?

Text as Mimicry

Brontë's narrator is often angry, only occasionally antic. Yet the playful impulse erupts at key moments. What confuses, perhaps, is the way Brontë's admiration for Thackeray's art coexists with criticism of his perspectives. The letter in which she identifies the author of *Vanity Fair* as "the legitimate high priest of Truth" continues in a reverential vein: "He, I see, keeps the mermaid's tail below water, and only hints at the dead men's bones and noxious slime amidst which it wriggles; but his hint is more vivid than other men's elaborate explanations" (*Correspondence* 224). Brontë echoes *Vanity Fair*'s narrator, who comments, "In describing this syren, singing and smiling, coaxing and cajoling, the author, with modest pride, asks his readers all round, has he once forgotten the laws of politeness, and showed the monster's hideous tail above water? No!" (617). Nonetheless, that narrator relishes a brief glimpse or two below the waterline, where the mermaid's tail is "writhing and twirling, diabolically hideous and slimy, flapping amongst bones, or curling round corpses" (617).

Dorothy Dinnerstein identifies the mermaid's threat with the element in which she lives, "the dark and magic underwater world from which our life comes and in which we cannot live" (5). That threat also lies in the oppositions she embodies: human/animal, charmer/destroyer. For all of his decorum, the narrator's alignment of Becky "shed-no-tears" Sharp with the mermaid reinforces a figurative economy in which woman's superficial charm conceals a deadly purpose: "They look pretty enough when they sit upon a rock, twanging their harps and combing their hair and singing, and beckon to you to come and hold the looking-glass; but when they sink into their native element, depend on it those mermaids are about no good, and we had best not examine the fiendish marine cannibals, reveling and feasting on their wretched pickled victims" (617). Who are "they"? Who is "you"? Who are "we"? "They" (mermaid/women) beckon "you" (men/the masculine narratee), and thus "we" (male narrator and readers-men/women?) must keep our bodies and minds above water. What happens to women caught and deformed in this syntax, as both third-person object/Other and first-person subject?

Staging the feminine—the stylization and parody of stereotypes and norms that is Irigaray's recommended tactic—becomes Brontë's strategy as she, too, introduces in *Shirley* the figure of the mermaid. First the narrator inexplicably describes her pure, meek heroine, Caroline Helstone, "combing her hair, long as a mermaid's . . . enchanted with the image" in her mirror (123). In light of her own letter of praise, it seems unlikely that Brontë has forgotten Thackeray's description of mermaids "combing their hair." The point seems to be that this enchantress enchants only herself. The man she dreams of winning resolutely resists her charms and proposes to a woman with money.

The mermaid figure returns when Shirley and Caroline plan a tour to the Faroe Isles; Shirley promises "seals in Suderoe, and, doubtless, mermaids in Stromoe" (248). The world Caroline longs to leave, the world of her uncle's rectory (rather than the mermaid's element) is here associated with "remnants of shrouds, and fragments of coffins, and human bones and mould" (248). Shirley spins out a fantasy of their nocturnal encounter with a mermaid: "an image, fair as alabaster" (249). Her features align her explicitly with Caroline: "The long hair . . . a face in the style of yours [Caroline's] . . . whose straight, pure lineaments, paleness does not disfigure" (249). She holds a mirror in her hand and serves herself as a mirror. Shirley exclaims: "Temptress-terror! monstrous likeness of ourselves!" (249). Whereas a man would "spring at the [mermaid's] sign, the cold billow would be dared for the sake of the colder enchantress," the two women "[s]tand safe though not dread-less." The mermaid "cannot charm" because they are like her, but "she will appal," again because they are like her.

The conflict between Thackeray's "they" and "we" has been resolved in Shirley's identification of woman with mermaid. Caroline demurs; Mrs. Pryor protests: "We are aware that mermaids do not exist. . . . How can you find interest in speaking of a nonentity?" (250). Shirley responds, "I don't know" (250), and the scene abruptly ends. It remains an unassimilable bolus, undigested by the narrative.

Such is Brontë's game. She assumes the feminine style and posture to uncover the mechanisms by which it exploits her; introduces, in short, the "patriarch bull . . . huge enough to have been spawned before the Flood" (249). This creature—not in traditional mythology—takes his place alongside the mermaid. Shirley comments to Caroline, "I suppose you fancy the sea-mammoths pasturing about the bases of the 'everlasting hills' . . . I should not like to be capsized by the patriarch bull." Isn't Thackeray just such a "patriarch bull" to Brontë, who defined his mind as "deep-founded and enduring" and who located in the concluding part of *Vanity Fair* "a sort of 'still profound' . . . which the discernment of one generation will not suffice to fathom" (*Correspondence* 224)? Isn't Thackeray just such a literary leviathan enjoying the authority of the patriarchal bull or, rephrased, the bull of patriarchal authority? He might indeed capsize Brontë's small craft.

All parodies risk being recuperated: "Parody by itself is not subversive, and there must be a way to understand what makes certain kinds of parodic repetitions effectively disruptive, truly troubling, and which repetitions become domesticated and recirculated as instruments of cultural hegemony" (Butler, *Gender Trouble* 139). Brontë's revisions of the marriage plot signal a parodic repetition not only of Thackeray's art but also of novel conventions in general. Indeed, Thackeray's own parody of marriage as fulfillment no doubt suggested the whole network of constricting codes, values, and beliefs distinctive to the culture that both he and Brontë inhabited; his iconoclasm in the face of those norms must have encouraged her further parody. At the same time, her novel's traditional conclusion, marriage, seems ultimately to recuperate the very values Brontë set out to parody. That is, we close with the romance we were initially advised to reject in favor of something "real, cool, and solid" (39).

But the parodic impulse is still at play. Although Brontë has not altered the plots in which women's lives are to be circumscribed, she has done something equally radical. She has changed the meaning of that plot, has altered the way in which the women's lives are to be understood. If we return once more to Thackeray's *Vanity Fair*, we recall that he opens his novel with the departure of his female protagonists, Amelia Sedley and Becky Sharp, from Chiswick Mall. They will make their way in the world, where the route to success is, essentially, marriage. Becky immediately and typically queries, "If Mr. Joseph Sedley is rich and unmarried, why should I not marry him?" (25). The narrator ironically asks whether "once land-ed in the marriage country, all were green and pleasant there" (250). But Thackeray embeds this question within the larger vanitas theme inform-ing his novel so that the question of *a woman's* fulfillment is not directly engaged.

Brontë's *Shirley* expends one-sixth of its length before it even introduces a major female character. Yet the novel clearly focuses on two women: Shirley Keeldar and Caroline Helstone. Why does Brontë so structure her novel? One immediate and frequently given answer is that we are to see the women's lives within the mercantile world of men and masters, both women and workers suffering from "the dehumanizing effect of patriar-chal capitalism" (Gilbert and Gubar 387). Such thematic observations are certainly valid, but the structure and events of the first several chapters also have the significant effect of beginning to unseat patriarchal ideolo-gies of womanhood through mimicry, a process that intensifies when the women are actually introduced.

Brontë opens with a male world devoid of women, except as servants. Women are negligible, insignificant, and ignored. The male world of guns and machinery and power is inaccessible to women or to women's influ-ence. Very subtly the text raises a question: What meaningful role can women have in men's lives and in a patriarchal culture? We are early vouchsafed an answer: the fable of Mary Cave. Mary Cave was the site of a contest and conflict between Yorke and Helstone. Helstone won her, "a girl with the face of a Madonna; a girl of living marble," "beautiful as a monumental angel" (81). This bride is no sooner invested with her offices as Victorian angel in Helstone's house than she begins a decline that ends in her death. Mary's demise is "scarcely noticed" by her husband because "she is of no great importance to him in any shape" (82). The Victorian myth of woman's regenerative moral sensibility is here mimicked and exploded.

This pattern is repeated when we focus on Robert Moore, the mill owner. He generally avoids his home where his sister, Hortense, presides:

"[I]ts air of modest comfort seemed to possess no particular attraction for its owner" (91). He prefers the snuggery and isolation of his separate quarters in his mill. After he is wounded by the would-be assassin's bullet, he is apparently transformed, a transformation signaled by his confession to his sister, "I am pleased to come home" (555). The narrator dryly comments, "Hortense did not feel the peculiar novelty of this expression coming from her brother, who had never before called the cottage his home; and to whom its narrow limits had always heretofore seemed rather restrictive than protective" (555).

The narrator builds on this kind of observation by associating both Louis and Robert Moore, the prospective husbands of Shirley and Caroline, with rock or stone. Louis is described as "cool as stone" and like "a great sand-buried stone head" (575). Robert asks Caroline, metaphorically, "if that rose should promise to shelter from tempest this hard, grey stone" (595). The reader inevitably recalls the narrator's angry summary of women's lives: "You expected bread, and you have got a stone; break your teeth on it and don't shriek because the nerves are martyrized" (128). Is the narrator suggesting that, in marrying Louis and Robert, the women have ingested stones that their "mental stomach[s]" must digest? That possibility recalls the metaphor of torture with which we began. The gap opened there has widened and exposed the Victorian ideologies of womanhood as dangerous romances, which, in Mrs. Pryor's words, "show you only the green tempting surface of the marsh, and give not one faithful or truthful hint of the slough underneath" (366).

Aggressively, the narrator titles her final chapter "The Winding-Up" and opens, "Yes, reader, we must settle accounts now" (587). The chapter is full of metalepses, or moments when the narrator transgresses the boundaries of the narrative, speaking directly to her characters. "Are you not aware, Peter," she asks of one, "that a discriminating public has its crotchets: that the unvarnished truth does not answer; that plain facts will not digest?" (587). Plain facts that don't digest recall stones that the women receive in place of bread, another indigestible morsel. A page later the narrator gloats: "There! I think the varnish has been put on very nicely" (588). Is the narrator varnishing the truth for men who don't wish to digest plain facts? The tendentious tone continues—"[Y]ou cannot know how it happened, reader; your curiosity must be robbed to pay your elegant love of the pretty and pleasing" (588). The narrator, in effect, tells us that the conclusion is varnish, put on to feed her narratee's love of "the pretty and pleasing." And Charlotte Brontë subverts our expectations that marriage can resolve the conflicts and fulfill our own narrative desires. The marriages, too, are a varnish "put on very nicely."

Thus, although the novel concludes with a pair of marriages, that ending should be read parodically. Brontë begins by promising us something called "reality" and concludes, laughingly, with something looking, at first glance, like "romance"! But that romance turns into a "manufacturer's daydreams," something that looks very much like garden-variety industrialization. The fairies and ladies disappear.

Thackeray, in contrast, begins with a puppet show—the Becky and Amelia dolls—and he concludes, ostensibly, with the same "game," as we children are admonished to "shut up the box and puppets." But who can forget the closing injunction: "Ah *Vanitas Vanitatum!* Which of us is happy in the world? Which of us has his desire? Or, having it, is satisfied" (666)? An ex cathedra pronouncement; a brilliant and pithy summa on the human condition; a magnificent moral gesture. One might want to argue, however, about whether Becky and Amelia have had their desires or have been had. Or, if one is Charlotte Brontë, one might want to try mimicry: "The story is told. I think I now see the judicious reader putting on his spectacles to look for a moral. It would be an insult to his sagacity to offer direction. I only say, God speed him in his quest!" (*Shirley*, finis).

Summa

This chapter has employed a variety of critical concepts, from mosaic to dialogue to discourse to theft to parody, in order to develop a theory of strategic intertextuality. Such a theory emphasizes not only the signature of the woman in the text, but also engages the transformative potential of woman, which it focuses by engaging the liberatory impulse implicit in certain concepts of intertextuality. Even a Foucauldian emphasis on discourse works to uncover and so destabilize the mechanisms by which one is subjected. My analysis has necessarily privileged Brontë's text over Thackeray's, yet I hope it has also engaged both texts in such a way as to make clear their currency within the general signifying practices of their culture. Assuming such currency provides the basis for any intertextual study, and it suggests the scope of Thackeray's own parodic impulse in the novel, which I have only minimally addressed. It also stresses the way influence and intertextuality become mutually entangled, the way one novel's engagement with another is not a simple process of transmission, but a dynamic encounter with the cultural values that saturate any literary object. That contestation of word with word, text with text, has the power to generate a productive friction that destabilizes the ground of meaning and so facilitates change.

I have devoted significant time in this first chapter to exploring Brontë's *Shirley* from a variety of theoretical perspectives to demonstrate that gender enters into and affects narrative in profound and transformative ways. My goal has been to capture the breadth of gender's importance to narrative, a breadth suggested by Robyn Warhol in "Guilty Gravings: What Feminist Narratology Can Do for Cultural Studies."[13] That is, we need to analyze narrative forms not only as they might involve us with "the gender of a character, an author, a narrator, a reader, or some combination of these figures" but also as those forms are "necessarily related to the era, class, gender, sexual orientation, and racial and ethnic circumstances of their producers and audiences" and so work to "structure gender within culture" (340–41). It is this scope—stretching from literary to cultural analysis—for which I have sought to lay a foundation in analyzing *Shirley.* In the next chapter's turn to Charlotte's sister Anne Brontë, we discover still other narrative strategies developed to express the younger sister's significantly different understanding of gender's role in culture.

CHAPTER 2

Dialogue and Narrative Transgression in Anne Brontë's *Tenant of Wildfell Hall*

exceeding limits

The intimacy of the Brontë household kept Anne closely acquainted with her sisters' work but did not persuade her to adopt her sisters' perspectives. We know from reading Anne's novels and poems that she often saw things in a very different light on Emily and Charlotte. Critics have often remarked the dialogic relationship subsisting between Emily's *Wuthering Heights* and Anne's *Tenant of Wildfell Hall,* even in such superficial matters as using identical initials for the two titular houses and a preponderance of male names beginning with H: Heathcliff, Hareton, and Hindley versus Huntingdon, Hattersley, Hargrave, and Halford. But critics have been less astute in discerning how Anne's novel persistently questions the values and premises of Charlotte's enormously successful *Jane Eyre.* As we will see, in numerous ways Anne signals that she is critical of what she perceived as her sister's romantic representations.

In a telling episode related in their letters, Anne and Charlotte impulsively rushed to London, walking eight miles "through a snowstorm to the station," to demonstrate to their publishers their female and separate identities (*Brontës* II, 251). As a strategy to boost sales, Anne's publisher, Newby, had been spreading rumors that two new books on his list—*Wuthering Heights* and *The Tenant of Wildfell Hall*—came from the same hand that penned *Jane Eyre,* which was published by Smith and Elder. Charlotte's integrity was impugned because she had promised her next book to Smith and Elder; thus, her passionate response is perhaps predictable. Anne's is less so. It invites us to consider what grounds she might have had for displeasure that her work should be confused with Charlotte's. Because Charlotte survived her sister, she has been able to claim, so to speak, the last word. It was a harsh one: Anne's novel was a "mistake": "[I]t was too little consonant with the character, tastes, and ideas of the gentle, retiring, inexperienced writer. She wrote it under a strange, conscientious, half-ascetic notion of accomplishing a painful penance and a severe duty" (*Brontës* III, 156). Despite the novel's enormous and immediate popular success during the nine months before Anne's death, Charlotte did not authorize its reprinting for the duration of her own life, that is, for ten years after Anne died. By then it was all but forgotten.

Dialogue

Charlotte would have been intensely aware of the relation Anne's novel held to hers. W. S. Williams, the reader for Smith and Elder, was immediately struck by the resemblance between Huntingdon (*The Tenant's* hero) and Rochester (*Jane Eyre's* hero) and wrote Charlotte to that effect. She responded emphatically, "there is no likeness between the two." She claimed that "Huntingdon is a specimen of the naturally selfish, sensual, superficial man . . . who is sure to grow worse the older he grows. Mr. Rochester has a thoughtful nature. . . . Years improve him; the effervescence of youth foamed away, what is really good in him still remains" (*Brontës* II, 244–45). Charlotte's favorable assessment of her own creation has been allowed to stand, and the dialogue Anne initiated has been silenced with the disappearance of her text. But it seems strange to let Charlotte have every last word on the two novels, especially because the composition of *The Tenant* followed that of *Jane Eyre*. In that regard, Anne always has the last word.[1]

At the core of both *Jane Eyre* and *The Tenant of Wildfell Hall* is a romance between a naive and innocent young woman, Jane and Helen respectively, and an older man, experienced in the world and partly corrupted by it. Both women are seen and see themselves as capable of redeeming the barrenness and waste of the man's earlier life, a life in which inadequate education has left him prey to certain vices and vicious tendencies. But whereas Jane Eyre is poor, obscure, and plain, Helen Graham is rich, prominent, and beautiful. The contrast suggests what Anne wanted to make explicit: With all the advantages in the world, no woman can easily reform a man whose habits are already established; far less can she undertake that task if she has the disadvantage of social inferiority. Helen marries her Huntingdon at the commencement of her story and is brought to a painful realization of her foolish idealism. For Helen, marriage is the beginning of growth; for Jane it marks the end. Jane's marriage to Rochester culminates her fairy-tale romance, as Charlotte's book must have seemed to Anne, a story wildly at odds with Anne's extensive and intimate experience with the gentlemanly class when she served as a governess at Thorp Green.

Rochester describes Jane in the exact terms that Helen Graham conceives her role with Huntingdon: "You are my sympathy—my better self—my good angel—I am bound to you with a strong attachment" (*Jane Eyre* 277). Huntingdon, too, speaks of Helen as his "angel" (163, 185). Rochester says of Jane:

> After a youth and manhood passed half in unutterable misery and half in dreary solitude, I have for the first time found what I truly love—I have found you. . . . I am bound to you with a strong attachment. I think you good, gifted, lovely: a fervent, a solemn passion is conceived in my heart; it leans to you, draws you to my centre and spring of life, wraps my existence about you. (*Jane Eyre* 227)

As if in echo, Huntingdon claims:

> My father, you know, was something of a miser, and in his later days especially, saw no pleasure in life but to amass riches; and so it is no wonder that his son should make it his chief delight to spend them, which was accordingly the case, until my acquaintance with you, dear Helen, taught me other views and nobler aims. And the very idea of having you to care for under my roof would force me to moderate my expenses and live like a Christian—not to speak of all the prudence and virtue you would instill in my mind by your wise counsels and sweet, attractive goodness. (*The Tenant of Wildfell Hall* 188)

These passages, so similar in idea yet so different in style and tone, take us to the heart of Anne's critique. Rochester's passionate "found what I truly love" and the italicized "you" contrasts with Huntingdon's tepid "until my acquaintance with you, dear Helen." Rochester claims that his torrent of emotion binds him to Jane, leans to her, draws her, wraps his existence about her. Huntingdon's shallow rill of feeling runs dry as he speaks of being forced to moderate expenses and live like a Christian. Rochester embraces Jane by describing her as "good, gifted, lovely"; Huntingdon holds Helen at arm's length by speaking of her "prudence and virtue," her "wise counsels and sweet, attractive goodness."

The romance in which Charlotte's readers are swept up receives a severe check in Anne's representation of Huntingdon, as she seems to question whether depth and profundity of feeling can coexist with licentiousness and dissipation. And from *The Tenant of Wildfell Hall*'s point of view, self-indulgent men are likely to adhere more tenaciously to their own pleasures than to the prospect of reform. Thus, Anne initiates a strongly revisionary view of what constitutes manliness, a revision underlined by her innovative use of narrative structure.

Transgression

The radical and indecorous subject matter of Anne Brontë's *The Tenant of Wildfell Hall*—a woman's flight from her abusive husband—shocked contemporary audiences. Yet the very indecorousness of the subject seems immediately undermined by the propriety of the form this narrative takes: The woman's story is enclosed within and authorized by a respectable man's narrative. Within the discourse of traditional analysis we would speak of the "nested" narratives of Anne Brontë's novel, one story enclosed within another. In this case, the woman's story, in the form of a diary, is nested within the man's narrative. The critical language I am employing here already suggests certain conclusions about priority and hierarchy. The woman's story must, it seems, be subsumed within the man's account, which is prior and originary. The presentation of her version of events depends upon his re-presentation. Within a traditional narrative analysis, then, Brontë's *Tenant* may tell an untraditional tale of a fallen woman redeemed, but it tells it in such a way that reaffirms the patriarchal status quo of masculine priority and privilege, of women's subordination and dependency. The radical subject is defused by the form. But such a traditional analysis that speaks of nested narratives is already contaminated by the patriarchal ideology of prior and latter and so cannot effectively question what I wish to question: the transgressive nature of the narrative exchange represented here.

Following Roland Barthes I propose that we recognize "[a]t the origin of Narrative, desire," because at the heart of narrative operates an economic system, an exchange. To Barthes, "[t]his is the question raised, perhaps, by every narrative. *What should the narrative be exchanged for? What is the narrative 'worth'?"* In his analysis of "Sarrasine," the exchange is a "night of love for a good story." Thus "the two parts of the text are not detached from one another according to the so-called principle of 'nested narratives.' . . . Narrative is determined not by a desire to narrate but by a desire to exchange: it is a *medium of exchange,* an agent, a currency, a gold standard" (1974 88–90). If we examine Anne Brontë's *Tenant of Wildfell Hall* in the light of narrative as exchange—of narrative within a narrative not as hierarchical or detachable parts but as interacting functions within a transgressive economy that allows for the paradoxic voicing of feminine desire—we discover the narrative innovation. Articulating this process is the remaining focus of this chapter. I also suggest here (to indicate larger implications of this analysis) that such narrative exchanges are common in Victorian stories of transgression, as in Barthes's example, Balzac's "Sarrasine" (the castrati as man/woman); in Emily Brontë's *Wuthering Heights* (the self as Other—"I am Heathcliff"); in Mary Shelley's *Frankenstein* (the human as monster); and in Joseph Conrad's *Heart of Darkness* (the civilized man as savage). Further, these novels also use nested narratives, written and/or spoken, to reveal how a transgressive perspective—whether Heathcliff's or the creature's or Kurtz's—can explode the conventional bounds that would frame it.

The ideas of feminine voice and feminine desire in Victorian England were oxymorons, in Roland Barthes's coinage, *paradoxisms,* a joining of two antithetical terms, a "passage through the wall of the Antithesis" (27). The patriarchal discourse of Victorianism coded terms such as masculine/feminine, desire/repletion, and speech/silence as opposites, as paradigmatic poles marked by the slash. Thus the feminine view, which was repressed, could have no voice, and passion, or desire, was the province of the masculine, a function of what Barthes calls the symbolic code.

Barthes elaborates, "The antithesis is a wall without a doorway. Leaping this wall is a transgression. . . . Anything that draws these two antipathetic sides together is rightly scandalous (the most blatant scandal: that of form)" (65). Barthes's formulation suggests the immense difficulty confronting the Victorian writer who wished to give voice to feminine desire. This transgressive act at its most blatantly scandalous depends on formal juxtaposition: something that "draws these two antipathetic sides together." I propose that we examine the transgressive possibilities inherent in the symbolic code itself and, further, that we look at the narrative within the narrative as a mode of juxtaposition, both of meanings and of focus.

In Brontë's *Tenant of Wildfell Hall* the subject is transgression—a woman's illegal flight from her husband.[2] Brontë uses the transgressive possibilities of narrative exchange to write her transgressive story, a story of female desire, and she uses the transgressive possibilities of the symbolic code to rewrite her transgression or "fall" as her triumph. A brief summary of the novel's plot will focus the central issues. A young and idealistic woman marries a man whose character is already in need of reformation. Believing herself called to this task, she begins optimistically only to discover that she is powerless to effect any changes that cannot be wrought by the force of moral suasion. She has no social or legal leverage. Ultimately, finding her son and herself sinking into the corruption generated by her husband, she plans to flee, only to be defeated on a first attempt when her husband, discerning her intention, confiscates all her property. Prompted by her husband's introduction of his mistress into the house as his son's governess, she succeeds at a second attempt, but she must carefully guard her identity from her inquisitive neighbors or she may be betrayed to her husband and forced to return.

These events, at the heart of the novel, are told only retrospectively. The novel is, in fact, doubly retrospective—Helen's narrative is nested within Gilbert's narrative, which is, in turn, a story told to his friend Halford. The novel opens in 1847, when Gilbert commences his correspondence with Halford. He has felt that he owes Halford a return for an earlier confidence and will now make good his "debt" with an "old-world story . . . a full and faithful account of certain circumstances connected with the most important event of my life" (34). Gilbert's narrative itself begins twenty years earlier, in the autumn of 1827, with the arrival of a new tenant at Wildfell Hall. Helen Graham, the mysterious tenant, is that woman who has transgressed Victorian social convention by leaving her husband, and her story—incorporated through her diary—begins on 1 June 1821. Brontë thus provides one model for Barthes's later theories by having Gilbert define narrative exchange as economic exchange. He writes to Halford: "If the coin suits you, tell me so, and I'll send you the rest at my leisure: if you would rather remain my creditor than stuff your purse with such *ungainly* heavy pieces . . . I'll . . . *willingly* keep the treasure to myself" (44). The monetary metaphors underline the novel's implicit insistence that one does not narrate simply because of a desire to narrate: narration enacts an exchange and a gain or loss.

Traditional literary criticism has faulted Brontë's *Tenant* for its clumsy device of Helen Graham's interpolated diary. George Moore, otherwise ardently enthusiastic over Brontë's talents, instigated criticism of her artistic "breakdown" in the middle of the novel. Moore regretted not the interpolated tale but the manner of exchange. He complained, "You must not let your heroine give her diary to the young farmer . . . your heroine must tell the young farmer her story" to "preserve the atmosphere of a passionate and original love story."[3] This distinction in the mode of exchange, telling versus writing, raises a question Barthes does not discuss, and it encourages further reflection. Were the heroine merely to speak her tale, then one kind of economic exchange would be confirmed: her story for his chivalric allegiance, something he is struggling to preserve in the face of society's calumny. Such a "telling" would "preserve the atmosphere of a passionate and original love story," as George Moore saw, because that story would be built on the tantalizing proximity of the two desiring bodies. Scenes of passion gain in intensity when readers are themselves enrapt by the representation; the focus is on emotion. But, I would argue, that story of passion between a man and a woman is not the one Brontë wanted to write. Helen's diary spans one-half of the novel, telling a different story and confirming another kind of economic transaction. Helen exchanges her story for the right to fulfill her polymorphous desire: to restore her reputation, to punish with impunity her first husband, and to marry a man who consents to be the object of her beneficence and affection.

Gilbert Markham opens his narrative with the arrival of Helen Graham at Wildfell Hall. She is immediately put into circulation as an object of community gossip, speculation, and horror that a "single lady" has let a "place . . . in ruins" (37). The community reads her character through this behavior, concluding she must be a "witch," a decoding that follows from an initial suspicion that she cannot be a "respectable female" (38, 39). Such suspicions unleash a barrage of one-way exchanges in the form of "pastoral advice" or "useful advice" (38, 39) as community members seek to circumscribe her within the usual sexual economies, to regulate "the apparent, or non-apparent circumstances, and probable, or improbable history of the mysterious lady" (39). The explicit oppositions in this passage emphasize the binaries that undergird Brontë's story from the outset, the excesses of which disrupt the seemingly simple love story of a young farmer and a beautiful stranger. As we have seen in Barthes's formulation, this is a function of antitheses or the symbolic code, which both separates and joins and thus allows for the transgression as well as the conservation of oppositions.

Is Helen Graham a witch-devil or an angel? Is she a wife or a widow, amiable or ill tempered? Is she pure or corrupt, a saint or a sinner, faithful or fallen? Her identity is made more problematic because her decorous appearance and religious devotion coexist with her claims that she has no use for "such things that every lady ought to be familiar with" and "what every respectable female ought to know" (39). Although civilized in manner, she appears to "wholly disregard the common observances of civilized life" (51).

It is immediately plain that Brontë is not giving us the traditional generic domestic comedy, that is, the story of a woman who focuses on making herself into a desirable object for a suitable man. That story is circumvented at the outset with Helen Graham's ambiguous status as widow/wife, and yet the pressure of that traditional narrative is such, and the cultural expectations for beautiful women are such, that Gilbert's story strives to become that narrative as he falls out of love with Eliza Millward and into love with Helen Graham and begins to write himself into the narrative as the rescuing figure of the maligned and misunderstood lady. Significantly, Gilbert's narrative at first tends to assign similar traits to Eliza and Helen despite their manifest differences. For example, Gilbert describes Eliza Millward as a woman whose "chief attraction" (like Helen's) lay in her eyes: "the expression various, and ever changing but always either preternaturally—I had almost said *diabolically*—wicked, or irresistibly bewitching—often both" (42). This assignment of traits aligns Eliza paradigmatically with Helen (she is already syntagmatically aligned since she is another love interest of Gilbert), and the effect is to domesticate Helen and her true strangeness because we rapidly perceive that Eliza is a very ordinary young woman who desires only to become the object of some man's affection. Thus, at this early point, Gilbert's narrative strives to interpret Helen Graham as it does Eliza Millward—as just another woman whose life could be fulfilled by connection with his.

By initially making Helen Graham an object of Gilbert's narrative and not the subject of her own, the text enacts what it also presents thematically: women's objectification and marginalization within patriarchal culture. Specific comments underscore our perception of this process. Helen Graham is criticized for making a "milksop," not a "man," of her little boy, who is supposed to "learn to be ashamed" of being "always tied to his mother's apron string" (52). Helen's energetic defense insists, "I trust my son will never be ashamed to love his mother," and "I am to send him to school, I suppose, to learn to despise his mother's authority and affection!" (55).

Women are paradigmatically all linked and consequently all marginalized by obsessive attention to men and their needs. Gilbert's sister complains, "I'm told I ought not to think of myself." She quotes her mother's words: "You know, Rose, in all household matters, we have only two things to consider, first, what's proper to be done, and secondly, what's most agreeable to the gentlemen of the house—anything will do for the ladies" (78). Mrs. Markham sums up the duties of husband and wife: "[Y]ou must fall each into your proper place. You'll do your business, and she, if she's worthy of you, will do hers; but it's your business to please yourself, and hers to please you" (79).

Gilbert Markham is suddenly and surprisingly enabled to articulate this process and his own benefits: "Perhaps, too, I was a little spoiled by my mother and sister, and some other ladies of my acquaintance" (5). He achieves this unusual self-knowledge partly to prepare for his ceding the position of subject to Helen and thereby crediting her story and the possibility of her desire. He tells his mother, "[W]hen I marry, I shall expect to find more pleasure in making my wife happy and comfortable, than in being made so by her: I would rather give than receive" (79).

We are also prepared for the narrative's change of focus by the extent of Helen Graham's difference from the women around her. A professional painter who supports herself and her son, she "cannot afford to paint for [her] own amusement" (69). She does not allow her painting to be interrupted by casual social calls, objects to Gilbert's "superintendence" of her progress on a sketch and to being the object of his appreciative gaze, and manifests an "evident desire to be rid of [Gilbert]" (89). A visit he pays her provokes his recognition, "I do not think Mrs. Graham was particularly delighted to see us," an indirect confession of his initial failure to accord primacy to her as desiring subject instead of desired object.

These thematic shifts anticipate and prepare for the narrative exchange that is about to take place as Gilbert cedes the story to Helen. In fact, such shifts proliferate just prior to the commencement of Helen's diary narrative. Gilbert begins to change his orientation toward Helen, focusing less on how she meets his desire and more on how he might meet hers. He confesses that his early behavior toward her made him "the more dissatisfied with myself for having so unfavourably impressed her, and the more desirous to vindicate my character and disposition in her eyes, and if possible, to win her esteem" (85).

Yet at the same time that Gilbert expresses dissatisfaction with his early behavior, he embroils himself in an embarrassing misunderstanding with Mr. Lawrence, whom he imagines to be another would-be lover of Helen because he is blind to the truth that Lawrence is, in fact, her brother. Markham here enacts a charade of the jealous lover—a charade marked by insults and, finally, by a physical assault on Lawrence. It is his nadir, the moment when he privileges the community voices and the "evidence of [his] senses" (145) over Helen's authority to speak her story. Although Gilbert Markham pretends to disregard the storm of rumor surrounding Helen Graham that the community circulates—characterized as "shaky reports," "idle slander," "mysterious reports," "talk," "the poison of detracting tongues," a "spicy piece of scandal," "the calumnies of malicious tongues," "vile constructions," "lying inventions," "babbling fiends" (96, 97, 102, 103, 120, 123, 124)—his behavior reveals that he accords rumor great authority. When he adds what he calls "the evidence of my senses," he feels his position is unassailable just at the point where it is most vulnerable. We, as readers, appreciate the limitation of Gilbert's perspective, the ways he, in focalizing events and other characters, has generated a cloud of misapprehension shaped by his own needs, fears, and desires. At this point his narrative is bankrupt, unable to provide answers to the questions generated by the text's hermeneutic code. Helen's voice intervenes at this point with greater narrative authority to silence the other proliferating voices. Her narrative must redeem Gilbert's and provide those answers, the final signifieds of the text's multiplying signifiers: the promise that the classic novel holds out.

I mentioned earlier that narratives of transgression often depend on narrative exchange. Whether we are dealing with the young lady in "Sarrasine," or Lockwood in *Wuthering Heights,* or Victor Frankenstein in *Frankenstein,* or the unnamed fellow in *Heart of Darkness,* or Gilbert in *The Tenant of Wildfell Hall,* the focalizer of events confronts an enigma born of a transgression of antitheses, and his explanatory power is momentarily exhausted. Answers to the enigma depend on a new viewpoint, a new focus—in this case, a new narrator or focalizer. I use the term "focalizer" deliberately to allow us to distinguish between the one who narrates and the one who sees or focuses the events (Genette 194–211). But the relationship between the two focalizers is always problematic because they offer competing narratives; each claims authority to tell the story, and the two versions cannot be simply supplementary. The relationship between the two focalizers may also become problematic because one of the narrators may become the focalizer of both narratives, which is what I believe happens in *The Tenant of Wildfell Hall,* and this collapse generates a narrative transgression—a confusion of outside and inside, primary and secondary, subject and object. Although Helen's story is enclosed within Gilbert's story and might seem, therefore, to be part of his, nonetheless, by providing the answers Gilbert and the reader seek, it subordinates his narrative to hers. Helen's narrative rewrites Gilbert's, stabilizing it within a particular hermeneutic pattern. Thus, it is her story but also his story, a conflation that Brontë plays upon after Helen's diary concludes and Markham resumes; it becomes impossible at times to determine which one is the focalizer of events, a process for us to examine after we explore the operation of the symbolic code in Helen's story.

Helen's narrative fully focalizes the paradoxism of feminine desire. Her diary, first of all, records the story of a young woman's falling in love and concomitant distraction and alienation from her common pursuits and ordered life. That is, hers is an often told tale of a young woman's newly aroused desire for a young man: "All my former occupations seem so tedious and dull. . . . I cannot enjoy my music. . . . I cannot enjoy my walks. . . . I cannot enjoy my books. . . . My drawing suits me best. . . . But then, there is one face I am always trying to paint or to sketch" (148). Helen's painting becomes an eloquent voice of her desire for Huntingdon because it reveals to him what her words deny. Indeed, Huntingdon pinpoints the connection between images and words, between hasty tracings and postscripts: "I perceive, the backs of young ladies' drawings, like the post-scripts of their letters, are the most important and interesting part of the concern" (172). And, as he reads the message of her desire in her sketch, Helen is mortified: "So then! . . . he despises me, because he knows I love him" (172). This recognition underscores a significant pattern already in place, that a young woman must disguise her physical desire for a man because expression of such desire only kindles contempt within a patriarchy.

Thus, Helen's perception initiates a process, first of dissembling her desire and then, more significantly, of coding a physical urge as a spiritual need. In the first move, the desire becomes a subterranean force, something not openly expressed; in the second move, the desire is no longer recognized or accepted for what it is. A woman sublimates her physical desire for a man; it becomes a need to reform him spiritually. So, women's physical desires, because illicit, are often encoded in literature as spiritual ones. The legion of female saviors in Victorian fiction testifies to this rewriting. Charlotte Brontë's Jane Eyre is to guide and protect a reformed Rochester; George Eliot's Dorothea Brooke and Mary Garth are to give a social focus to the self-indulgent desires of Will Ladislaw and Fred Vincy. Anne Brontë allows her heroine to be more vocal and articulate about her sublimated desire. In justifying her marriage to Huntingdon, Helen argues, "I will save him from" his evil companions, "I would willingly risk my happiness for the chance of securing his," and, finally, "If he has done amiss, I shall consider my life well spent in saving him from the consequences of his early errors" (167). She sighs, "Oh! if I could but believe that Heaven has designed me for this!" (168). Helen is so indoctrinated by this myth that, when she believes Huntingdon has committed adultery with Annabella Wilmot, she claims, "It is not my loss, nor her triumph that I deplore so greatly as the wreck of my fond hopes for his advantage" (178). The failure of this rosy scenario is anticipated in her aunt's summation: "Do you imagine your merry, thoughtless profligate would allow himself to be guided by a young girl like you?" (165). That, of course, is precisely the Victorian myth and ideology. While Helen quietly gloats, "[A]n inward instinct . . . assures me I am right. There *is* essential goodness in him;—and what delight to unfold it!" (168), we are already apprised of her mistaken apprehension by the retrospective structure of the narrative that testifies to the fiction she is projecting.

What does it mean, then, that Brontë's Helen fails in her efforts at spiritual reform? And not only does she fail, but Huntingdon also succeeds to an extent in corrupting her. Such failure and reversal inevitably shift attention from the spiritual realm back to the physical one, in the traditional antithesis of body and soul. Not surprisingly, reviewers of *Tenant* were outraged because the novel concentrated so heavily on sensual indulgences and abuses. Perhaps more threatening, however, *Tenant* explodes the myth of woman's redemptive spirituality and insight, and it opens the door to the unthinkable transgression, feminine desire. The force of Helen's love is now channeled into hatred; a desire to redeem becomes a desire to punish. Helen admits, "I hate him tenfold more than ever, for having brought me to this! . . . Instead of being humbled and purified by my afflictions, I feel that they are turning my nature into gall" (323).

Again, Barthes's symbolic code helps to articulate the process. The symbolic code represents meaning as difference through antithesis that appears inevitable. And, as we have seen, "every joining of two antithetical terms . . . every passage through the wall of Antithesis . . . constitutes a transgression" (Barthes 26–27). Brontë insistently deploys such oppositions as love/hate, redemption/punishment, saint/sinner, angel/devil, female/male to set up the conditions for transgression. At this point the text works to privilege and to legitimate one binary term over another. But, inevitably, due to the operation of the symbolic code, the text also becomes the site for exposure, multivalence, and reversibility. The pivotal event is Helen's return to nurse her injured husband. Does she return to redeem or to punish? Does she go out of love or out of hatred? Is she a ministering angel or a vengeful devil? Is she a holy saint or a common sinner?

In returning to Huntingdon, Helen passes through the wall of antithesis to transgress and to collapse differences that were seemingly inviolable.

Huntingdon ejaculates at her return, "Devil take her," even as Markham
extols the man's good fortune to have "such an angel by his side" (428,
444). Huntingdon perceives his returned wife as a "fancy" or "mania" that
would "kill" him. Helen insists his mania is the "truth." She asserts she
has come "to take care" of him, to "save" him. He answers, "[D]on't tor-
ment me now!" He interprets her behavior as "an act of Christian charity,
whereby you hope to gain a higher seat in heaven for yourself, and scoop
a deeper pit in hell for me." She states she has come to offer him "comfort and assistance," whereas he accuses her of a desire to overwhelm him
"with remorse and confusion" (430). Huntingdon recognizes her act as
"sweet revenge," made sweeter because "it's all in the way of duty" (433).
He complains that she wants to "scare [him] to death"; she responds that
she does not want to "lull [him] to false security" (434). Helen characterizes herself as his "kind nurse," while Huntingdon regrets that he has been
abandoned to the "mercy of a harsh, exacting, cold-hearted woman" (439,
445). He is the object of her "solicitude"; she is no longer the object of his
cruelty. Save/kill, care for/torment, angel/devil, truth/fancy, duty/revenge,
kind/harsh, lull/scare, heaven/hell, higher seat/deeper pit—the signifiers
slide, distinctions collapse, meaning erodes. Feminine desire expresses
itself in the resulting vacuum of meaning. In the novel's hermeneutic, the
fallen woman of Victorian life becomes the paragon, the exemplum, and
revenge becomes a fine duty.

At the point that Helen returns to Huntingdon's bedside, Gilbert
Markham has resumed the narration, but he has not assumed the authority to focus the bedside events. His narrative contains frequent letters
from Helen, and she is as often the focalizer of the events as he is; indeed,
it is often impossible to determine who the focalizer is. Gilbert's perspectives merge with Helen's as he incorporates her letters into his narrative—
sometimes the literal words, sometimes a paraphrase—until the reader
cannot distinguish between them. One narrative transgresses the other,
distinctions between narrators collapse. For example, in chapter 49
Gilbert Markham writes, "The next [letter] was still more distressing in
the tenor of its contents. The sufferer was fast approaching dissolution"
(449). Theoretically, he is summarizing. But suddenly we are in the midst
of a scene between Helen and Huntingdon in which present tense mixes
with past to convey immediacy: "'If I try,' said his afflicted wife, 'to divert
him from these things . . . , it is no better'.—'Worse and worse!' he groans.
. . . 'And yet he clings to me with unrelenting pertinacity'" (450). We are
then immediately immersed in dialogue:

"Stay with me, Helen. . . . But death will come. . . . Oh, if I could believe there was nothing after!"

"Don't try to believe it. . . . If you sincerely repent—"

"I can't repent; I only fear."

"You only regret the past for its consequences to yourself?"

"Just so—except that I'm sorry to have wronged you, Nell, because you're so good to me." (450)

The "afflicted wife" of Gilbert's narrative merges with the "I" of Helen's reportage and the "you" of the dialogue. The shifting persons stabilize in the "I" of the scene's final sentence, which also stabilizes the meaning: "I have said enough, I think, to convince you that I did well to go to him" (451). The narrative exchange and transgression allow for Helen's behavior here to signify duty instead of willfulness or perversity, to signify her elevation from fallen woman to paragon. Gilbert anticipates this closure: "I see that she was actuated by the best and noblest motives in what she has done" (435). He rejoices: "It was now in my power to clear her name from every foul aspersion. The Millwards and the Wilsons should see, with their own eyes, the bright sun bursting from the cloud—and they should be scorched and dazzled by its beams" (440). His story has, in fact, become her story.

Through the transgressive possibilities of the symbolic code and antithesis, Helen's desire to punish has been enacted as a wish to succor, and, through narrative exchange and transgression, the enigma surrounding her life has been seemingly penetrated, and Gilbert's resumed narrative now seemingly conveys the "truth." The meaning of Helen's behavior—as triumph rather than fall—is therefore stabilized by Gilbert's narrative. Although it may seem strange to speak of a novel that imbeds a woman's story within a man's as "giving voice" to a woman's desire, we can now appreciate the techniques through which Brontë enacts this process.

Yet a final, difficult aspect of the expression of feminine desire in this text remains unexplored: the representation of courtship and marriage between Gilbert and Helen. As we saw earlier, Gilbert's narrative at first strives to become the traditional story of a male subject's desire for the female as object. That narrative movement is thwarted when Helen becomes the speaking subject of the diary portion of the novel, but it could easily reassert itself as Gilbert regains narrative control in the novel's concluding pages. Indeed, many critics have been dissatisfied with women's novels that must, it appears, conclude with the traditional wedding bells reaffirming the status quo. To what extent, we must ask, does Brontë elude that resolution in *The Tenant of Wildfell Hall*?

Clearly we hear wedding bells, but the status quo is destabilized by certain subversive tendencies in the narrative. Huntingdon's death, which allows the meaning of Helen's behavior to be stabilized, radically destabilizes the relationship between Helen and Gilbert, which had been perforce limited to "friendship." She is now capable of becoming an object of courtship, but Huntingdon's death has altered the relationship in a more significant manner by making her a wealthy widow, as Gilbert realizes: "[T]here was a wide distinction between the rank and circumstances of Mrs. Huntingdon, the lady of Grass-dale Manor, and those of Mrs. Graham the artist, the tenant of Wildfell Hall" (454). The class distinction supersedes the gender difference and subverts the gender hierarchy. Gilbert becomes silent, submissive, passive, and acquiescent. He resolves to wait several months and then "send her a letter modestly reminding her of her former permission to write to her" (456). Only his receiving news that Helen is about to remarry goads him out of his passivity.

Again, Gilbert enacts the part of an ardent suitor, determined to save Helen from a bad marriage, but, as he takes on this more active role, we are reimmersed in the world of antitheses. He imagines himself in the role of heroic savior even as he recognizes he might pass "for a madman or an impertinent fool" (465). He goes to her, "winged by this hope, and goaded by these fears" (466). When he discovers he has been mistaken in his information, he resolves to find Helen and speak to her. He seeks her at Grass-dale Manor (Huntingdon's estate) and is impressed by the "park as beautiful now, in its wintry garb, as it could be in its summer glory" (472). He discovers that Helen has removed to Staningly, her uncle's estate, and that she has become even more remote from him through inheriting this property as well. He now feels himself to be indeed on a madman's or fool's errand and resolves to return home without seeing Helen. Their fortuitous encounter leaves him silent and forces upon her the role of suitor. She must propose to him and so transgress the boundaries of the masculine and feminine. She plucks a winter rose—a paradoxism particularly within a literary economy that metaphorically aligns the rose with youth and innocence, not with age and experience—and says, "This rose is not so fragrant as a summer flower, but it has stood through hardships none of *them* could bear. . . . It is still fresh and blooming as a flower can be, with the cold snow even now on its petals—Will you have it?" (484). The paradoxism of a winter rose, the transgression of customary antithesis, prepares for the paradoxism of the assertive woman expressing feminine desire.

In addition, although Gilbert is narrating, Helen is the focalizer of the scene. Gilbert, here a very diffident suitor, hesitates to understand the meaning of the rose, and Helen snatches it back. Finally she is forced to explain, "The rose I gave you was an emblem of my heart," but he is so backward that he must ask, "Would you give me your hand too, if I asked it?" (485). Though he still worries, "But if you *should* repent!" she utters definitive words, "It would be your fault. . . . I never shall, unless you bitterly disappoint me" (486). She has focalized the meaning of this event. Her wishes dominate; he is *subject to* her desire, and he is the *object of* her desire.

At the same time that Helen expresses her desire, she closes off the meaning of this story and proleptically concludes all subsequent ones; if she repents, it will be his fault. Gilbert writes his story as her story. She has been defined—and now predefines herself—as the paragon, an exemplar among women. Whereas the angel could only fall in the previous narrative controlled by Victorian ideology, here only Gilbert can fall. However, a tension underlies this resolution. Because the expression of feminine desire depends on transgression and exchange, the stabilization of the narrative in closure seems simultaneously to close off the space for that expression. Not surprisingly, Brontë destabilizes her conclusion by focusing on exchange: Gilbert exchanges the final installment of his narrative with Halford, and he simultaneously anticipates the exchange of Halford's visit.

It is appropriate in a world of antitheses and in the context of their transgression that the ending of the narrative should be just such an advent. Gilbert writes, "We are just now looking forward to the advent of you and Rose, for the time of your annual visit draws nigh, when you must leave your dusty, smoky, noisy, toiling, striving city for a season of invigorating relaxation and social retirement with us" (490). The implied antithesis of country and city gives way to the explicit paradoxisms of "invigorating relaxation" and "social retirement" in the last line of the novel. And "this passage through the world of Antithesis," by keeping open the possibility for transgression, also keeps open a possible space for feminine desire (Barthes 27). If this seems a fragile and tentative resolution—one threatening to reassert the status quo—it is also a radically important one in refusing to postulate an essential female desire existing outside of and independent of the discursive practices that construct women's lives. Further, to return to the initial dialogue between Anne's and Charlotte's novels, it is a resolution that grounds that fulfillment of desire in a less idealized evaluation of female salvatory potential and a less romantic assessment of a rake's potential for reform.

My goal in this chapter was to expand our understanding of how two writers—both women and both sharing similar circumstances as sisters—might nonetheless represent gender in narrative and gender in culture quite differently. It is not only women, of course, who felt and struggled to articulate the burden that cultural expectations placed upon them. In the next chapter on Thomas Hardy's *Jude the Obscure,* we explore the pressure to reconceive masculinity exerted by changing conceptions of femininity.

CHAPTER 3

Becoming a Man in Thomas Hardy's *Jude the Obscure*

Because Thomas Hardy's representations of women, by and large, exceed the simple stereotypes scholars initially identified as characteristic images of women, feminist critics early turned to his novels. Although those first studies opened up possibilities of a rewarding feminist approach to Hardy, recent work looks more broadly at gender, exploring the problem of masculinity as well as femininity. Poised between centuries (nineteenth and twentieth), between cultures (rural and urban), and between classes (peasantry and middling), Hardy engaged profound social dislocations in ways that disturbed the stability of gender classifications. His representation in *Jude the Obscure* of the social and material construction of masculinity and femininity reveals something that feminist and gender critics have begun exploring more fully: the extent to which patriarchal constructions of masculinity become constrictions and, when inflected by class, create contradictions for individual males. To speak of "patriarchy" in this way exposes a basic truth. Patriarchy (like the resistance to it) is not only outside but also inside, structuring language, logic, our very understanding of human subjectivity. Part of the novel's brilliance derives from Hardy's ability to represent Jude's battle with the class and gender self-constructions his culture offers him. His embattlement gives the novel its richness and generates its tragic denouement.

The novel articulates Jude's dilemma of identity largely through his conflicting responses to his cousin, Sue Bridehead. This interpretation of *Jude the Obscure* turns attention away from questions of the authenticity of Sue's character—where it has often focused[1]—and queries instead Sue's place in the construction of Jude's masculinity, her role as catalyst for the text's trenchant critique of gender and class paradigms. In an earlier article I have demonstrated that Sue as character is filtered almost entirely through Jude's perspective.[2] Thus, she is known to us through his experience and interpretations of her. I argue here that Jude increasingly embraces a relationship with his cousin as a means of self-fulfillment.[3] He seizes upon her as an answer to the difficulty of "growing up," his feeling that "He did not want to be a man" (1.2.15). Through kinship and twin-ship with Sue, Jude seeks an alternative to the frustrating constructions of his masculinity that his culture holds out.[4]

By linking issues of self-definition to cultural practices, discourses, and institutions, Linda Alcoff provides a way of thinking about a human sub-ject "constructed through a continuous process, an ongoing constant renewal based on an interaction with the world . . . [defined] as experi-ence. 'And thus [subjectivity] is produced not by external ideas, values, or material causes, but by one's personal, subjective engagement in the prac-tices, discourses, and institutions that lend significance (value, meaning, and affect) to the events of the world.' "Alcoff goes on to note that this is the process "through which one's subjectivity becomes en-gendered" (423).

We may merge this concept of subjectivity with a Bakhtinian distinc-tion between authoritatively persuasive and internally persuasive dis-courses that interact in the historical and cultural construction of a sub-ject. Often, Bakhtin explains,

> an individual's becoming, an ideological process, is characterized precisely by a sharp gap between these two categories: in one, the authoritative word (religious, political, moral; the word of a father, of adults and of teachers, etc.) that does not know internal persuasiveness, in the other internally per-suasive word that is denied all privilege, backed up by no authority at all, and is frequently not even acknowledged in society (not by public opinion, not by scholarly norms, nor by criticism), not even in the legal code. The struggle and dialogic interrelationship of these categories of ideological dis-course are what usually determine the history of an individual ideological consciousness. (342)

Bakhtin offers an important dialogical model of an individual's engage-ment with the world, the struggle between the authoritatively persuasive and the internally persuasive word. In the wide gap between the two, however, he locates idealistically the possibility of individual choice and control over one's destiny.

In contrast, I would agree with Alcoff that authoritative discourse often takes on the aspect of the internally persuasive word, if not at first then at last (Alcoff 428–33). De Lauretis explains further: "Self and identity, in other words, are always grasped and understood within particular discur-sive configurations. Consciousness, therefore, is never fixed, never attained once and for all, because discursive boundaries change with historical conditions" (8). Such a theory allows us to account for Jude's initial embrace, rejection, and final recuperation of his culture's religious, political, sexual, and moral discourses: the authoritative word of a father, of adults, of teachers. Jude's longing for Sue Bridehead is culturally embedded within this dynamic: He interprets her as that which his culture forbids. As an alternative to authoritative discourses, she embodies the internally persuasive voice.

It is a striking detail of the novel that Jude longs for Sue before he sees her, before he has even seen a picture of her. Why? Sue is introduced early in the novel in Aunt Drusilla's comments to a neighbor overheard by Jude. She links her two foster children through their love of books—"His cousin Sue is just the same" (1.2.9). Yet, she also contrasts Sue, a "tomboy," to Jude, a "poor useless boy," who has the sensibility and frame of a girl. Slender and small, Jude weeps easily and feels pain keenly: "[H]e was a boy who could not himself bear to hurt anything," a tendency the narrator terms, only half-ironically, a "weakness of character" (1.2.13). Jude feels the assaults of his life so sharply that he wishes "he could only prevent himself growing up! He did not want to be a man" (1.2.15). Jude's desire to evade the constraints of manhood leads him to posit an alternative that he reifies in the character at once like and unlike him, his cousin, Sue.[5]

The problem of becoming a man and the prohibition of Sue Bridehead are linked in Jude's mind by the early events at Marygreen and Aunt Drusilla's comments on the tragic issue of Fawley marriages. If marriage is fatal to one Fawley, the same blood flowing through two linked individuals must culminate in tragedy. Sue is therefore forbidden to Jude. Hardy encodes that prohibition as a function of fate or nature. Aunt Drusilla warns, "Jude, my child, don't *you* ever marry. Tisn't for the Fawleys to take that step any more" (1.2.9). Hardy himself defined his concern in the novel as "the tragic issues of two bad marriages, owing in the main to a doom or curse of hereditary temperament peculiar to the family of the partners" (Purdy and Millgate 93). The idea of hereditary taint reproduces in the narrator's attitudes the same conflicts that doom Jude. Such fatalistic discourse disguises the extent to which actual institutions coerce and thwart individuals, a process traced throughout the novel, which contemporaneous critics rightly recognized as a trenchant attack on authoritarian social practices and institutions.

That attack begins in the early events of the novel, when Jude is hired to scare away the rooks come to peck the grain in Farmer Troutham's field.

"His heart grew sympathetic with the birds' thwarted desires" (1.2.11), and he lets them feed until surprised by his angry employer, who beats him. That beating, which chastens desire, initiates Jude's reluctance to become a man, at least a man fashioned after the class models most readily available to him.

In the process of formulating his identity, Jude fastens on Christminster and becoming a "university graduate," "the necessary hallmark of a man who wants to do anything in teaching" (1.1.4). Both are associated with Mr. Phillotson, his early model, and both are utterly distinguished from his current life, substituting as they do a middle-class for a lower-class model of manhood. Ironically, his aunt puts the idea in his head that such an occupation might suit her "poor boy." After Troutham fires Jude, she complains: "Jude, Jude, why didstn't go off with that schoolmaster of thine to Christminster or somewhere?" (1.2.14). He reverently anticipates that "Christminster shall be my Alma Mater; and I'll be her beloved son, in whom she shall be well pleased" (1.6.41). Although the Latin makes the school his mother, in fact, by entering Christminster, Jude would embrace an established patriarchal tradition, a fact underscored in the Biblical passage that Jude's rhetoric echoes: "This is my beloved Son, in whom I am well pleased" (Matthew 3:17).

Hardy frames the larger issue of Jude's struggle with social codes by stressing his desire to learn the languages of the past. Jude will master Latin and Greek with the goal of ultimately being authorized to speak as an educated, middle-class man. Latin, in particular, holds power over him even before he knows anything about it except its ascribed value. His longing for that authority culminates in a fanciful idea of Christminster as a "new Jerusalem" (1.3.20) and as a "mistress" (1.3.22) who is beckoning him to his fulfillment. The intensity with which Jude applies himself to these dead languages reveals their power, which is not simply the authoritatively persuasive word of his "fathers" and of the past, but quickly becomes an internally persuasive word guiding Jude's first major struggle toward self-definition. His ability to understand and to use Latin will determine his behavior at later moments of crisis.

Until he is nineteen, Jude's sexual impulses are held completely in abeyance by his infatuation for the scholastic life. But his encounter with Arabella Donn temporarily displaces the authority of intellectual discourse with another ideology. Generally, Jude's distraction has been interpreted as a capitulation to his natural sexual instincts, what the narrator characterizes as "The unvoiced call of woman to man, which . . . held

Jude to the spot against his intention—almost against his will" (1.6.44). But sexual desire is not, in fact, what traps Jude. Notably, he is never the sexual aggressor with Arabella; she sees all his advances as "rather mild!" (1.7.52), and she has to plot rather cleverly to bring him to the point.

Two cultural paradigms of masculinity motivate Jude's divided drives. The first dictates that a "natural" man will find the stimulus of a proximate woman sufficient to arouse strong sexual desire, and it cuts across classes. The second involves the rhetoric of chivalric or honorable love and courtship and belongs more properly to the middle and upper classes. According to the first essentialist discourse, men are sexually different from women.[6] Even Phillotson, a middle-aged, staid scholar, can consummate and reconsummate his marriage with a rigid and unresponsive Sue Bridehead. He, after all, is a "man." Thus, although the rhetoric of the novel presents Jude's weakness for women as a fault, it also insists on that weakness or susceptibility as important evidence of manliness. When Jude fails to live up to other discursive formulations of his masculinity, this one never fails him, as we shall discover in the crucial final scenes of the novel.

Surprisingly, this rhetoric of manliness is not undercut by the behavior of Arabella Donn, who is always equally ready to engage in sexual relations. We may attribute that curious gap to the presence of the second authoritative discourse we have identified. When Jude becomes sexually involved with Arabella, he simultaneously becomes entangled in another discourse of manliness whose hallmark is romance, chivalry, and honor: "It was better to love a woman than to be a graduate, or a parson; ay, or a pope!" (1.7.53). These two discourses cooperate to construct the "gentleman," a middle-class ideal. Notably, Phillotson is as bound by the second discourse as Jude; it initially determines his decision to let Sue leave him to go to Jude. He justifies his decision to Gillingham in the following way: "I don't think you are in a position to give an opinion. I have been that man, and it makes all the difference in the world, if one has any manliness or chivalry in him" (4.4.278).

Jude's susceptibility to the chivalric code of helpless women and protective and honorable men allows Arabella to use her claim of pregnancy to trap him into marriage. In spite of the fact that Jude knows too well "that Arabella was not worth a great deal as a specimen of womankind," "he was ready to abide by what he had said, and take the consequences" and "save [her] ready or no" (1.9.65, 70). His susceptibility to this discourse—a function of his middle-class aspirations—distinguishes Jude's "finer" aspirations and sensibilities from the "peasant cynicism" of country women such as Arabella and Aunt Drusilla. According to their discourse, he is a "simple fool" (1.9.65) and "poor silly fellow" (1.9.66). When Arabella's plot is revealed, Jude vaguely ponders not his own folly but "something wrong in a social ritual" (1.9.70). In fact, Jude's construction of manliness betrays him because he applies a middle-class ethic to Arabella's classic peasant ruse.

After Jude should have learned the bankruptcy of this patriarchal code of male honor and female victims—in its inapplicability to his relationship with Arabella, where he is the defenseless innocent and she the practiced seducer—it seems inexplicably naive of him to persist in it. Yet such persistence provides another example of the ways in which authoritative discourses becomes internally persuasive. Indeed, Jude clings to such constructions both because they define him as middle class and because they define him as masculine (not simply as male). Jude learns from Arabella not to question the adequacy of such formulations but only to "feel dissatisfied with himself as a man at what he had done" (1.10.76).

Such class and gender constructions of his masculinity come to seem essential to Jude's identity. When Arabella and Jude separate at her instigation, Jude returns to his dream of education in Christminster, motivated by another pair of self-images. First, he reaffirms his dream of modeling his manhood and embourgeoisement on those of the schoolteacher, Phillotson. In addition, he pursues an elusive superiority and gender neutrality figured by his middle-class cousin, Sue Bridehead, whom he has seen only in a photograph. The narrator explains this new motive as "more nearly related to the emotional side of him than to the intellectual, as is often the case with young men." It really is surprising that Jude should be led to Christminster by a photograph, especially after his disastrous marriage. But we accept the motive, I believe, because we recognize that Sue offers an alternative version of his problematic self. She is like Jude, after all, also "of the inimical branch of the family" (2.1.90).

Entering Christminster at evening, Jude immediately feels himself in the presence of "those other sons of the place" (2.1.93), a kind of patrillineage that seems to promise accommodation for a humble laborer. But in the morning, "he found that the colleges had treacherously changed their sympathetic countenances. . . . The spirits of the great men had disappeared" (2.2.97). Although Jude is momentarily impressed by the dignity of manual labor, what the narrator calls a "true illumination"—that the "stone yard was a centre of effort as worthy as that dignified by the name of scholarly study within the noblest of colleges"—he soon loses this impression "under the stress of his old idea" (2.2.98). Ironically, this discourse of manual labor's dignity stems from the middle-class intellectual elite, and the very condescension implicit in the perspective undermines its validity. So the narrator reproduces in his own rhetoric the conflicts that will doom Jude. Because Jude will *be* a manual laborer denied access to scholarly pursuits, the gap opened up will lead him increasingly to Sue as an authentic alternative. Not surprisingly, then, no sooner is Jude aware of the gap between his aspirations and his pursuits than his passion for Sue intensifies. He insists his aunt send his cousin's portrait, "kissed it—he did not know why—and felt more at home. . . . It was . . . the one thing uniting him to the emotions of the living city" (2.2.99).

This extraordinary scene of alienation and "at homeness" makes Sue pivotal to the construction of Jude's identity. Jude's claim of blood and emotional kinship (she "belongs" to him) suggests that his investment in her is deeply tied to his gender identity (2.2.103). Before meeting her, Jude has already internalized Sue's being as essential to his own subjecthood, a process intensified by his aunt's prohibition that "he was not to bring disturbance into the family by going to see the girl" (2.2.99). Sue represents what is in him but also what he is not to seek in himself, which is here coded as the feminine. His desire to discover that alternative, of course, results from his frustrations with both lower-class social definitions of manhood and the conflicts introduced by middle-class codes. When he first locates Sue, he "recognized in the accents certain qualities of *his own voice*" (2.2.103) [my emphasis]. Later Jude sees Sue, dressed in his clothes, as "a slim and fragile being masquerading as himself on a Sunday" (3.3.173). He affirms, "You are just like me at heart!" (4.1.243). Phillotson corroborates the "extraordinary sympathy, or similarity, between the pair. . . . They seem to be one person split in two!" (4.4.276). Jude appropriates Sue to ground his floundering self in her "social and spiritual possibilities" (2.3.107).

Jude alternates between reflections on Sue as an "ideality" or a "divinity"—totally divorced from the coarse Arabella—and sexual longings for her. The tension in Jude's view has often been interpreted as stemming from Sue's "inconsistency"—her waxing hot and cold, her frigidity coupled with her desire for attention. But this approach to her character as a charming neurotic tends to ignore her fictional, cultural, and tendentious construction. I propose instead that the tension within the narrator's depiction of Sue reflects Jude's complex investment in her, which also causes him to hide from her his marriage to Arabella.

The urgent need Jude feels for Sue stems from his increasingly precarious sense of masculine identity and social significance. Comparing Christminster's "town life" to its "gown life" (2.6.139), he characterizes the former as the "real Christminster life" (2.7.141). The text implies that, if Jude were not possessed by "the modern vice of unrest" (2.2.98), not a "paltry victim of the spirit of mental and social restlessness" (6.1.393–94), he might be able to have a more authentic existence, that is, one grounded in a secure sense of who and what he is. At such moments, the narrator seems implicated in the same ideological illusions and conflicts that condemn Jude. The idea of an authentic existence is problematic in the text. Thus, Jude flounders among social markers for masculine identity and increasingly turns to Sue as the source of his meaning, finally concluding "with Sue as companion he could have renounced his ambitions with a smile" (2.6.137). Of course, Jude is naive to believe he can easily renounce his ambitions; they are already too important to his self-concept, as we shall see.

In the novel's first half, Jude progresses from would-be intellectual, to honorable young husband (Marygreen), to would-be intellectual again (Christminster), to would-be ecclesiastic (Melchester)—each stage dominated by a particular authoritative discourse that promises to make a man of him. All the while he keeps in reserve his dream of Sue as a means to construct a self outside unsatisfactory patriarchal models: "To keep Sue Bridehead near him was now a desire which operated without regard of consequences" (2.4.121). Only the force of his need explains why Jude cannot tell Sue of his marriage to Arabella and must instead project his failure and secretiveness onto her as her inconsistency. When he finally and belatedly informs her and lamely excuses himself—"It seemed cruel to tell it"—she justly rebukes him, "To yourself, Jude. So it was better to be cruel to me!" (3.6.198).

When Jude finally reveals his marriage to Arabella, he also begins to generalize about Sue as a "woman." Such generalizations characterize the two points in the narrative when Jude must defend himself against separation from Sue, first here and then at the end of the novel. Previously Sue has been represented in a more gender-neutral way, as a "tomboy" who joins boys in their exploits or as a "comrade" with a "curious unconsciousness of gender" (3.4.179) who mixes with men "almost as one of their own sex" (3.4.177). Impelled to defend his own sexuality, Jude now stresses Sue's need to exercise "those narrow womanly humours on impulse that were necessary to give her sex" (3.6.200). Sue both is and is not a typical woman depending on Jude's psychosocial investment in her. At those points when he fears he will lose her, he tends to brand her typical of her sex to distance himself from his need for her. He repeats this distancing act at Susanna's marriage to Phillotson: "Women were different from men in such matters. Was it that they were, instead of more sensitive, as reported, more callous and less romantic?" (3.7.209).

Sue's self-generalizations as woman have a somewhat different textual function. She says, for example, in reference to herself, "some women's love of being loved is insatiable" (4.1.245). Such comments reinforce Jude's characterizations of Sue as an asexual "spirit," a "disembodied creature," a "dear, sweet, tantalizing phantom—hardly flesh at all" (4.5.294). The spiritualization preserves her as the endlessly desired object, a Shelleyan Epipsyche. The text demands, above all, "the elusiveness of her curious double nature" (4.2.251).

The last half of the novel focuses the tension between Jude's need to be the man his culture demands and his desire to locate a more fulfilling existence outside custom and convention. When Jude argues his similarity to his cousin—"for you are just like me at heart"—he demurs, "But not at head." And when he insists, "we are both alike," she corrects him, "Not in our thoughts" (4.1.243). Their disagreement arises because Sue's attractiveness disrupts but cannot displace the categories of masculinity Jude has already internalized. He is drawn in two directions because he can never fully abandon the categories of thought he has imbibed from his culture.

Constructed as an outsider to patriarchal culture, Sue can articulate social tensions that Jude can then increasingly recognize. She argues, "the social moulds civilization fits us into have no more relation to our actual shapes than the conventional shapes of the constellations have to the real star-patterns" (4.1.246–47). When Sue asks Jude, hypothetically, whether a woman who feels repugnance for her husband ought "to try to overcome her pruderies," he responds in contradictory ways, "speaking as an order-loving man . . . I should say yes. Speaking from experience and unbiased nature, I should say no" (4.2.252). Shortly thereafter, under pressure of his love for Sue, Jude announces, "my doctrines and I begin to part company" (4.2.258). After he passionately kisses Sue, Jude realizes that "he was as unfit obviously by nature, as he had been by social position, to fill the part of a propounder of accredited dogma." Yet barred by Sue's marriage to Phillotson and his own marriage to Arabella, Jude has recourse to the category of "woman" to explain his difficulties: "Strange that his first aspiration—toward academic proficiency—had been checked by a woman, and that his second aspiration—toward apostle-ship—had also been checked by a woman. 'Is it,' he said, 'that women are to blame?'"(4.3.261).

The conclusion, "women are to blame," lodges Jude's reasoning within a traditional framework that takes him back to the Garden of Eden, Genesis, and Eve's temptation and fall. Although Jude should reject a discourse so inadequate to his experience, instead he reauthorizes its tenets on women. Such constructions are so essential to his subjectivity that they cannot be completely abandoned. Indeed, it is important to Jude that "he might go on *believing* as before but he *professed* nothing" (4.3.262, my emphasis).

The role of women as temptresses in this narrative corresponds to an ideology of masculinity that suggests sex is, for a man, a snare that leads first to entrapment, then disillusionment, and even damnation. As we have seen, a deep ideological subtext of the novel argues that a "man" is inherently disposed toward sexual relations and will find women a lure to physical intimacy. The fact that sexual familiarity may culminate in contempt does not prevent his being ready to behave sexually on the next encounter. A companion ideology stipulates that, whatever his feelings, a "gentle-man" will then behave honorably toward the "victimized" woman. The logic of these interlocking ideologies supports Jude's sexual relations with Arabella, both initially and following a chance encounter after several years' separation.

Jude's embrace of the gentlemanly ethic allows the lower-class Arabella repeatedly to exploit him. Similarly, when Arabella later appeals to Jude to follow her to her hotel to hear her story, and Sue objects, Jude argues: "I shall certainly give her something, and hear what it is she is so anxious to tell me; no man could do less!" (5.2.318). Arabella pronounces, "Never such a tender fool as Jude is if a woman seems in trouble" (5.2.324).

All of Jude's justifications of his behavior produce essentialist views of men and women. When Sue asks, "Why should you take such trouble for a woman who has served you so badly?" he responds, "But, Sue, she's a woman, and I once cared for her; and one [a man] can't be a brute in such circumstances" (5.2.319). In response to Sue's accusation that his behavior is "gross," Jude replies, "You don't understand me either—women never do!" (4.5.293). By generalizing from "you"—Sue—to "women,"

Jude also implicitly generalizes from "me"—Jude—to "men." Women do not understand men or male sexuality.

Jude's determination to fulfill a "man's" obligations to Arabella exerts a sexual coercion on Sue, who precipitously agrees to sleep with Jude to erase Arabella's claims on him. When Sue capitulates, Jude transfers to her his sexual allegiance and chivalric code. Arabella is no longer "a woman" but her clever self: "You haven't the least idea how Arabella is able to shift for herself" (5.2.322).

The sexual possession of Sue marks a crux in the novel and in Jude's self-construction. It permits him to define his male nature as one given to sensual indulgence—wine, women, and blasphemy. But he also aspires to a value outside a carnal construction of his masculinity that he locates in his relations with Sue. He tells her: "All that's best and noblest in me loves you, and your freedom from everything that's gross has elevated me, and enabled me to do what I should never have dreamt myself capable of. Or *any man,* a year or two ago" (5.2.320, my emphasis). The kinship Jude feels for this female self allows him to move beyond the patriarchal imprimatur, defining an identity he had not believed accessible to himself or any man. In the "nomadic" phase of their life together, Jude "was mentally approaching the position which Sue had occupied when he first met her" (5.7.373).

Their kinship will be undermined by the cultural codes that define Jude's masculinity. Although Jude is represented as sharing Sue's anxiety about the constraints of marriage, his behavior is simultaneously shaped by Biblical injunctions on manhood: "For what man is he that hath betrothed a wife and hath not taken her?" (5.4.338). And although the couple is exquisitely happy in their life together—returned, in Sue's words, to "Greek joyousness" (5.5.358)—Jude reveals his continuing attraction to Christminster in the model of Cardinal College he and Sue have made for the Wessex Agricultural Show. Despite the narrator's insistence on Jude's independence of thought, he chooses to bake "Christminster cakes" when he is pressed for employment after his illness. Arabella neatly pinpoints his continuing obsession and slavery to his former ideals: "Still harping on Christminster—even in his cakes. . . . Just like Jude. A ruling passion." Sue admits: "Of course Christminster is a sort of fixed vision with him, which I suppose he'll never be cured of believing in. He still thinks it a great centre of high and fearless thought, instead of what it is, a nest of commonplace schoolmasters whose characteristic is timid obsequiousness to tradition" (5.7.376).

Arabella's accidental meeting with Phillotson, immediately following
her rencontre with Sue, sets the stage for the series of reversals or "returns"
that conclude the novel. Arabella's crude invocation of Old Testament law
and learning as a model for contemporary behavior prepares us for the way
in which Jude, as well as Phillotson, will be drawn back to the authority
and consequence held out to them as men in a patriarchal society. Arabella
states: "There's nothing like bondage and a stone-deaf taskmaster for tam-
ing us women. Besides, you've got the laws on your side. Moses knew. . . .
'Then shall the man be guiltless; but the woman shall bear her iniquity'"
(5.8.384). Arabella's addendum—"Damn rough on us women; but we
must grin and put up wi' it!"—comfortably accepts a damaging gender
bifurcation that Jude and even Phillotson have struggled to overcome in
their response to Sue Bridehead. When Sue questions, "Why should you
care so much for Christminster?" Jude replies: "I can't help it. I love the
place. . . . it is the centre of the universe to me, because of my early dream.
. . . I should like to go back to live there—perhaps to die there!" (5.8.386).
Part 5 culminates with the realization of his dream to return there; Part 6
culminates with the realization of his dream to die there.

We, too, ask Sue's questions: Why does Jude suddenly develop a passionate desire to return to Christminster for this Remembrance Day, and
why does he return in a way so entirely forgetful of Sue and his children?
Then, why does Jude persist in his resolve to seek work in Christminster
after it has become the scene of his grotesque tragedy and can serve only
as a reminder of that tragedy? In fact, the text occludes these questions
and shifts focus to Sue Bridehead's intellectual, sexual, and emotional
degradation. But there are significant ideological implications in that textual strategy. These breaks and shifts reveal their inner logic if we keep our
eye on Jude's alternating evasion and pursuit of manhood.

Jude's return to Christminster spells a rejection of Sue and a reembrace
of the patriarchal discourse that originally attracted him. Whereas on one
level it seems absurd to say that Jude has rejected Sue since he pleads for
her emotional and physical return to him, the subtext of the novel argues
differently. By returning to Christminster, Jude privileges a hierarchic
order in opposition to his more egalitarian relationship with Sue. Indeed,
by delaying the search for housing, he shifts the burden of their relationship onto Sue, who bears the visible evidence of their three children and
her pregnancy while he again becomes, in effect, the unencumbered
novice who first entered the city several years earlier. When he again seeks
lodging in his old quarter, Beersheba, he continues to replicate his earlier

patterns. The unbearable poignancy of the novel's last section derives not only from the representation of Sue's collapse but also from the painful tension between Jude's embrace and rejection of Sue, a rejection that demands the collapse of her textual function as a significant alternative.

Jude longs for the spirit of the law but is drawn to the letter as primary ground of his identity. He finally seeks an authority to define the meaning of his life, and he must do that from within the system, from a position that validates the system and its judgments of him as a failed man who has "missed everything." This final need for authority explains Jude's return to Christminster. Jude wants that intellectual milieu to frame the tragic limitation of his manhood. If, as Sue says, Christminster is only a "nest of commonplace schoolmasters," then Jude's life is a relative success. To give his life the tragic cast he favors, he must reauthorize Christminster. Relationship with Sue originally provided a focal point for a critique of authoritative discourse. Now that relationship, in its domestic and quotidian aspects, cuts away the ground of meaning necessary to Jude's "tragedy." The triumphant tragedy of Jude's life is apparent only when inscribed within the dominant, authoritative discourse of Christminster. Under that authority he can echo Shakespeare's *Romeo and Juliet* in summarizing his life: "However, it was my poverty and not my will that consented to be beaten. It takes two or three generations to do what I tried to do in one" (6.1.393).

The narrative sequence supports a reading of Jude's return to Christminster as a rejection of Sue Bridehead. First, Jude chooses to return on Remembrance Day, when the city is teeming with visitors. Upon arrival he initially insists that "the first thing is lodgings," but he quickly abandons that goal in his desire to hurry to the procession, ignoring Sue's demurral: "Oughtn't we to get a house over our heads first?" Although "his soul seemed full of the anniversary," Jude announces that Remembrance Day is really "Humiliation Day for me!" a "lesson in presumption," an image of his own "failure" (6.1.390). Of course, to see his failure is also to see the possibility of success, to see that he might have become "a son of the University." The Alma Mater as paterfamilias. As it begins to rain and "Sue again wished not to stay," Jude grows more enthusiastic as he rediscovers old friends and reevaluates his life. He says he is "in a chaos of principles—groping in the dark—acting by instinct and not after example" (6.1.394), thereby grounding his identity in the context of Christminster and its definitions of success. Through that prism he reexamines his life, granting to Christminster authority to write his "romance," the middle-class tragic romance of the common man: "I'm an outsider to the end of my days!" (6.1.396).

Throughout the entire day, through thunderstorms and drenchings, Jude ignores his pale, reluctant wife and his several children to bask once more in the reflected glory of Christminster, "to catch a few words of the Latin," and so, in spirit, to join the fraternity that has otherwise excluded him. He may tell Sue that "I'll never care any more about the infernal cursed place," but as they belatedly begin to search for lodgings, Jude is drawn to "Mildew Lane," close to the back of a college, a spot he finds "irresistible" and Sue "not so fascinating" (6.1.396). She is finally housed outside Sarcophagus and Rubric Colleges, Hardy's symbolically appropriate names, and she contemplates "the strange operation of a simple-minded man's ruling passion, that it should have led Jude, who loved her and the children so tenderly, to place them here in this depressing purlieu, because he was still haunted by his dream" (6.2.401). Jude's pursuit of his "dream" has left Sue and the children terribly exposed, and the events culminate in Father Time's suicide and murder of the other two children. Sue claims responsibility for these tragic events, and neither the narrator nor Jude disputes her interpretation, yet responsibility really belongs to Jude, who, in returning to Christminster, rejected Sue and his children for his old "dream."

Sue now takes on the narrative function of justifying Jude: "My poor Jude—how you've missed everything!—you more than I, for I did get you! To think you should know that [the chorus of the *Agamemnon*] by your unassisted reading, and yet be in poverty and despair!" (6.2.409). There is nothing in the narrative that contradicts Sue's assessment. Thus the text can endorse the position that Jude "missed everything" whereas Sue, in getting Jude, apparently "got" what she wanted. It is ironic that she, who was supposed to be what he wanted, now stands debased, as the coin he received for his labors, an emblem of what riches he has missed.

It is a further irony that the only blame Jude accepts is for "seducing" Sue, a grotesque reinterpretation of his desire for her. He claims, "I have seemed to myself lately . . . to belong to that vast band of men shunned by the virtuous—the men called seducers. . . . Yes, Sue—that's what I am. I seduced you. . . . You were a distinct type—a refined creature, intended by Nature to be left intact" (6.3.414). The idea of Jude as seducer presents an absurd reduction of their complex relationship with its twin fulfillments of independence and happiness. But a reconstruction of the scenario with himself as seducer serves the function of reconstructing yet another social aspect of Jude's manhood.

As Jude adopts these conventional, middle-class gender terms, he deprives Sue of any meaningful textual role outside parallel gender stereotypes, which dictate that the chaste but violated female move toward self-sacrificing, punitive, masochistic degradation. We return, once more, to the generalizations about women that were absent during the long emotional and sexual intimacy between Jude and Sue: "Is woman a thinking unit at all, or a fraction always wanting its integer?" (6.3.424). The text's positioning of comments such as this one suggests that Sue's function as desirable other, a space free from the socially coded and rigid definition of manhood, has been exhausted or used up. In order for Jude to reclaim the construction of his manhood implicit first in Christminster and then in his relationship with Arabella, Sue must be reinterpreted as merely a pathetic woman whose mind has become unhinged. Hence, her "inconsistency."

This strict sexual bifurcation figures in the novel's closing rhetoric. Sue says to Jude, "Your wickedness was only the natural man's desire to possess the woman" (6.3.426). And, on Sue's return, Phillotson says ominously, "I know woman better now" (6.5.442). Sue accounts for her own role in the relationship by admitting to an "inborn craving which undermines some women's morals . . . the craving to attract and captivate, regardless of the injury it may do the man" (6.3.426).

Jude returns to the twin evils of his life, his "two Arch Enemies . . . my weakness for womankind and my impulse to strong liquor" (6.3.421). He embraces in his Christminster dreams and the cruel reality of marriage to Arabella the same constricting construction of his manhood that figured prominently in the opening pages of the novel. Although drunk, Jude calls up the established discourse of manliness to justify remarrying Arabella: "I'd marry the W— of Babylon rather than do anything dishonourable. . . . marry her I will, so help me God! . . . I am not a man who wants to save himself at the expense of the weaker among us!" (6.7.461–62). By sacrificing himself to the sham of this "meretricious contract with Arabella," Jude, of course, preserves a definition of manhood essential to his identity.

The honor, the rectitude, the righteousness, and the learning that Jude claims as the hallmarks of his middle-class manhood allow him to die with the words of Job on his lips: "Let the day perish wherein I was born, and the night in which it was said, There is a man child conceived" (6.11.488). Such an invocation accords well with the other discourses Jude has previously embraced.

In *Jude the Obscure,* Hardy has given us a novel in which the authoritatively persuasive word ultimately becomes the internally persuasive one in the construction of one man's subjectivity. In the process, Hardy has revealed masculinity as a cultural and social class construct, one that coerces and limits individuals even as it holds out the irresistible promise of conferring definitive meaning on their lives. In Jude's longing for Sue, Hardy has made us feel the poignant desire for a self free from such coercive definitions, the need for some more flexible way to confront the problem of "growing up . . . to be a man," for some way to feel satisfied with himself as a man (1.2.15). In Sue's emotional and intellectual collapse, which proleptically justifies Jude's return to the Christminster way, he has made us feel the virtual impossibility of anyone defining him- or herself in opposition to society's dominant culture. Jude's death and Sue's degradation, the events concluding the novel, arrest but do not resolve the text's testing of discursive formulations of gender paradigms. The anticipated unfolding of a subject proves to be an involution, a collapse inward resisted only by social practices and discourses that mock the idea of individual self-determination and locate self-fulfillment in death.

Early in her relationship with Jude, Sue Bridehead claims that "We are a little beforehand, that's all" (5.4.345). In fact, she is only partly right; Jude and Sue are constructed by the very terms they seek to transcend. The lingering sadness of this novel lies in its apprehension of the ways destructive cultural self-constructions ultimately reach out to claim them, the ways, indeed, they are always already within, crucial to the formation and development of individual subjecthood and therefore perilous to reject. This modern understanding of the problematic subject and the material basis for subjectivity allows Hardy to give us a trenchant interrogation of the cultural construction of gender paradigms and their often contradictory inflections by class. It also allows him to generate a new form of tragic irony in the disparity between what we can understand and aspire to and what we can ultimately become—undermined, as we are, from within. Hardy's depiction of this ineluctable dilemma of identity gives him a distinctive place in the Victorian canon and suggests significant links with a modern sensibility that has been acknowledged in his poetry but not so readily in his novels. In this regard we may recognize Hardy as both the most modern of Victorians and, in the poignancy of his final novel, the most Victorian of moderns.

The first three analytical chapters of this book have concentrated on reading texts and illuminating the subtle and complex ways in which gender enters into narrative and shapes the tale that is told. The next chapter on Wilkie Collins and Mary Elizabeth Braddon continues with that close reading but also concentrates greater attention on the narratives a culture tells about itself. Specifically, I focus on how an abstraction such as space also bears the imprint of gendered subjectivities. Further, an expansion to space further illuminates a question only partially answered in this chapter: that is, why Jude remains fatally attracted to Christminster. This is the place that he associates with his own humiliation, yet he is determined to risk his family's and his own destruction to return. "Why should you care so much for Christminster?" Sue asks Jude. "Christminster cares nothing for you, poor dear!" (254). In Jude's travels and the novel's movement expressed in the titles given to its parts—at Marygreen, at Christminster, at Melchester, at Shaston, at Aldbrickham and Elsewhere, and at Christminster Again—we discover a geopolitical reality of disenfranchisement that finds its bitter echo in Father Time's final assessment: "It would be better to be out o' the world than in it, wouldn't it?" (263). In short, at the same time that Hardy's novel beautifully delineates how gender definitions are inflected by class, its structure is revealing space as crucially shaped by both gender and class, that is, representing space as contested, political, and socially produced.

CHAPTER 4

Gendered Geographies:
The Lady and the Country House in Wilkie Collins's *Woman in White* and Mary Elizabeth Braddon's *Lady Audley's Secret*

In the late eighteenth and early nineteenth centuries, a new series of enclosure acts allowed landowners progressively to annex public lands, the commons, producing a proportionately small number of wealthy country estate owners and a larger number of the landless and disinherited. In this chapter, I explore the relationship between the enclosure of lands and the enclosure of bodies reflected in descriptions of the country houses, which are architectural, domestic sanctuaries that function as visible signs of the social order. In the process of enclosure, upper-middle-class women were positioned unevenly: on the one hand, they enjoyed certain class and gender privileges; on the other, as symbols of those privileges, they found themselves confined and circumscribed by their demands. Whereas domestic novels governed by the conventions of realism often obscure the resulting tensions, the very sensationalism of sensation fiction allowed it to expose not only the conflicting passions of middle-class women but the dark side of domesticity itself. And Wilkie Collin's *Woman in White* and Mary Elizabeth Braddon's pioneering sensation novel, *Lady Audley's Secret,* took the lead in foregrounding this dialectic between freedom and enclosure, privilege and confinement that structures the lives of upper-middle-class women.

Although Wilkie Collins's *Woman in White* (1860) preceded and has generally been credited with influencing Braddon's 1862 *Lady Audley's Secret,* the relationship between them cannot be reduced to simple influence on the one hand and borrowing on the other. In the intertextual relationship between these two sensation novels, we discover patterns similar to those we found governing Charlotte Brontë's rewriting of W. M.

Thackeray. In this case, Braddon took key plot elements from Collins, such as the conflated identities of two women, one living and one dead, but she reconceived both characters and events to produce a more morally ambiguous tale than Collins's. And although Braddon ostensibly produced the conventional conclusion of evil punished at the end of her story, the representation of Lady Audley complicates a traditional reading of that conclusion. Indeed, in *Lady Audley's Secret* Braddon carried out a significant rewriting of Collins's novel, one that allowed her to solidify interest in this new subgenre while subtly expanding and redirecting its focus to illuminate further the persistently troubling links between country house and madhouse and to expose the connections between the ideal upper-middle-class lady and childishness associated, on the one hand, with asexuality and, on the other, with madness.

Collins's novel illuminated for Braddon the suggestive connection between country house and asylum. *The Woman in White* focuses on the attempts of an impoverished baronet, Sir Percival Glyde, to procure a wealthy wife in Laurie Fairlie and then to appropriate her fortune to his own uses by substituting her identity for that of a woman, Anne Catherick, for many years confined to an asylum and, therefore, certified as "mad." Anne, who closely resembles Laura, suffers from a heart condition, and her escape, recapture, and timely death allow the baronet and his ally, Count Fosco, to replace her with Laura, announce Laura's death, and confine the real Laura in the asylum as Anne Catherick. Although Laura's release is procured and her identity ultimately restored, she retains traces of the imbecility she has suffered as a result of her incarceration in the asylum. Collins thus foregrounds the relationship between the country house and the asylum, and he is astute about the ease with which upper-class men can confine women in both country houses and asylums.[1]

In playing on the double and conflicting meanings of asylum, Collins further exposes the way in which the country house can be a place of confinement.[2] In its positive connotations, an asylum is a sanctuary, a place of refuge from oppression, providing safety from threatening forces without. This is, in fact, the meaning that the novel first employs when Hartright reveals that his Italian friend Pesca has adopted, as "the ruling idea of his life," the belief that "he was bound to show his gratitude to the country which had afforded him an asylum and means of subsistence, by doing his utmost to turn himself into an Englishman" (3). A scant few pages later Hartright meets the woman in white, whom, he is told, has just escaped from an asylum, and he confesses to the horror, "the idea of absolute insanity which we all associate with the very name of an Asylum" (22). This is, of course, the alternative meaning of the word, associated now with confinement of those who pose a danger to the safety of others. The country house and the insane asylum, the lady and the madwoman, are syntactically and semantically linked when Hartright realizes the "ominous likeness between the fugitive from the asylum and my pupil at Limmeridge House" (51). Subsequently, when Laura is married to Sir Percival Glyde, Miriam queries him: "Am I to understand . . . that your wife's room is a prison, and that your housemaid is the gaoler who keeps it?" He responds that, "Yes; that *is* what you are to understand. . . . Take care my gaoler hasn't got double duty to do—take care your room is not a prison, too" (267). Prompted by this outrage, Miriam urges her reluctant uncle to "turn Limmeridge House into an asylum for [his] niece and her misfortunes" (316).

The country house cycles back and forth between asylum as confinement and asylum as refuge, and Laura's experiences as wife and inmate do not differ materially. In both spheres she is deprived of her freedom and wits. However, Collins's novel retreats from the implications of these connections by concluding with Laura's seemingly joyous restoration to Limmeridge House, where she and her half-sister, Miriam, serve as vessels and props for the new heir of Limmeridge. But it looks suspiciously like the old order, and, arguably, the asylum of Limmeridge House remains as much a confinement as a sanctuary.[3]

It is not only women who are imaged in terms of confinement. Collins begins his novel with the arrival of middle-class Walter Hartright at Limmeridge House, where he has been hired as a drawing master for the ladies. His inferior class status allows his employer, Philip Fairlie, to frame his position as a kind of possession. He welcomes Hartright to his employment with the words, "So glad to possess you at Limmeridge" (33), and Hartright picks up the verb when he reflects later that, "Throughout the whole of that period, Mr. Fairlie had been rejoiced to 'possess' me, but had never been well enough to see me for a second time" (96). What Hartright fails or refuses to recognize is that having bought and possessed him, Mr. Fairlie need not give him a second thought. More ominously, having possessed his nieces at Limmeridge, Mr. Fairlie sees them no more often; after all, they have nowhere else to go.

Braddon's *Lady Audley's Secret* refuses to mystify this dialectic that is obscured in the closing pages of Collins's novel.[4] Whereas Collins retreats from his initial insights, leaving them ultimately unexplored, Braddon pursues the connections through representing the subtle parallels in the position of both country house and asylum.

A brief analysis of the impact of those Enclosure Acts passed principally in the last half of the eighteenth and first quarter of the nineteenth century begins to illuminate Braddon's achievement.[5] Although enclosure had been part of the socio/political landscape of Britain since early modern England, the later acts gave a distinctive character to the landscape of Victorian England, a subject usefully addressed by Raymond Williams in *The Country and the City.* Williams illuminates the effect of concentrating "nearly a quarter of the cultivated lands" in the hands of four hundred families, in conjunction with other processes such as rack renting, on the class configuration of nineteenth-century England. Just as the appropriation of surviving open field villages and common rights put general economic pressure on small landowners and eliminated marginal lands on which lower classes could eke out an independent livelihood, so, too, that appropriation set in motion new ways of symbolizing power through possession of land, crowned by the English country house, which focalized the possession and power. Williams comments, "What had happened was not so much 'enclosure'—the method—but the more visible establishment of a long-developing system . . . a formal declaration of where the power now lay" (107). That "formal declaration" was most manifest in the country house. Williams elucidates:

> What these "great" houses do is break the scale, by an act of will corresponding to their real and systematic exploitation of others. . . . These were chosen for more than the effect from the inside out. . . . They were chosen . . . for the other effect, from the outside looking in: a visible stamping of power, of displayed wealth and command: a social disproportion which was meant to impress and overawe. (106)

Whereas Williams brilliantly illuminates the effect of enclosure on class configurations, he does not turn his lens on the way that enclosure impacted the position and representation of upper-middle-class women, who functioned centrally in the process of signifying wealth and class. And, ironically, often the owners' coffers were emptied not in developing the lands, which could have produced greater profits, but in augmenting the size and grandeur of the house, which could yield no profit.

Thus, enclosure in nineteenth-century England was as much about signifying wealth as producing it, and women played a key role in that process of signification. In Austen's *Pride and Prejudice,* written in 1813, Elizabeth Bennet recognizes that displayed wealth and command, that "social disproportion," when she views Darcy's estate for the first time and acknowledges that, "to be mistress of Pemberley might be something!" (167). Later, in responding to Jane's inquiry about when she began to love Darcy, Elizabeth laughingly punctures the social grasping after position that would lead many women to accept the man to get the estate—"I believe it must date from my first seeing his beautiful grounds at Pemberley" (258). Despite Elizabeth's self-irony or, we might say, because of her self-irony, we discover that the social motive can never be wholly discounted, even for the most disinterested young lady.

Indeed, to become mistress of an estate like Pemberley or Limmeridge House or Audley Court *is* something. But the role brings with it explicit social expectations, which are given full development in Braddon's novel. Mark Girouard's *Life in the English Country House* lays out the implications of country house life in the Victorian era. Girouard entitles his chapter on that period "The Moral House: 1830–1900," and argues that, "an essential part of the new image cultivated by both new and old families was their domesticity; they were anxious to show that their houses, however grand, were also homes and sheltered a happy family life" (270). To this end, the mistress was essential; she was the primum mobile of that self-contained world, and her values and their successful embodiment in organization and decor were on display for the world.[6] Indeed, in this regard, the country house functioned as would have Bentham's prospective Panopticon, a space in which one could be under continuous anonymous surveillance. The house metaphorically and metonymically stood for power and one's moral entitlement to that power. Because it operated most effectively through its continual visibility, it was thus open to random visitors, and even its most intimate spaces could be penetrated with impunity, as we will see. And at the center of that visible structure stood the lady of the house, whose motions were precisely regulated by etiquette practices such as morning calls, afternoon teas (instituted in the 1840s), and elaborate dinners that put her continually on display.[7]

Recent studies in the history of architecture suggest that the gendering of space and the spatializing of gender are not new. Drawing on Alberti's classic and canonical fifteenth-century treatise, *On the Art of Building in Ten Books,* Mark Wigley argues that its fifth book, "discussing the delight of 'private' houses, contains an overt reference to architecture's complicity in the exercise of patriarchal authority by defining a particular intersection between a spatial order and a system of surveillance which turns on the question of gender" (332). He continues,

Women are to be confined deep within a sequence of spaces at the greatest distance from the outside world while men are to be exposed to that outside. The house is literally understood as a mechanism for the domestication of (delicately minded and pathologically embodied) women. (332)

Wigley cites Alberti, who clarifies that, "The woman, as she remains locked up at home, should watch over things by staying at her post, by diligent care and watchfulness. The man should guard the woman, the house, and his family and country, but not by sitting still" (334). And, as Wigley notes, Alberti's text is closely following Xenophon's fifth-century treatise *Oeconomicus*. This long architectural history provides the foundation for Wigley's claim that "the house is involved in the production of the gender division it appears to merely secure," and "the role of architecture is explicitly the control of sexuality" (336). One might argue that *plus ça change, plus c'est la même chose*.

Wigley focuses his argument almost exclusively on gender questions and on the relationship of patriarchal control to household architecture. But the class implications of these architectural treatises are equally available for analysis and provide us with a model for thinking about the crucial intersections of class and gender constraints in the architecture of the English country house. With the advent of enclosure in England, domestic architecture increasingly secured class as well as gender relations, allowing a growing gentry, or upper-middle class, to define itself apart from the prosperous merchant and professional middle classes immediately beneath it and the poor, far below. It is true of class as well as gender to say that the wife "is one of the possessions whose status the house monitors and is exposed by the structure of the house she maintains. It is this exposure by a system of classification, rather a simple enclosure by walls, that entraps her" (Wigley 341). The lady of a house is trapped within interlocking systems of sexual and class management.

But the logic of class demands the visibility of even private spaces, so the lady, like the house with which she is identified, is subject to continual scrutiny. It is Braddon's astute articulation of this relationship between lady and country house that is remarkable in *Lady Audley's Secret*. Present are all the key architectural elements: enclosure securing wealth and power; the maintenance of wealth and power demanding continual visibility; continual visibility justifying the penetration of even private spaces; and private space gendered feminine so that the woman who is most protected by the architecture is also most exposed by it.

Lady Audley's Secret opens with an extensive description of Audley Court, which emphasizes exclusiveness tied to exclusion:

> It lay down in a hollow, rich with fine old timber and luxuriant pastures; and you came upon it through an avenue of limes, bordered on either side by meadows, over the high hedges of which the cattle looked inquisitively at you as you passed, wondering, perhaps, what you wanted; for there was no thoroughfare, and unless you were going to the Court, you had no business there at all. (1).

Everything about the house bespeaks enclosure. Its wall "bordered with espaliers . . . shut out the flat landscape, and circled the house and gardens with a darkening shelter," and "the principal door was squeezed into a corner of a turret at one angle of the building, as if it were in hiding from dangerous visitors, and wished to keep itself a secret" (1). Described as a "glorious old place," its glory seems to consist in the yearning which it provokes "to have done with life, and to stay there forever" (2). However, the very seclusion of the spot, which allows it to function as a sanctuary, also and ominously facilitates its function as confinement: "A noble place: inside as well as out, a noble place—a house in which you incontinently lost yourself if ever you were so rash as to attempt to penetrate its mysteries alone" (2). Braddon has picked up on the dual meanings of asylum and bodied both forth in Audley Court, at once sanctuary and confinement. The avenue that heralds the approach to the house, is "so shaded from the sun and sky, so screened from observation by the thick shelter of the overarching trees that it seemed a chosen place for secret meetings or for stolen interviews; a place in which a conspiracy might have been planned or a lover's vow registered with equal safety; and yet it was scarcely twenty paces from the house" (3). The narrator continues throughout this descriptive balance of a seclusion at once protective and ominous: "The very repose of the place grew painful from its intensity, and you felt as if a corpse must be lying somewhere within that gray and ivy-covered pile of building—so deathlike was the tranquillity of all around" (17). George Talboy's shortly thereafter echoes this description in remarking of the approaching avenue that "it ought to be an avenue in a churchyard. . . . How peacefully the dead might sleep under this somber shade!" (44).

Despite the seclusion provided by ancient trees and walls, Lady Audley's private spaces are curiously vulnerable to penetration. Audley Court provides her with little protection, as it both limits her range of motion and opens to visibility all of her activities, much like a Panopticon. Even those things that Lady Audley tries to hide from prying eyes are almost immediately exposed to view. Within the first few pages of the novel, Lady Audley's maid has invited her brutish lover to "see my lady's rooms" and offered to show him her jewels. They penetrate her jewel casket even to the secret drawer and discover sufficient evidence of her past to blackmail her during the remainder of the novel.

But it's not only her maid, with her legitimate access to her lady's chambers if not to her jewelry casket, who can penetrate those seemingly private spaces and her very identity. To avoid exposing her face to George Talboys's view, Lady Audley cleverly evades the social etiquette that demands she invite her nephew and his friend to dinner. However, she cannot prevent their illicit entry to her private chambers or keep their prying eyes from viewing her portrait. The secret passages and chambers that formerly hid suspect persons and activities from view, now lead straight to Lady Audley's exposure. Sir Michael Audley's daughter, Alicia, confides to her cousin, "if you don't mind crawling upon your hands and knees, you can see my lady's apartments, for that passage communicates with her dressing-room. She doesn't know it herself, I believe" (45). Ironically, the locks and keys, secret passages and drawers that should secure her secrets from penetration, prove no defense against the social expectation of continual and invited visibility.

What we discover is the seamless interpenetration of the house and its lady. Ironically, Phoebe does not intend to expose her mistress, and it is not Alicia's intention to expose her new step-mother; they assume, as does everyone else, that there can be nothing to expose, that both Lady Audley and Audley Court are available for public viewing, part of that economy that Williams identified in which the house and its occupants stand in for social power and moral entitlement to that power. Operating most effectively through continual visibility, the house and its lady secure the economic status quo.

More than being simply available to viewing, Lady Audley is herself decked out to invite scrutiny, her garments and jewels metonyms for class privilege, luxury, and idleness. As she plays the piano, Robert Audley lingers by her side:

He amused himself by watching her jeweled, white hands gliding softly over the keys, with the lace sleeves dropping away from her graceful, arched wrists. He looked at her pretty fingers one by one; this one glittering with a ruby heart; that encircled by an emerald serpent; and about them all a starry glitter of diamonds. From the fingers his eyes wandered to the rounded wrists: the broad, flat, gold bracelet upon her right wrist dropped over her hand, as she executed a rapid passage. She stopped abruptly to rearrange it; but before she could do so Robert Audley noticed a bruise upon her delicate skin. (59).

Because everything about her is structured to invite the gaze that secures class standing, she becomes, in spite of herself, a constantly available text as Robert sets out to penetrate the mystery of George Talboys's disappearance. His licit scrutiny allows him to discover the signs of her illicit activity.

Further, the confinement of the lady's legitimate activities within a limited sphere keeps her virtually under continual surveillance. When she will be away from home, she must declare where she is going, how long she will be absent, and when she will return. She cannot move without accounting for her whereabouts. The surveillance under which she lives in her role as lady contrasts most dramatically with the virtual invisibility of George Talboys. He enters Audley Court, departs, sets out for Liverpool with the intention of returning to Australia, and ends up in America, but his tracks are impossible for Robert Audley to trace. His very invisibility allows him to be presumed dead and therefore justifies the relentless pursuit of a highly visible Lady Audley.

There is, readers will note, a tension between the very visibility of a lady and her sexualized, because privatized, body. If we return now to Wigley's argument about gendered space, we can appreciate the significance of these interlocking systems of surveillance by following through the connections he lays out between architecture and gender. Domestic space, Wigley argues, produces "sexuality as that-which-is-private" (346), so that a "privacy within the house developed beyond the privacy of the house" (347). Hence, the logic of separate bedrooms/chambers for the master and mistress.

Indeed, one would expect a lady's chambers to be penetrable, like her body, only by the master. How can her private spaces be penetrable by the public if what they produce and secure is her sexualized body? In a gendered scheme, as we have already seen above in the architectural treatises, the private spaces should be inviolate. But once visibility is necessary to the logic and economy of enclosure, then that class discourse must (re)produce the Victorian lady as asexual.

Thus, Braddon's novel enables us to revise radically our understanding of Victorian prudishness, produced less it would seem, *pace* Foucault, by the discourse of sexuality than by the discourse of class. Of course, Foucault does recognize the way that sexual discourse flows from the upper-middle classes down to the lower-middle and lower classes throughout the nineteenth century, but what his analysis misses is the extent to which class claims demand the continually visible and, therefore, asexual or sexually immature female body.

This logic ties enclosure and visibility to the childishness that marks both Collins's Laura Fairlie and Braddon's Lady Audley. Class visibility requires that their bodies be produced as asexual or sexually immature, belonging to a child. The child woman can have nothing to hide. Walter Hartright's early impression on viewing Laura of "something wanting," expresses not only her "ominous likeness" to the woman from the asylum but also confirms her childishness and asexuality. In the sexuality that marks Miriam's face and form, Hartright had already found, and been repulsed by, the something he had wanted. And the childishness that characterizes Laura's behavior marks her off limits as an object of Hartright's *sexual* interest. She exists as an embodiment of an ideal, and Walter's determination to have her recognized again as an heiress suggests that she is a locus for his class ambitions rather than his sexual desires.

Just as Laura's childishness is tied to the mental vacuity of madness, so, too, her detention in the insane asylum produces a further infantilization and seems further to equip her for her future life as mistress of Limmeridge. The "quaint, childish earnestness" that was initially only a part of her character becomes, after her incarceration, its defining feature: "She spoke as a child might have spoken; she showed me her thoughts as a child might have shown them" (43, 403).

Like Laura Fairlie, Lady Audley is defined by her idealized asexual beauty and her childishness. Despite having married her and fathered her child, George Talboys recalls leaving "my little girl asleep with my baby in her arms" (12). As Lady Audley, she is described as "irretrievably child-ish," acting in her own "childish, unthinking way," as possessing a "win-ning childish smile," as speaking in a "pretty musical prattle" (32, 37, 43, 58). Even her penmanship is childish, as are her every whim, mood, desire, and motivation.

And Lady Audley, like Laura, is found to have "something wanting," ominously linked to madness. Robert concludes of his uncle's passion for his wife: "I do not believe that Sir Michael Audley had ever *really* believed in his wife. He had loved her and admired her; he had been bewitched by her beauty and bewildered by her charms; but that sense of something wanting . . . had been with him" (232). Just as Collins sets up a relationship between childishness and madness, so does Braddon. Although we are tantalized with the prospect that Lady Audley's "secret" focuses on illicit behavior—she is a bigamist, a murderess, an arsonist—in fact, she is hiding from the world a tendency to madness inherited from her mother. It is That predisposition causes her to flee her father and child to pursue employment as a governess after her husband abandons her to pursue wealth in Australia. What is infantile is also, potentially, mad. That is what she confesses when Robert Audley confronts her as "the demoniac incarnation of some evil principle" (227). She taunts him: "It is a great triumph, is it not—a wonderful victory? You have used your cool, calculating, frigid, luminous intellect to a noble purpose. You have conquered— a MAD WOMAN!" (227). She continues: "When you say that I killed George Talboys, you say the truth. When you say that I murdered him treacherously and foully, you lie. I killed him because I AM MAD! . . . Bring Sir Michael; and bring him quickly. If he is to be told one thing let him be told everything; let him hear the secret of my life!" (227). Ironically, of course, Lady Audley has not killed her first husband; he has survived his tumble down the well with only a broken arm and absconded for America. And one might argue that she is more sinned against than than sinning in taking Sir Michael Audley for her husband after George Talboys abandons her with no prospect of returning unless he strikes gold. But Talboys is absolved of guilt whereas Lady Audley must play out the play. Her mother was mad and institutionalized, and, under duress, she, too, is destined for a similar fate. That this is to be her fate is written in her childish aspect. Although Lady Audley fears to find her mother a "distraught and violent creature," she discovers instead "no raving, straight-waist-coated maniac, guarded by zealous jailers, but a golden-haired, blue-eyed, girlish creature, who seemed as frivolous as a butterfly, and who skipped toward us with her yellow curls decorated with natural flowers, and saluted us with radiant smiles, and gay, ceaseless chatter" (230).

The relationships between asexual childishness and the ideal lady of the house and between childishness and madness underscore the homology between country house and Panopticon, between country house and madhouse, the juxtaposition with the latter calling into question the freedoms of the former. Both Laura Fairlie and Lady Audley can be transferred against their wills from their estates to asylums. And the very qualities that have led to their idealization as ladies facilitate their condemnation as madwomen. And if Lady Audley is not the innocent she pretends to be—if, in fact she has a past to hide—then her visibility becomes a liability rather than an asset, and she must be transferred from public view without a ripple.

D. A. Miller perceptively notes in *The Novel and the Police* that madness as a diagnosis "lies in wait to 'cover'—account for and occlude—whatever behaviors, desires, or tendencies might be considered socially deviant, undesirable, or dangerous" (169). He continues:

> The "secret" let out at the end of the novel is not, therefore, that Lady Audley is a madwoman but rather that, whether she is one or not, she must be treated as such. . . . The doctor's double-talk ("the cunning of madness, with the prudence of intelligence") will be required to sanction two contradictory propositions: 1) Lady Audley is a criminal, in the sense that her crimes must be punished; and 2) Lady Audley is not a criminal, in the sense that neither her crimes nor her punishment must be made public in a male order of things. (169–70)

However, it is not specifically or singly a "male" order of things; it is also a class order of things that facilitates this seamless transfer from country house to madhouse. Robert Audley wants to avoid at all costs "the necessity of any exposure—any disgrace" (250). The class entitlement of a Sir Michael rests on his visible presence, as Girouard argues, of the moral order. It is thus extraordinarily convenient that the lady who fails that moral order should be susceptible to private "burial" from sight instead of the public exposure of a trial. Lady Audley claims that she goes to a "living grave," a sentiment confirmed by the doctor's promise to Robert that, "If you were to dig a grave for her in the nearest churchyard and bury her alive in it, you could not more safely shut her from the world" (256, 250). That we should have been prepared from the beginning for this transfer is suggested by the way Braddon's description of the "maison de santé" at the end ironically echoes the early descriptions of Audley Court, with its darkening shelter, its intensely painful repose, and its deathlike tranquillity provoking a "yearning wish to have done with life" (1, 2, 16, 17).

In conclusion, the lurid sensationalism of this new subgenre facilitated Braddon's articulating the subtle connections between country house and madhouse and disclosing how the class and gender position of the upper-middle-class lady might simplify her private transfer from one sphere to the other. By returning Laura Fairlie to Limmeridge House and her senses at the end of *The Woman in White,* Collins ultimately deranges the archaeology through which we expose knowledge of those connections. Mary Elizabeth Braddon, however, lets the logic of asylum and Asylum play itself out in Lady Audley's fate. Moreover, she exposes how the lady's mandatory visibility secures the class system and thus requires that her deviance be marked as madness and the lady be buried alive.

In this chapter, I have only begun to introduce ideas that receive more extended discussion in the next. Particularly, I more fully theorize the concept of space, which has been assumed, by and large, to function as an empty, neutral vessel waiting to be filled rather than as a phenomenon under constant production and negotiation, empowering some and disempowering others. We have seen in Lady Audley's fate that her "privacy" is socially produced to secure certain gender and class arrangements. The next chapter turns to the experiences of working-class women, whose disenfranchisement takes different but subtly related forms that further elaborate the gendering of space in Victorian England.

CHAPTER 5

Private Space and Public Woman: Victorian Working-Class Narratives

As is evident in the trajectory of this volume, my interest in gender and narrative led me first to the Victorian domestic novel and then increasingly to large questions about the configuration and gendering of space in the Victorian Age. Feminist critics have engaged this issue from the standpoint of the separate spheres that developed at the time of the industrial revolution: a private domain of the home, associated with women, and a public domain of work, associated with men. This chapter continues with ideas introduced in the preceding one, focusing on how spatial configurations situate knowledge and so reflect, initiate, and solidify gender and class distinctions in the Victorian Age.

Historians, geographers, and sociologists are remarkably unanimous in postulating an epistemic shift in early Victorian England. The combined forces of industrialism, capitalism, imperialism, growing urbanism, and individualism worked together to impact dramatically the social production of space. New wealth and an increasing tendency to locate work at a site some distance from the house—a function of the advent of reliable rail travel, improved roads under a national system of building, and the development of suburban spaces distinct from urban workplaces—turned the house into a new kind of social space that renegotiated relations between men and women. The overall change may be summed up briefly as marked by a separation of classes that had previously cohabited, the separation of places of work from those for leisure, and an articulation of male versus female spaces, all supported by a new ideology of public and private spheres, unprecedented in its scope, authority, and power to mystify social relations between men and women, adults and children, and middle and working classes.[1]

Many feminists have pointed to the problematic hierarchy in the terms private and public; for some, it is *the* dichotomy founding women's oppression. Recently there has been a new outpouring of critical and theoretical work by feminist legal theorists, historians, and political scientists.[2] Private and public, of course, refer to many things—from space to legal definitions pertaining to the legitimacy of state intervention, to commercial transactions and the organization of a market economy.[3] This mutability of the terms suggests we need to be careful to define the way in which we are using them. For example, taking issue with an early rhetoric of "the personal is the political" that focused on the political implications of what happened in private life, many feminist political theorists believe that the pendulum has swung too far in the direction of conflating the private with the public and now legitimately want to reclaim for women the space of the private as something appropriately outside the realm of political interest.

I want to wed the questions feminists are asking about what is private and what is public with the perspectives articulated by sociologist Henri Lefebvre in *The Production of Space,* particularly his idea that space is socially produced. Lefebvre points to the problem with discussions of private and public spheres as they generally exist today, that is, that they tend to proceed as if space were properly treated as an abstract entity waiting to be filled. He notes that our conception of space has been governed by the illusion of transparency: "Here space appears as luminous, as intelligible, as giving action free rein. . . . The illusion of transparency goes hand in hand with a view of space as innocent, as free of traps or secret places" (27). Lefebvre, in contrast, encourages us to reconceive space as socially produced: "The successful unmasking of *things* in order to reveal (social) relationships . . . was Marx's great achievement" (81). "A [similar] . . . approach is called for today . . . which would analyse not things in space but space itself, with a view to uncovering the social relationships embedded in it" (89).[4]

My goal is to bring together the work of scholars from several disciplines—sociologists, geographers, historians, and literary theorists—to produce a new and, I think, more troubling reading of Victorian working women's access to spaces termed both private and public.

Conceiving space as socially produced and not as a passive receptacle enables us entirely to reconceptualize our understanding of individuals' access to and control over the spaces they inhabited. It enables us further to grasp the mystifying effects of the rhetoric of private and public spheres that dominated Victorian life. In the previous chapter I explored the way that representing the middle-class home as a mistress's private sphere disguised the disappearance of autonomy and control from her life. In this chapter, which focuses on working-class women, examining the social production of space enables us to perceive how an ideology of privacy elides a collapse of so-called private spaces into public space. That is, Victorian working women could not lay claim to any spaces that were genuinely private in the sense that they could function freely and autonomously within them.

It is somewhat difficult to assess the impact of the social production of space on working-class women because of the scarcity of documents written by those from the laboring classes. I focus on recorded testimony in debates about the Contagious Diseases Acts and contemporaneous narratives of workhouse and lower-class life from three personal memoirs: Emma Smith's *A Cornish Waif's Story,* Kathleen Woodward's *Jipping Street,* and Hannah Cullwick's *Diaries.* I also briefly examine two fictional representations of working women: Charles Dickens's Betty Higden from *Our Mutual Friend* and Wilkie Collins's Hester Dethridge from *Man and Wife.* Although these narratives are to some extent shaped (and perhaps compromised) by middle-class perspectives, the first three, particularly, draw significantly on the words and represented experiences of members of the working classes.

For working women an ideology of the home as private site at a distance from work was entirely problematic. Not only were working women employed in large numbers to *work* in middle-class homes, but the very fact that they worked away from their own homes complicated their relationship to their places of employment, the streets they had to traverse to get to work, and the places to which they returned after work. I've chosen the group of narratives that follow to point up these difficulties.

The Contagious Diseases (CD) Acts of the 1860s represent a significant moment in legislative history in that they impacted solely women and, notably, women of the lower classes. Briefly, their intention was to curb the spread of venereal disease in seaport towns by allowing officials to arrest women suspected of being prostitutes and to subject them to gynecological examination. Suspicion was enough to detain a woman, and evidence of venereal disease sufficed to commit her to a lock hospital while her infection was treated. Because men—sailors and members of the militia— who populated these towns were not subject to arrest, forcible examination, or restraint, no real prospect existed for arresting the spread of VD. In short, for women the private domain of their bodies could become publicly accessible to search simply because they appeared in the public streets. The CD Acts intervened in women's private lives in unprecedented ways, as we see implicitly in this argument mounted by William Acton over a debate on extending the CD Acts to the civil population:

> I have no hesitation in admitting that the private life of the individual, so far as it does not affect society at large, is the concern of the individual

alone, and in no way whatever of the state, and that any attempt on the part of the legislative to control the individual, whether man or woman, is incompatible with the freedom which is the birthright of every person born in this country. This, however, is a very different case. . . . The title of the Act sufficiently indicates that no infringement of individual freedom is intended, except so far as such freedom infringes on the public health.[5]

Private citizen, public health. Again we must question why men were exempt from such examinations because *their* individual freedoms also impinged on public health. In this debate a woman alone on the public streets, whatever her business, could readily be redefined as a public woman, or prostitute, endangering public health, and her rights to hold her body free from intrusion of the most intimate kind could be abridged. This massive violation of civil liberties is an inevitable consequence of mystifying the power relations implicit in concepts of private and public and of identifying women's privacy with a gendered place: the home. That move implicitly makes "public" any woman unaccompanied on the public streets, which would be the condition of most working women. And, predictably, working women were often subjected to these examinations although they had done nothing more than walk down a public street.

The irony of this procedure as a remedy for venereal disease is apparent in testimonials from other contemporaneous observers. James John Garth Wilkinson observed that, "In general results, this forcing open of women's bodies with the speculum is useless; and indeed is a mode of propagating contagion. The parts seen at the bottom of the speculum are seldom the seat of venereal sores; and in the early stages these sores when they exist internally, are seldom detectable" (3). The point seems, precisely, to be as much about controlling women and their access to space as about controlling the spread of disease. One woman who was detained described the assault on her body that followed:

> It is such awful work; the attitude they push us into first is so disgusting and so painful, and then these monstrous instruments,—often they use several. They seem to tear the passage open with their hands, and examine us, and then they thrust in instruments, and they pull them out and push them in, and they turn & twist them about; and if you cry out they stifle you with a towel over your face.[6]

The examination appears to be a virtual rape of the intimate spaces of women's bodies, and this exam could then be followed up with incarceration in a lock hospital. The effect was to encourage women to remain both sequestered in their homes and chaperoned everywhere else. The very idea of chaperone—a protector of person and reputation in public places—cancels the notion that one has real privacy or personal autonomy.

To examine further this forcible conversion of private affairs to public regulation among poor and working-class women, let me turn to another rhetoric of spaces in Victorian narratives, that governing dialogues about the workhouse. Designed to provide shelter—a home, if you will—for the poor and indigent, workhouses and their routines were also constructed to stigmatize their inhabitants. As a physical presence on the landscape, workhouses were forbidding places. They were developed in the 1830s to meet public concerns over the idle poor. In November 1834 the Poor Law Commissioners described the workhouse system as "the only remedy which can be entirely depended upon for the mitigation and ultimate extinction of the various evils which have been generated through the faulty administration of the Poor Laws."[7]

Even ardent supporters of the workhouse system were frank about their punitive versus eleemosynary function. Assistant Commissioner Sir Francis Head explained: "The very sight of a well-built establishment would give confidence to the Poor Law Guardians . . . and dignity to the whole arrangement, while the pauper would feel it was utterly impossible to contend against it."[8] Geographer Felix Driver cites contemporaries who described the new workhouses as intended as a "terror to the able-bodied population," who found their "prison-like appearance . . . inspires a salutary dread of them" (59). Readers of Charles Dickens's novels will remember his castigation of workhouses in classics such as *Oliver Twist* and *A Christmas Carol.* When Scrooge refuses to give a small donation to charity, he asks in self-justification: "Are there no workhouses?" When he learns that there are "plenty," he responds: "Let the poor go there then. My taxes support those institutions." Whereat the philanthropists cry out, "Many would rather starve first," a fate preferable to the treatment the poor received in workhouses.

Separating husband from wife, child from parent, workhouses felt more like prisons than refuges. In 1865 the *Social Science Review* published anonymously an essay entitled "The English Bastille," which described the effect of the workhouse upon children: they "neither laugh as ordinary free children do, nor move like them; when they laugh they tremble, when they run they shuffle, and when they come in obedience to a call they cringe" (197).[9]

Small wonder that the accounts we have universally stress their delete-
rious effects on all of their inhabitants and question the justice of impos-
ing such a system on innocent victims such as children and elderly or
disabled widows. *Workhouses and women's work,* a pamphlet published in
1858, noted that workhouses "are less comfortable than prisons, and that
the latter are preferred as places of abode by the lower classes," an assertion confirmed by Henry Mayhew's conversations with the poor.[10] Emma
Smith, author of *A Cornish Waif's Story: An Autobiography,* writes movingly of how residence in a workhouse stigmatized her and how that
stigma attached to her individual, private body. Because children in workhouses were dressed in the equivalent of prison uniforms and given distinctive haircuts to signify their social condition, Smith was vulnerable to
taunts even when she was returned eventually to her grandmother's home:
"[M]y happiness was clouded over at times by the ridicule of other children who, because of my cropped head, would call after me, 'old Union
maid'. Children can suffer untold humiliation through such things" (22).
At another point, the children attack "that old Union maid" with the cry
"let's roll her in the hay" (24), a process that almost suffocates her.
Initially, Emma has relished the cleanliness and order of these institutional homes—like the Salvation Army Home and the Bramshot Home
for wayward girls—as an alternative to living in one-room squalor and
sleeping on a "heap of dirty rags" crawling with bugs and vermin, vulnerable to sexual predators. However, as she grows up, she learns their terrible cost:

> [M]y outdoor clothing, all black and plain, told all and sundry that I had
> come from a Home [capital "H"]. . . . Now here at last it was rubbed into
> me that it was something to be very ashamed of that I had been an inmate
> of the Home at Bramshot. . . . 'Why, oh why,' I kept asking myself, 'has my
> life been so full of stigmas?—first illegitimacy, then my place of birth being
> a workhouse, and now for the rest of my life I must always be trying to hide
> the fact that I have spent years in a penitentiary' (153, 154, 156).

From her middle-class perspective, the reformer Frances Power Cobb
confirms the way such Homes as these, by making one's private life a subject for public display, destroy the very people they are meant to save:

> The poor workhouse girl is the child of an institution, not of a mother of
> flesh and blood . . . only one of a dreary flock driven about at certain hours

from dormitory to schoolroom and from school room to workhouse yard. . . . Even her hideous dress and her cropped hair are not her own! . . . I can affirm one thing on my own experience of England, and that is this— that one of the largest channels through which young lives are drained down into the Dead Sea which lies beneath all our vaunted civilization is the Workhouse! (8–9)

Sociologist Pierre Bourdieu has identified the distinctive ways that class impinges on one's bodily posture so that, after years of being treated as socially inferior, one will adapt a posture expressing that condition, what Bourdieu calls one's bodily "hexis."[11] The production of a workhouse hexis has in this case the status of a clearly legible text marking institutional history on individual bodies. It is initially manifest externally in clothes and a haircut. Then it becomes internalized in the body's very rhythms and responses, revealing the difficulty in Victorian England of erecting for the working classes, and especially for girls and women, any kind of meaningful boundary between something called private life and something else called public life. The public script of workhouse habitation has been permanently inscribed on the private body.

In personal accounts of workhouse life, representations powerfully produce their spaces as de facto public spaces; graphically described physical sensations reveal the negation of privacy in all its connotations. Kathleen Woodward's *Jipping Street: A Childhood in the London Slums,* published in 1928, details her girlhood in the 1880s.

As in Emma Smith's account from a child's perspective, Kathleen Woodward's representation of old age in the workhouse bespeaks the effacement of personality and individuality in the interest of inscribing a cautionary social tale, a publicly legible text on women's bodies. At the same time, the environment is constructed to facilitate complete institutional control of bodies and persons. Inmates of the workhouse suffer a spatial and temporal disorientation that renders them docile subjects of the state. Woodward testifies that visitors to the workhouse "were permitted only on Sunday afternoons" (48); otherwise, days are indistinguishable to the inhabitants. One workhouse resident Woodward visited speaks of "the uninterrupted days and the long nights in the workhouse; of the monotony so sustained that it defied the times of the day, no less than the seasons of the year—she could not tell, she said, 'whether it was Monday or Thursday'" (52). The temporal disorientation finds its match in the spatial dislocation:

Through the workhouse gates we went, down a long stone corridor which had walls of green bricks, glazed, and clammy to the touch. Soon we found ourselves in a room of bewildering space; it seemed at first that the space had swallowed everything else, but presently I picked out little black objects huddled together in regular intervals about the walls; and I saw that there were forms to sit on round the room, and there were texts on the walls, in such dressy letters that it was not easy to read them. The place filled me with a sickening fear—confused, inarticulate—and I clutched at Jessica's shawl as if she, too, would be swallowed up in so much space, or succumb to the intangible but no less chilly and hateful influences that seemed to brood over everything.

I smelled the smell of very washed old ladies, a dry sad smell mixed up with the smell of newly washed clothes not put out to air.

The room was barren without corner or recess, so clean that the east wind might have swept bleakly through it just before we came; bleak and barren the room was, and at first sight, the old ladies seemed a part of its bleak barrenness—cruelly clean and garnished, dressed uniformly in gray frocks which buttoned down the front and were stiffly voluminous, which served to mark and heighten their lean shriveled bodies. (49–50)

All that the word "home" comprises of privacy, dignity, autonomy, self-determination, independence, and freedom has been utterly and deliberately effaced. The workhouse poor women must publicly signify their personal economic failure within a laissez-faire economy of self-help and self-made men. The space of the workhouse and its political organization express social relationships eloquently; this is Lefebvre's maxim.

That any individual with pride would struggle against this ideological inscription is perhaps only too obvious. And a reader searches for evidence that working-class people made choices, asserted themselves, and refused the conversion of their lives to publicly legible texts. Woodward represents such choice and self-assertion in the figure of her mother, who stands at the center of her narrative. She is not an idealized angel in the house; the very language in which Woodward depicts her captures the way she occupies and is occupied by the social spaces of poverty. "Fearless and without hope mother was, flinty, enduring, strong, proud; she did not ask and she did not receive; the suffering had bitten in until it was itself impotent against the granite it laid bare" (5). Woodward speaks of indissoluble ties to her mother but confesses that "she had no love to give us and, thank God, she never pretended what she did not feel; but children miss the pres-

ence of love and wilt, when they are not embittered, in its absence"
(21–22). This mother supports five children and her chronically ill husband by taking in washing and, when work is slack, she must request relief
from the local Guardians. Rice is the form of relief they provide, and when
the family is "sick from eating rice," they appeal for a change in their
unvarying diet. As a result they are "summoned peremptorily before the
Board of Guardians, mother and we five" (17). This graphic representation
of her mother's frustrated attempt to preserve her own dignity powerfully
captures the private family's erasure within the logic of public welfare:

> I recall how the bleak, uncompromising light of that November morning
> dealt mercilessly with the faces of the 12 men and women Guardians; how
> mother's face whitened and hardened as the board fired question after ques-
> tion and she grew more dogged, and less able to show cause why we should
> not continue eating rice. . . . Life might have been less difficult for my
> mother if she had been able to relax her pride, if she had been more hesi-
> tating, more diffident in the presence of her 'superiors'. (18–19)

Through an unvarying diet of rice for Woodward and her family, the
Guardians viscerally remind beneficiaries that their poverty has annulled
their right to even a modicum of freedom and self-determination.
Woodward recognizes that her mother could improve her position by per-
forming her inferiority publicly, but she refuses to do so, with the result
that the Guardians remind her viscerally and daily that she depends on
them for welfare by forcing her family to continue to eat rice. In short, it
would have been more conducive to her ends if her mother had adopted
the bodily hexis of the social inferior and welfare recipient. But that she
cannot do. Little wonder that she experiences life as a "long drawn-out
agony of uncertainty, rounded off by death and possibly the workhouse,
which was worse than death" (7).

Charles Dickens represents in his fictional character Betty Higden,
from *Our Mutual Friend,* that same determined pride. Therefore, as she
ages, her "highest sublunary hope" is "patiently to earn a spare bare living, and quietly to die, untouched by workhouse hands" (523). Unlike the
working-class autobiographical writings we have seen, Dickens's fictional
treatment can frame those humiliating experiences within the narrator's
outrage. The narrator charges that "we have got things to the pass that
with an enormous treasure at disposal to relieve the poor, the best of the
poor detest our mercies, hide their heads from us, and shame us by

starving to death in the midst of us" (523). As she approaches death, feeble Betty Higden refuses an institutional Home and embraces the priva-
tions of the open road and the "track in which her last home lay, and of
which she had last had local love and knowledge" (524). Always she flees
the prospect of being "charitably clutched off to a great blank barren
Union House, as far from old home as the County Jail . . . and in its
dietary, and in its lodging, and in its tending of the sick, a much more
penal establishment" (526). Even as her physical strength and intellect fal-
ter under duress, her purpose to "die free" of the Parish remains firm; she
is determined to "die independent" (529, 531). That purpose is attained
when, her strength expiring, she arranges herself where she will be discovered, dead, "by some of my own sort; some of the working people"
(532)—all this in order to avoid the public exposure of the workhouse.

If the workhouse offers an extreme example—and certainly one not
common to the working classes in general—it nonetheless paves the way
for a more critical assessment of working-class spaces, about which it is
impossible to generalize. Differences among dwellings in rural areas, villages, towns, industrial cities, and metropolitan London abound. What is
more generalizable, perhaps, is middle-class expectations that cleanliness,
order, and privacy—meaning, here, the separation of adults from children, boys from girls—should be priorities in their organization of homes.
The intersection of ideologies of home with the concrete material realities
of those accommodations affordable by the working classes produces what
I call the social space of working-class habitations. Although working-
class families could not afford the kind of space that would provide privacy for each family member, they were often judged by the middle classes as choosing to live in intimate and immoral proximity—boys and girls
in the same bed, the entire family in one room. As a result, the middle
classes felt free to intrude with their so-called philanthropy upon the
spaces of the poor and working classes, further eroding any sense of privacy they might have had.

That middle-class ideology of the domestic and private home is evident
in the retrospective accounts of their lives by both Emma Smith and
Kathleen Woodward. Smith recollects that the furnishings of her grandmother's cottage were "wonderful . . . at least they seemed wonderful to
me. . . . It was the contrast between these simple homely sights and my
other life at the Union that has so firmly embedded them in my mind,
and with such affection" (20). Poignantly, the only song she remembers
from her childhood labor with the organ grinder is a paean to home:

Oh it's nice to have a home of your own,
And to sit by your own fireside,
if you've only got a table and a chair,
It's your own, and you're welcome there. . . .
What more do you want
When you've got your wife and children
And a nice little home of your own? (65)

Woodward similarly longs for that room of her own; she grows up feeling torn between the loathsome alternatives of the Union workhouse on one hand and, on the other, the river of humanity that flows relentlessly down Jipping Street. "I hardly know," she records, "if there is much to choose between being born in sin—or in Jipping Street" (22). She longs for a room of her own, "my citadel. Oh, the inexpressible balm of its bareness" (141):

How I sickened of people, loathing them! From morning until night, and again in the morning; people, people, in travail with their insufferable burdens. . . . I shrank from them because they scattered and refuted my dreams, with their tired eyes and indomitable endurance: subtle, insidious enemies of revolt, with their forlorn, wooden acceptance of the intolerable burden of life in Jipping St. Going on and on . . . to the grave, or to the workhouse . . . which was worse than the grave. (54)

For Woodward, the ubiquitous presence of Jipping Street as a thronging public space crowds out any possibility of a private life. She envisions her desired room not only as a private place away from the public crowd but also as a spare, uncluttered space in contradistinction to "those things which made up the real Gethsemane of my childhood": "odds and ends . . . cheap china pieces with inflexible countenances . . . photographs [and] stuffed chairs smelling with age and the need for fresh air" (141). Woodward's reference to the "swarming knickknacks in her [landlady's] parlor" (142) simultaneously captures what was characteristic of Victorian middle-class interior design and aligns that idealized interior with the constant press of human life that characterizes working-class and slum life *tout court*. Privacy does not exist for Woodward, whether in her home or in the world at large. She disavows the "swarming" interior as an extension of intrusive lower-class street life and obliquely implies a new perspective on how that cluttered interior functioned for middle-class women. I suggest that the busyness of the rooms may have compensated for the lady's increasing isolation and expressed more her loneliness than her comfort. Thus, many middle-class women found their enforced sequestration in the home not the achievement of desired privacy but the realization of their lack of access to public life.

Woodward's preference for spareness bespeaks her telling disavowal of the values that structure her world from top to bottom. Another working-class woman, Hannah Cullwick, expressed a different but related perspective toward the interior spaces of the middle-class homes in which she was employed as servant. For Cullwick, as for Woodward, "privacy," as we are engaging that term here, freedom from intrusion, does not and cannot exist. Although Cullwick inhabits the rooms of middle-class homes in which she labors, and often does so in isolation, yet they do not afford her what she calls "self-possession," which is founded on economic possession:

> Still, I felt that nothing could be done without self-possession, & which I've found out is the' great difference 'twixt a lady & a servant, & which I must own too is scarcely possible for a thorough servant to have except in her own kitchen. And even there she must be what I call a presumptuous one except with the servants under her, 'cause it shows that she forgets the kitchen is not her own. Yet I pity the servants who always remember it, no one can tell her feelings who does remember that & forgets that she's working & earning all her wages. I went out to service too soon, before I really understood the meaning of it. (282)

What the so-called privacy of the bourgeois home guaranteed, in fact, was freedom from intrusion for only one person: master of the house. The mistress and her servants could not finally control, limit, or prevent access to any household spaces. Further, under the aegis of privacy, the home became a potential site of vulnerability for both women and servants. So we must ask on behalf of Victorian middle-class women: Can one have privacy if one cannot choose to leave it for the public sphere? Does a prisoner have privacy in his cell? And on behalf of the Victorian working woman, we must ask: Can one have privacy if one's home and body are not free from public surveillance and intrusion? Again, does a prisoner have privacy in his cell?

Cullwick's insight into the structure of the domestic arrangements determined by social power dynamics finds articulation and elaboration in Wilkie Collins's *Man and Wife*. In this novel of sensation, Collins depicts a working-class woman, a servant, Hester Dethridge, whose talents as a cook have procured for her a certain measure of indulgence with her eccentricities. In particular, she refuses to speak, and she writes anything she wants to say on a slate that hangs around her neck. In addition, periodically she simply disappears for a time without explanation. We subsequently learn the explanation for her behavior, as she becomes an increasingly prominent character in the novel's development. Previously married to a man who squandered their resources on drink and beat her, she earlier sought protection from his alcoholism and brutality in the law. Repeatedly told that, as this man's wife, she has no protection from him under the law—all that she owns is his—she takes the law into her own hands and murders him. The cleverness of her stratagem enables her to escape detection, and she imposes on herself the penalty of living a "separate and silent life: to dedicate the use of [her] speech to the language of prayer only . . . when no human ear could hear [her]" (603–4). She is, however, haunted by an apparition, a "visionary Thing" that appears irregularly and urges her to kill some proximate person (636). This is the cause of her periodic absences from her employment, as she flees this frightening command and her overpowering urge to execute it. Hester has confessed her secret in writing to a manuscript that she carefully sequesters in her breast until one night, under the power of the apparition, she leaves it lying on a table in the house bequeathed to her at her brother's death. The manuscript is discovered by her renter, a gentleman who seeks to rid himself of his wife with impunity. He blackmails Hester into helping him.

The circle is complete. Hester has been initially expelled by her husband from the first home she owned, purchased and furnished with her legacy. She has been cheated of her wages by his drunkenness and robbed of her positions by his brutality. She has no space she can call her own, where she can be free from his intrusion. Her "home" is simply a site in which he can beat and cheat her with impunity. The law holds private her relationship with her husband and will not interfere between them, even though her privacy—or freedom from his violent intrusion—is utterly cancelled by his rights over her as a man and master. She frees herself only by killing him but pays the penance of uncontrollable visions and urges. In a sense, her body has been colonized by this "visionary Thing," a punishment for claiming a private space for herself. Finally, even her volition is appropriated by the gentleman who wants his wife murdered. The narrator describes Hester's role in the intended murder in this way: "She was standing motionless in the middle of the room—not like a living woman—like a machine waiting to be set in movement. . . . With slow step and vacant face—moving as if she was walking in her sleep—she led the way" (627). The intended victim is spared, however, when the apparition urges Hester to kill the murderous husband instead. Hester ends her life confined to an asylum, "unconscious of her dreadful position, incapable of the smallest exertion of memory, resigned to the existence that she leads, and likely (in the opinion of the medical superintendent) to live for some years to come" (639). The confinement of her marriage with its dreadful consequences has been literalized in her final incarceration in the asylum, little different from her early experiences of "home." There is a bitter irony that this chapter on working-class women and the previous one on middle-class women should both close with images of incarcerated women. In both, we recognize that the concepts of privacy and the private sphere are often meaningless for women; the social production of the home as private domain functioned instead as a mystification that helped to sustain both gender and class relations in Victorian England.

In this chapter I have been able only to begin interrogating concepts of private and public space in Victorian England, particularly their differential impact on women of the lower classes. Space was configured in ways that fostered and maintained existing power alliances. Working women enjoyed few, if any, entitlements to the places they inhabited; even their bodies were not sacrosanct. We owe it to them not to be enthralled by an ideology that idealizes the private, domestic sphere. And it is our challenge to continue to uncover how gender and class relationships and the power dynamics that flow from those relations are embodied in the particular spaces we inhabit and from which we come to know our worlds.

In the next chapter I turn to another cultural narrative—that of value—that also had a differential impact on women. Although I seemingly take a very different focus here, one more concerned with aesthetics than politics, it will not surprise my readers to learn that the aesthetics I examine is implicated in politics and that similar mystifications help to produce a similar disenfranchisement for the woman writer.

CHAPTER 6

Cultural Capital and the Gendering of Values: Victorian Woman Writers

.

This chapter encompasses two interconnected issues: the way gender enters into judgments of artistic value and the production of cultural capital in nineteenth-century England. I draw the term "cultural capital" from the work of sociologist Pierre Bourdieu, who identifies kinds of capital other than material capital (money, property, etc.), which is the one we all recognize. These other kinds of capital that have value include, for example, social capital and cultural capital, the one that concerns me here; previously, however, I have argued for the importance of social capital in Victorian England. In *Nobody's Angels* I claimed that certain kinds of social capital possessed by middle-class women and manifest in mastery of etiquette practices, conventions of dress, and so on, cooperated with material capital—a man's income—to produce the middle-class household in Victorian England. In other words, it was not enough to possess the fortune to qualify for a certain position in society; if one did not also possess the signs—that is, the social capital—by which middle-classness is recognized, then one would not find acceptance within the elite circles to which one aspired. Controlling the production of meanings yields social capital just as controlling the means of production realizes material capital, and the two are integrally tied to each other.

My interest here is in another kind of capital that circulates and produces value in an economy, one that impacts on aspiring writers: cultural capital. Bourdieu defines cultural capital as an "elaborated taste for the most refined objects," and he seeks to uncover its operation in society (1984, 1). Arguing that the "economy of cultural goods . . . has a specific logic," Bourdieu traces how "art and cultural consumption are predisposed, consciously and deliberately or not, to fulfill a social function of legitimating social differences" (7). That is, taste—or the ability to make aesthetic distinctions between one object and another—functions to validate social or class distinctions. Whereas Bourdieu focuses on social *class* differences, he leaves unexplored those social distinctions determined by gender, which are surely as significant in legitimating social differences as is class. Both class and gender figure prominently in my analysis, particularly how, in the realm of taste, gender influences and informs what is regarded as cultural capital and so influences the fate of women writers.

Since the early 1970s we have witnessed a veritable explosion of interest in women writers across centuries and cultures. Women's texts have been recovered, women's writing has found a publisher's market, courses in women's literature have been created, and some might even argue that curricula are beginning to be transformed by the inclusion of women writers. Three of the novels I discussed earlier have benefited from this surge of interest: Charlotte Brontë's *Shirley,* Anne Brontë's *Tenant of Wildfell Hall,* and Mary Elizabeth Braddon's *Lady Audley's Secret:* the first a less frequently discussed novel of a major Victorian woman novelist, the other two, recovered texts, garnering sustained critical attention for the first time. Recent scholarly attention these works have attracted obviously reflects an increase in their cultural capital. And I suggest that its source lies in what Nancy Miller has called (in a passage I cited earlier) the "embodiment in writing of a gendered [or, we might amend, a racialized or classed or queer] subjectivity." With the advent of gender, ethnic, and cultural studies, interestedness, as opposed to disinterestedness, has a new cultural cachet. Value seems to reside now in the particularity of social and economic dispositions rather than in the claims to universality.

A question remains as yet unanswered: How widespread and enduring are these changes? Several years ago I enthusiastically greeted the reprinting of some novels by Margaret Oliphant—one focus of this chapter—only to find them out of print again within a couple of years. And although women's studies courses thrive on campuses across the United States, in many places they haven't yet successfully transformed "traditional" curricula. Further, despite one publisher's claim to me that any title including the word "woman" was sure to find print, excellent books on those termed "minor" writers, women and men alike, still struggle to find publishers. Thus, when forced by a tough job market to be pragmatic, I have advised my students to broaden the appeal of dissertations on figures such as Rhoda Broughton, Mary Elizabeth Braddon, Margaret Oliphant, Sarah Grand, or George Egerton. The advent of cultural studies has both facilitated and encouraged ways of thinking about these writers that potentially lend broad interest to projects that include them. In the past, however, "broadening the appeal" meant including a chapter or two on a so-called canonical writer in order to be more competitive for jobs.

In part, the very insights that were to liberate women writers from the chains of convention have at best simply sawed off the shackles, leaving women writers as a group unfettered but still disadvantaged, at the bottom of a Mount Parnassus whose aesthetic summit has already been claimed by primarily white, male writers. That is to say, some of the most brilliant writing on the subject of values has established only that values and value judgments are contingent, "the product of the dynamics of a system, specifically an *economic system*" of publication, dispersal, and markets rather than universal and absolute (30). I am citing here Barbara Herrnstein Smith's book *Contingencies of Value,* which opens with an acknowledgment to feminist criticism—both what it has accomplished and what it has not. Herrnstein Smith wrote in 1988,

> Recent moves in the direction of opening the question of value and evaluation in the literary academy have come primarily from those who have sought to subject its canon to dramatic revaluation, notably feminist critics. Although their efforts have been significant to that end, they have not amounted as yet to the articulation of a well-developed noncanonical theory of value and evaluation. (24)

Herrnstein Smith draws attention to the fact that much of the early energy of feminist critics went into justifications of two kinds: first, to arguing that certain women writers properly belonged in the traditional canon, or second, to establishing a countercanon, one questioning and challenging the established values of the "canon": those "monuments more durable than brass." For Herrnstein Smith, to retain the language and logic of canons is to perpetuate systems in which certain writers will always be disadvantaged vis-à-vis others. And it leaves unexposed the very contingency of all values. She argues, "Beguiled by the humanist's fantasy of transcendence, endurance, and universality, [American critical theory] has been unable to acknowledge the most fundamental character of literary value, which is its mutability and diversity" (28). Herrnstein Smith's astute analysis not only diagnoses obstacles that lie in the way of developing a theory of literary value: it also questions the very possibility of deriving such a theory for a practice built on "mutability and diversity." And, we might add, this difficulty is exacerbated by the increasing emphasis put on diversity and mutability by gender, ethnic, and cultural studies.

What has always been a sufficiently difficult task of selecting among major and minor canonical works for anthologies of British and American literatures has been enormously compounded in recent years by demands for a greater representation of perspectives. And the erosion of a theory of literary value puts pressure on anthology editors to adopt comprehensiveness as a standard, resulting in a multiplication of pages and authors.

Herrnstein Smith's argument that "Of particular significance for the value of 'works of art' and 'literature' is the interactive relation between the *classification* of an entity and the functions it is expected or desired to perform" (32) has enabled feminist critics to pose trenchant questions that challenge claims of value for a particular piece of art, questions such as "valuable for whom?" and "valuable in what contexts and under what circumstances?" This awareness of the contingency of value has emboldened critics to dispute the disinterestedness of the status quo and to expose its *interestedness*, illuminating how aesthetic values are entangled with social and political values in troubling ways.

Although Herrnstein Smith's persuasive analysis of the contingency of values facilitates questions about the particular bases on which an aesthetic object has been valued in the past, it cannot produce any rationale for valuing one piece over another. Herrnstein Smith acknowledges that "relativism, in the sense of a *contingent* conceptualization *that sees itself and all others as such,* cannot found, ground, or prove itself, cannot deduce or demonstrate its own rightness, cannot even lead or point the way *to* itself" (183). We may not be troubled by the triumph of relativism were all things equally relative. But certain texts continue to enjoy institutionalized priority conferred by earlier canonical status, even though the grounds for that priority have certainly been eroded. And, as I suggested earlier, those who have claimed Mount Parnassus already cannot be seriously challenged by an argument from contingency. At best, one can celebrate "the sense of a conception of the world as continuously changing, irreducibly various, and multiply configurable" (183). The relativist may find some other people "who conceptualize the world in more or less the same way she does" (184), but this final picture of a plucky relativist, always glad "for a bit of company," stops short of generating a new analytic framework equal to the task to be done.

This relentless move toward the relativism of all values removes pressure for change because one has license to continue preferring values that have already been institutionalized as preferable. One has not instituted a critique of how aesthetic judgment is constituted. As a result, the idea of universality continues routinely to inform aesthetic judgments today. For example, Peter Keating recently reviewed the new anthology of *Victorian Women Poets* for the *Times Literary Supplement*. In response to its editors' claim that this volume "offers nothing less than a complete refiguring of the Victorian poetic canon," Keating replies that these "women poets . . . are only fleetingly a match for their male counterparts" (27). Both the volume's editors and Keating are gesturing to the authority of the canon. Pertaining to Keating's analysis just cited, Herrnstein Smith's analytic allows us to ask only: In what *terms* and for *whom* are Victorian women poets only "fleetingly a match"? These are important but limited questions.

I do not wish, however, to appear to scapegoat Keating here. I myself have made similar claims, and the desire to do so must be the dilemma of every critic who finds value in a work and writes about it, which is an implicit declaration that these values have general application and should be shared. My remarks in the preceding chapter about Braddon's relationship to the modern canon is a claim about how Braddon has been evaluated in light of certain standards in the past and how we might valuably reread *Lady Audley's Secret* through perspectives highlighted by recent gender and feminist theorists.

Further, thinking about my own scholarship, I recognize that my choices of what to study have been motivated by a general value I place on works that problematize gender, sexual, racial, class, and ethnic identity markers instead of leaving identity unmarked or simply celebrating a particular identity *tout court*. Even as I reflect on works I read before feminism and other developments gave a defining cast to my scholarly interests, I gravitated to those works that grappled with identity as a problem, and such works have come from every period and from many hands. It is the assumption, of course, of universality that currently makes the canon, often described derisively as "dead white male writers," a convenient whipping boy. Current interest, in contrast, now often focuses on cultural, social, and economic particularity.

Drawing on the work of Pierre Bourdieu, John Guillory proposes to go further than Barbara Herrnstein Smith; in his book *Cultural Capital*, Guillory notes that the judgment of aesthetic value alone is never sufficient because "judgments with canonical force are institutionally located" (1993, 29). Thus, he sets out to redefine the "object of our critique" not as taste but rather "as the institution of the school" (38) where the distribution of cultural capital reproduces the structure of social relations, and the process of canonical selection mirrors the process of social exclusion

(6). Guillory's analysis, then, anticipates mine in setting forth the economic and social base of cultural distinction with the goal of producing
not another critique of aesthetic value but rather a "sociology of judgment" (xiv). In his conclusion Guillory cites Bourdieu, who explains that
"to denounce hierarchy does not get us anywhere. What must be changed
are the conditions that make this hierarchy exist, both in reality and in
minds. We must—I have never stopped repeating it—work to *universal-
ize in reality the conditions of access* to what the present offers us that is
most universal" (339–40). Following Bourdieu's trenchant insight,
Guillory argues that, "Insofar as the debate on the canon has tended to
discredit aesthetic judgment, or to express a certain embarrassment with
its metaphysical pretensions and its political biases, it has quite missed the
point. The point is not to make judgment disappear but to reform the
conditions of its practice" (340). For Guillory, that reformation means
universalizing access. That solution does not, however, address past exclu-
sions—my focus. Nonetheless, Bourdieu's attention to the conditions of
access does suggest one profitable avenue of approach to cultural distinction and the constitution of aesthetic judgment in Victorian England.

For Bourdieu, aesthetic practice has generally privileged distance,
detachment, disinterestedness, and indifference. He writes, "Aesthetic
theory has so often presented these as the only way to recognize the work
of art for what it is, autonomous, *selbständig*, that one ends up forgetting
that they really mean disinvestment, detachment, indifference, in other
words, the refusal to invest oneself and take things seriously" (1984, 34).
As exemplifying a traditional aesthetic practice, Bourdieu cites Virginia
Woolf, so often hailed as the radical foremother of feminist theory and a
preeminent figure in the women's countercanon. Bourdieu positions
Woolf's practice so that she above all is seen to have maintained the very
standards by which women writers have traditionally been excluded.
Woolf's "incandescence," celebrated in *A Room of One's Own,* is precisely
a cultural capital borne of certain kinds of educational and social capital
as well as distance from economic necessity. Hence, Woolf's famous five
hundred pounds a year.[1]

Despite her own aesthetic practice, which favors more traditional standards of canonicity, Woolf is nonetheless made honorary head of a countercanon of women writers simply because she is a "woman." Moreover,
she herself has helped foster the emergence of an identity politics in
speaking so movingly of our artistic foremothers. John Guillory has com-
mented that contemporary canon revision has by and large depended on

such an identity politics: That is, one's gender or one's race has been the central criterion for inclusion within an evolving countercanon.[2] Thus, the practice of amalgamating figures such as Virginia Woolf, Phyllis Wheatley, and Margaret Oliphant, for example, has not been seriously troubling to feminist theorists. But Woolf's own aesthetic practice would exclude many, if not most, of the female literary figures with whom she is routinely grouped today on the basis of gender. That Woolf resides comfortably under the same umbrella with Margaret Oliphant reveals that the hard questions about cultural distinction and the way aesthetic judgments are constituted have yet to be asked. The inherent incoherence of such a grouping points only more forcibly to the inadequacy of an identity politics in challenging traditional aesthetic claims, such as those Woolf made. That is, it is inadequate and ultimately ineffectual to oppose identity to a long-standing aesthetic practice.

To move beyond such limitations and inadequacies, Bourdieu analyzes the circumstances through which people attain cultural capital, how they acquire the "specifically artistic competence" and the "aesthetic disposition" that give them a claim to the dominant aesthetic (50).[3] He cites several contributing factors beginning with familial capital or the kinship network into which one is born. Social capital—or class position—plays an important role, as does educational capital, or schooling, which may partially but not wholly compensate for insufficient social capital. Bourdieu identifies a strong correlation between educational capital and an "aesthetic disposition" or the propensity to appreciate a work independently of its content (53). But the aesthetic disposition is also dependent on "past and present material conditions of existence" or "distance from necessity" (53). In short, the aesthetic disposition depends also on economic power, or a "power to keep economic necessity at arm's length" (55). Thus, the accumulation of cultural capital is built on a withdrawal from economic necessity (54).

Cultural distinctions, then, reflect class differences, "the infinitely varied art of marking distances" (66). And high culture defines itself in part by its disdain for what others on a lower economic level regard as culture (59–60). Throughout, Bourdieu interrogates the notion of "natural taste" that has informed aesthetic theory. He argues that "the ideology of natural taste owes its plausibility and its efficacy to the fact that, like all the ideological strategies generated in the everyday class struggle, it *naturalizes* real differences, converting differences in the mode of acquisition of culture into differences of nature" (68).[4] Thus, for Bourdieu, such natural taste "finds its real basis in a set of aesthetic principles which are the uni-versalization of the dispositions associated with a particular social and economic condition" (443).

Although he does not theorize what the basis for a new aesthetics might be, Bourdieu provides an important window on bases for previous exclu-sion. Particularly, he adumbrates significant connections between, on the one hand, aesthetic values and, on the other, social, political, and economic values. Thus, Bourdieu's are powerful insights to bring into a debate about women's literature although he himself is seemingly unconscious of gender in his discussion of cultural capital. My goal, then, broadly conceived, is to begin to gender Bourdieu's insights with the objective of reforming, or re-informing, the conditions under which we practice our judgment of both male and female writers in the Victorian age. More particularly, I am focusing on one "noncanonical" woman writer in Victorian England, Margaret Oliphant, in contrast to two often canonized authors: Anthony Trollope and George Eliot. My goal is not to elevate Oliphant at the expense of Trollope or Eliot, rather to illuminate the different economic and social dispositions that structure their novels and so begin to trace links between those dispositions and their aesthetic valuations.

I begin by developing further an argument that I flirted with in *Nobody's Angels* but ultimately found tangential to my thesis, that is, that many texts positioned as counterhegemonic in their representations have often bought into the dominant economy in so positioning themselves. It is an argument that has implicitly shaped my earlier analyses of Charlotte Brontë and W. M. Thackeray and of Mary Elizabeth Braddon and Wilkie Collins. The discussion that follows also reflects on my exam-ination of intertextual relationships between the work of two other Victorian women novelists, Charlotte and Anne Brontë.

My example for this more extended analysis of aesthetic value is George Eliot's *Middlemarch.*[5] In the process of reading Margaret Oliphant's novel *Miss Marjoribanks* in relation to George Eliot's *Middlemarch,* I encoun-tered Q. D. Leavis's important essay (1989), which claims Oliphant's text as an influential precursor of Eliot's and finds Oliphant's protagonist, Lucilla, much more attractive and likable than Eliot's Dorothea. That arti-cle opened my way to speculation about how canonical value is estab-lished, specifically about the canonical status afforded Eliot's novel and denied Oliphant's.

Let me state my argument baldly at first and then proceed to make it more nuanced. That Gilbert and Gubar's monumental *Madwoman in the*

Attic (1979) found core exempla of its thesis in the works of already canonical writers such as the Brontës and George Eliot is not surprising when we consider that this study takes as foundational women's rage at a patriarchal system that disenfranchises them while it marginalizes and trivializes their efforts. Focusing on women's rage endorses representations of social reality that stress the emptiness of women's lives and the plenitude of men's. By complaining that "women need a field for their efforts, just as men do" (*Jane Eyre* 95), a novelist such as Charlotte Brontë validates representations of the inconsequence of women's lives and the deeper importance of men's. In fact, this *is* the hegemonic perspective, with the lens significantly adjusted to register women's dissatisfaction with the status quo rather than their acquiescence.

George Eliot's representations of women's lives collude equally and, because of the intensity of her novels' "reality" effect, perhaps more effectively in depicting the meaninglessness of life, especially for ladies. Eliot's *Middlemarch* minimizes and even erases women's role as household managers, protoprofessional positions that demanded the skills required to run any small business: acumen in hiring, supervising, and disciplining workers along with financial accountancy expertise. Little of this is represented in *Middlemarch,* where a lady such as Dorothea Brooke finds only ennui in the idleness and triviality of her life.

Significantly, George Eliot does not represent middle-class women as class managers; Margaret Oliphant does. George Eliot's heroines chafe under the social restrictions that keep them confined to the home; Margaret Oliphant's pragmatically gather into their hands the reins that allow them to control local society and effect class management. If anything, George Eliot's heroines are deemed too good, too idealized in their ultimate self-abnegation and resignation to the status quo, whereas both contemporaneous and more recent readers of Oliphant's novels have characterized her heroines as "hard" and "unpleasant" for calculating strategies through which to amass power and influence, disdaining romantic love in favor of shrewd political alliances and lucrative marriages.

George Eliot's dismay that she should be suspected of writing one of the *Chronicles of Carlingford* certainly helped to keep Oliphant humble, and Eliot's art has subsequently set the standard by which Oliphant's seems less significant. If we reverse the focal optic, however, Oliphant's politics of domesticity reveal Eliot's commitment to politics of a different sort. Class relations are inscribed in Eliot's *Middlemarch* in ways that reinforce the depiction of women's disability within patriarchy, that is, class and gender representations emerge as complementary or congruent discourses. In her representation of middle-class life, George Eliot omits key aspects of the semiotics of social life, which generate distinctions of rank and class. By omitting the very semiotic that Oliphant foregrounds, Eliot seems to naturalize both social differences and economic conditions so that what the novel represents seamlessly accords with an aesthetic practice that naturalizes taste and cultural distinction. In short, this general observation about Eliot's novels bears out Bourdieu's insight into the link between what a novel represents and the cultural distinction it is accorded. In tying educational capital and an aesthetic disposition to a propensity to appreciate a work independently of its content—independently, that is, of its social and economic dispositions—Bourdieu illuminates the process through which works by disenfranchised members of a society are devalued.

As I noted earlier, particular social and economic circumstances are in fact primary foci of texts by women and marginalized others and a significant source of the anger that often marks and mars their texts, as, for example, Virginia Woolf feels it mars Charlotte Brontë's *Jane Eyre*.

George Eliot early developed an aesthetic theory congruent with a representational practice that distinguished details leading to a general, higher knowledge from those that were local and semiotically variable. Disdaining the world of etiquette and related domestic discourses that figures prominently in Oliphant's work, Eliot identified these discourses as marks of "silly novels." In her scorn for what she regarded as certain "unessential" details—or as G. H. Lewes put it, "*detailism* which calls itself realism"—Eliot grounded her own philosophy of realism in emphases shared by Lewes and John Ruskin. Of Ruskin, Eliot argued that "the truth of infinite value that he teaches is *realism*—the doctrine that all truth and beauty are to be attained by a humble and faithful study of nature, and not by substituting value forms, bred by imagination on the mists of feeling, in place of definite substantial reality" ("Art and Belles Lettres," 626). This praise, linking fidelity to nature and definite substantial reality, privileges detail as a ground for higher knowledge in contradistinction to detail as semiotically variable. Lewes implied a similar value in distinguishing detailism—the inessential—from essential detail: "The painter who devotes years to a work representing modern life, yet calls for even more attention to a waistcoat than to the face of a philosopher, may exhibit truth of detail which will delight the tailor-mind, but he is defective in artistic truth, because he ought to be representing something higher than waistcoats."[6] The contrast Lewes establishes is telling: waistcoats versus philosophers' faces. Both are signs, but Lewes refuses status to the former; it cannot produce "artistic truth." In essence, he fundamentally refuses the instability of semiotics, arrogating artistic truth to certain signs but not to others. What George Eliot and G. H. Lewes argue, in short, is that details differ in essence rather than in ideological construction.[7] Some conduce to artistic truth and some do not. Both thinkers contemn the detailed semiotics of social life—of interest to tailors and upholsterers but not, apparently, to novelists.

Thus, key details that might lead us to a fuller grasp of how social and economic distinctions operate in a milieu to produce class differences are elided in Eliot's work because they are deemed inimical to artistic truth or the achievement of cultural distinction. This connection between class and cultural distinction in Eliot's aesthetic recalls Bourdieu's comment that natural taste "finds its real basis in a set of aesthetic principles which are the universalization of the dispositions associated with a particular social and economic condition" (1984 443).

Dorothea's life, as represented, stands in stark contrast to what Margaret Oliphant portrays of the life of her protagonist, Lucilla Marjoribanks, who, occupied with household and social management, has no time even for a husband. Oliphant dramatizes how women's roles as household and social managers helped produce and reproduce class differences, significant roles that have been elided by conventional and more traditional representations of figures such as the angel in the house—a passive, idle, dependent creature. A closer look at the economy of middle-class life and the forces that subtend it reveals how Oliphant's novel institutes a critique of the social dispositions that feed the kind of cultural distinction, or canonical status, we accord to a work.

A comparison of Oliphant's *Phoebe Junior* with Anthony Trollope's *The Warden,* which it rewrites, is also instructive on this point because Trollope's novel enjoys a stature not accorded Oliphant's. Whereas a comparison between the novels and their relative statures would usually be referred to matters of aesthetic taste, following Bourdieu I want to foreground the different social and economic propositions to which each novel asks us to assent.

Briefly, both novels deal with a position as hospital warden, which is basically a sinecure. That is, the position pays generously for minimal work. Trollope's fictional newspaper, *The Jupiter,* puts the question bluntly: "Does [the warden] ever ask himself, when he stretches wide his clerical palm to receive the pay of some dozen of the working clergy, for what service he is so remunerated?" (59). In this case, one John Hiram in 1434 provided monies in his will to establish a retirement home for super-annuated workers to be superintended by a warden. Over the centuries the original bequest has grown to provide over eight hundred per annum to the fortunate clergyman named warden, so that it has become "one of the most coveted of the snug clerical sinecures attached to our church" (4). Trollope is not unaware of the complexities of the issue, but he choos-es to defend "privilege and the old ways by the back door" (Gilmour 1984, xxi) as opposed to a kind of "moral imperialism" that insists on being right whatever the cost to those involved. But, of course, posing the question in this antithetical way facilitates the defense of privilege.

When Mr. Harding's own conscience finally expels him from his Eden at Hiram's Hospital, the novel makes plain that the old pensioners who have been agitating for a more equitable distribution of the income are losers by his departure. Indeed, throughout the novel, Mr. Harding stands as an emblem of individual conscience and integrity as opposed to the general cupidity that animates his old pensioners, men of the working classes who, broken by their labors, have had the good fortune to arrive at Hiram's Hospital.

Mr. Harding's continuing concern with being truly "right," despite legal entitlements to his income, sets him apart from the many people contending on all sides. And critics have focused on Trollope's representa-tion of that integrity in discussing the novel's aesthetic excellence.[8] Yet critics do not adequately foreground the way in which such "integrity" is already secured against disastrous consequences because of the kind of social capital that Mr. Harding has readily at his disposal. He will never starve for his conscience; he will not even suffer hunger pangs. His influ-ential friends stand ready to cushion any blow—with income to provide for his bodily needs and titles to bolster his dignity.

All of the actions are represented within a social context that in fact informs our aesthetic practice. It is easy for us to applaud Mr. Harding's integrity because it confirms the moral superiority of his educated and cultivated class. Those who attack him, such as the lawyer John Bold, lack his sensitive discrimination of spirit, and the old men who have com-plained about the income's distribution are represented as lacking his moral rectitude and cultivation. But that rectitude and sensitivity flow from the warden's social and economic privilege, which provides a rich soil for the flowering of his moral superiority. This is another case in which cultural distinction originates in social and economic conditions that are then elided so as to naturalize issues of taste.

Although this process is mystified in Trollope's text, other canonical writers have uncovered it, and it is useful to consider the operation of one such unmasking in Thackeray's *Vanity Fair,* notably when the narrator represents Becky Sharp's machinations: "And who knows but Rebecca was right in her speculations—and that it was only a question of money and fortune which made the difference between her and an honest woman? If you take temptations into account, who is to say that he is better than his neighbour? A comfortable career of prosperity, if it does not make people honest, at least keeps them so" (410). Thackeray invites us to share and to understand Becky's economic and social perspective. And she, like Oliphant's heroines, may appear "hard" and "mercenary" to readers, but there's a significant difference. The narrator and implied author share that judgment of this protagonist whereas Oliphant's do not. Becky's desire to marry wealth is understandable but culpable; Phoebe Junior's, as judged by the narrator, is realistic and admirable.

Trollope himself is sufficiently aware of class issues to depict them, but he does so in ways that downplay the consequences of wealth and social standing in determining one's moral behavior and cultural preferences. Trollope's bedesmen under the warden's care are routinely treated to or subjected to (depending on one's point of view) Mr. Harding's concerts on the violoncello, which he dearly loves to play. Mr. Harding's distinction consists in a cultured appreciation for music that heralds a refinement of conscience. The narrator comments: "I will not say that [the old men] all appreciated the music which they heard, but they were intent on appearing to do so; pleased at being where they were, they were determined, as far as in them lay, to give pleasure in return" (18)—a kind of quid pro quo in which the price for well-being instead of destitution is a pretended enjoyment of culture. Even Bunce, the most loyal of Harding's pensioners, who is said to "enjoy the moment, or acted enjoyment well," is damned with faint praise (19). Bunce is valuable to Mr. Harding precisely because he knows his place; the warden is "not ashamed, occasionally, when no other guest [is] there, to bid him sit down by the same parlour fire, and drink the full glass of port which was placed near him" (19). Bunce, sensible of the distinction afforded him, takes a second glass but never a third because "he knew the world too well to risk the comfort of such halcyon moments, by prolonging them till they were disagreeable" (19).

The text of class difference and cultural distinction is there for us to read, if we wish, but it is muted. Furthermore, the narrator seems to suggest that the old men who reside at Hiram's Hospital inhabit their sphere because their natures are coarser, less refined than the warden's. And when their complaints culminate in the departure of Mr. Harding, the narrative heaps coals of fire upon their heads. Mr. Harding has the triumph of an "innocent revenge" in which he forgives them all, while they are denied any monetary supplement they might have hoped for: "poor wretches! who had been so happy, had they but known it! Now their aged faces were covered with shame" (176). They are afflicted with "faint hearts" for "having returned so much kindness with such deep ingratitude" (177). And they are forced to swallow the humiliating lesson that their "position could hardly be improved" (178). But their suffering is not confined to those evaluative insults; they must also endure the injury of a bishop who, in his pique, refuses to appoint a successor to Mr. Harding, so that the old men are left both dependent on the bounty of the hospital and bereft of the superintendence necessary to maintain it and its occupants. At the end of the novel, "the whole place has become disordered and ugly. The warden's garden is a wretched wilderness" (182–83). The costs of Mr. Harding's clear conscience sadly are borne almost exclusively by the poor old men.[9]

This is a serious message about how social and cultural distinction operate in the world and whose shoulders bear the burden. And it is precisely this message, elided in Trollope's novel, that Oliphant foregrounds, which makes ironic critics' claims that Oliphant, "in her rapid, capacious way . . . had undoubtedly helped herself to details" from Trollope (Fitzgerald 1989, xi) or that the novel's "sub-plot . . . fairly blatantly imitates the main plot of *The Warden*" (Williams 1986, 84). This is imitation of a curious kind that launches a broadside at values Trollope's novel endorses.

Margaret Oliphant's fiction foregrounds the social and economic arrangements supporting the privileges of conscience enjoyed by a Mr. Harding. We may pose the same question we asked in the context of George Eliot: Is there a correspondence between the way critics have formed aesthetic judgments about her work and the way Oliphant unfolds the material and social privileges that inform cultural distinction?

Oliphant introduces the question of a church sinecure in the context of women's labor—the very antithesis to a sinecure. If a sinecure rewards slight work with significant income, women's labor involves significant work for no income. Reginald May, the young, Oxford-educated son of the high church rector of Carlingford, is offered a position as warden, but he strenuously objects to taking it because it pays him 250 a year "for doing nothing." He asks his envious sisters, "how do you suppose I can be pleased? Thrust into a place where I am not wanted—where I can be of no use. A dummy, a practical falsehood. How can I accept it? . . . I tell you it is a sinecure!" (66). Reginald's sister Ursula regards the matter rather differently, wishing that "there were sinecures which could be held by girls. But no, in that as in other things 'gentlemen' kept all that was good to themselves" (73). The contrasts between male and female labor and the value accorded each structure Oliphant's tale so that whatever Reginald is doing "the girls respected his occupation as no one ever thought of respecting theirs" (105).

Oliphant's representation of Victorian domestic life emphasizes two key economic and social dispositions as they are influenced by gender. First, women work, but their labor is unvalued. Mr. May rails about girls "who are of no use" or "useless impedimenta" (108). The mythos of the angel in the house, which subtends Mr. May's rhetoric, tends to disguise female labor in many Victorian novels, Trollope's prominent among them. A frustrated Ursula cries out, "if *I* had the chance of two hundred and fifty pounds a year! there is nothing I would not do for it. . . . I would do anything, the dirtiest work" (111). But, of course, nothing she does can procure that income because women's labor is, by definition, valueless. Second, when Reginald is ultimately forced to swallow his pride and accept the sinecure, the novel acknowledges that such material fruits are distributed independently of merit and that they depend on certain kinds of social and educational capital encapsulated in the phrase "Oxford man." His sisters urge him to recognize that he can indeed find "plenty of work to do," "plenty of work in the parish." When they ask, "What do the fellows do at Oxford that they get that money for? I have heard you say you would be very glad to get a fellowship" (112), he responds, "That is different, that is a reward of scholarship." Ursula's rebuts, "Well, and so is this too. . . . You would be a really educated man, always ready to do anything that was wanted in Carlingford. Don't you see that was their meaning? They pay you for that which is not work, but they will find you plenty of work they don't pay for" (112). She has sketched out a system wherein monetary rewards of a certain kind both result from and confer social and cultural distinction.

Not surprisingly, this novel about labor, value, gender, and class has a subplot in which the impecunious upper-middle-class rector, Mr. May,

forges the signature of the prosperous lower-middle-class tradesman, Mr.
Tozer, as guarantor on a loan, and the novel's eponymous heroine privileges social and cultural distinction over blood in rescuing the elegant and
cultivated Mr. May from social humiliation and her crass grandfather's
wrath. Oliphant keeps very near the surface of her novel issues that
remain buried in Trollope's: how the value of work is assessed and how
matters of integrity and conscience ultimately rest on a bed of social and
cultural capital—Woolf's "incandescence" if you like—supported by
invisible but omnipresent social safety nets.

This is not to claim that any literary work whose values share the social
and economic dispositions of the dominant class becomes, ipso facto,
canonical. Issues of form and structure, characterization, and style all
enter into our appreciation of a work of art. I would argue for the validity of emphasizing particular social and material values in a comparison of
Trollope and Oliphant because in other narrative dimensions—such as
crafting of plot, representation of character, stylistic expressiveness, and
philosophical reach—there is substantial parity between their novels.

Interesting as these comparisons are between novels that bear a revisionary relationship to one another, we do not, of course, have definitive
or conclusive proof that the factors to which I have pointed are the ones
operating to exclude one work from and include another within the
canon. That is not my goal. Instead, I wish to highlight the applicability
of Bourdieu's theories of cultural distinction to these two Victorian novels, where one novel, deemed canonical, subtly supports ideas of culture
and value that are intrinsic, inborn, and innate and the other, lodged outside the comforts of canonicity, persistently traces the contributions of
material, educational, and social capital in the formation of high culture
and value.

Nonetheless, it is important to remember that raising questions about
the grounds for one kind of aesthetic practice does not automatically legit-
imize another. The question remains of what values might found a revised
canon.

We discover equally marked contrasts between aesthetic practices—
both inside and outside of their novels—when we consider Margaret
Oliphant in relation to George Eliot. If we follow Bourdieu's logic that
cultural capital derives principally from social capital and certain kinds of
educational capital that facilitate the universalizing of certain dispositions, then Victorian women writers are, from the beginning, seriously
disadvantaged. Bourdieu's analyses allow us to deepen our grasp of what

it means for one woman to employ a male pseudonym and the other to term herself "Mrs. Oliphant." Cultural distinction is not simply a generic refinement of manner that is coded as the outward manifestation of inner taste; it is also gendered masculine, as George Eliot's commentator in *Middlemarch* succinctly and ironically alleges: "A man's mind—what there is of it has always the advantage of being masculine,—as the smallest birch-tree is of a higher kind than the most soaring palm,—and even his ignorance is of a sounder quality" (16). Presumably, his ignorance is of a sounder quality because it is educated ignorance.

George Eliot was fashioning an aesthetic practice that generally underwrote a conventional logic of culture. For example, those who produce high culture should have a fund of educational capital on which to draw. A level of education might be generally conceded for a man of a certain class but could never be assumed in a woman. Thus, Eliot's *Middlemarch,* for example, demonstrates from chapter to chapter the extraordinary bank of educational capital on which its author can make generous drafts. Epigraphs are drawn not only from Cervantes, Milton, Spenser, Chaucer, Dante, Pascal, and Shakespeare but also from Blake, Ben Jonson, Goldsmith, Beaumont and Fletcher, Burton, Donne, Alfred de Musset, Italian proverbs, and so forth. A knowledge of Italian art, classical music, German higher criticism, and philosophy in general, French, German, and Italian languages, contemporary science, and the literatures of several nationalities constitutes only a part of the erudition that informs the narrator's commentary.

Social or class capital also has its subtle but pervasive presence. As Bourdieu points out, members of a superior class will always disdain the pleasures of the class or classes beneath them. And the "Keepsake" album that Ned Plymdale proudly presents to Rosamond Vincy as the "very best thing in art and literature" can be sneeringly dismissed by Lydgate as "sugared invention" (198–99). It is the narrator who places each participant in this comic social drama of cultural distinction, and that narrator already has also framed Lydgate within that scene as one who is "so ambitious of social distinction" that the "distinction of mind which belonged to his intellectual ardour" cannot save him from confusing acquiring substantial material possessions with the "attainment of true culture" (111).

A final refinement of universalizing certain dispositions as natural, aesthetic taste enables the cognoscenti to recuperate for high taste what the populace deems vulgar. A justifiably memorable example of this process in Eliot's canon occurs in *Adam Bede*. In the well-known chapter titled "In

Which the Story Pauses a Little," the narrator reflects on the difficulty of representing truth and then remarks that "It is for this rare, precious quality of truthfulness that I delight in many Dutch paintings, which lofty-minded people despise" (152). Although ostensibly pointing to her own simplicity in preferring "an old woman bending over her flower-pot, or eating her solitary dinner" to "cloud-borne angels . . . prophets, sibyls, and heroic warriors," she in fact asserts her cultural distinction to those who sneer, "Foh! . . . what vulgar details! What good is there in taking all these pains to give an exact likeness of old women and clowns? What a low phase of life!—what clumsy, ugly people!" (152). The narrator's cultural distinction allows her to perceive the aesthetic value in representations of vulgarity, which, to those lacking her distinction, are merely vulgar.

Bourdieu's theories, then, offer some plausible explanations for George Eliot's achievement of the cultural distinction signified by canonicity. This is neither to fault nor to celebrate her works; rather, it simply foregrounds some factors that may have contributed to their elevation.

On Oliphant's claims to cultural distinction, I can be rather brief. She does not bank on any educational capital of the kind found in Eliot, and it is easy to dismiss her novels because they do not scorn plebeian tastes. In fact, early identified as Queen Victoria's favorite novelist, Margaret Oliphant has had her educational capital fixed at a low estimate: bourgeois woman's novelist.

Middlemarch, as we have seen, strategically lays out its claims to high culture, just as representations of the author's life lay claim to a social and economic distinction free from the worries of getting and spending. We know, in fact, that Eliot supported herself with income produced from her writing, but portrayals of her life often suggest a leisured withdrawal from such monetary concerns. She terms novel writing her "true vocation," speaks of her books as "deeply serious things to me," "something worth living and suffering for," and celebrates her success in writing a novel that "people say has stirred them very deeply."[10] Contrasting her own life with George Eliot's, Oliphant picks up on this narrative, complaining, "How I have been handicapped in life! Should I have done better if I had been kept, like her, in a mental greenhouse and taken care of?" (*Autobiography* 5). Ironically, Eliot early suffered many slights for her irregular union with G. H. Lewes, but she has by and large expunged the resulting anger from her art. The image of a "mental greenhouse," upon which Oliphant seizes, bespeaks Eliot's own representation, one might say misrepresentation, of her artistic career.

Oliphant represents her own life in dramatically different terms.[11] And here I touch only on the received truisms about that life because, as I wish to argue, it is precisely those truisms that have diminished her aesthetic capital as a writer. The key details are these: Oliphant wrote too fast and too much because she needed money. The mercenary motive, Oliphant's obsession with her income, and the fact that she claims that "it was necessary for me to work for my children" (4), seem to disqualify her as an artist and turn her into a hack writer of sorts. That Oliphant also enjoyed certain social luxuries, such as first-class travel and silk dresses, further jeopardized her stature as an artist, as if an austere lifestyle fostered great art and material prosperity were inversely related to cultural capital. Perhaps Virginia Woolf led the way, memorably encapsulating Margaret Oliphant's career in *Three Guineas:* "Mrs. Oliphant sold her brain, her very admirable brain, prostituted her culture and enslaved her intellectual liberty in order that she might earn her living and educate her children" (1938, 91–92). Strains of incandescence return in this unabashed linking of economic, social, educational, and cultural capital. Thereafter, the anecdotal Margaret Oliphant became a figure who "wrote her way out of debt" (Trela 1990, 32), was "addicted to the trappings of a genteel style of life" (O'Mealy 1991, 247), "never traveled other than first class . . . always wore silk" (Haythornthwaite 1988, 39), and continually hounded her forbearing publishers for advances. Not surprisingly, we arrive at this characteristic final estimate: "[A]ll her books are flawed by speedy and careless writing" (Haythornthwaite 38). The aesthetic judgment of the novels flows from an assessment of the novelist's economic and social dispositions.

The very paucity of jobs for women meant that writing, one of the few ways to produce income, figured very differently for women than for men in Victorian culture. That is, the economic imperative does not seem to operate so strongly as a disqualifier of artistic merit for men because of the subtle way that artistic labor is gendered in nineteenth-century England. Certainly, Charles Dickens supported his family through his writing. But a man who did so operated within the tradition of the starving artist who, free to choose from an array of lucrative jobs, takes up art as the nobler and less prosperous enterprise. Far from being mercenary, he is celebrated for the sacrifices he makes for art. In contrast, women who wrote were faulted for their economic motives.[12]

Thomas Hardy offers a nearer parallel to Margaret Oliphant in suffering similar economic pressures that forced him to write quickly. Further, we know that Hardy struggled all his life with a sense of his inferiority to his university-educated peers. Bourdieu's analysis and argument, of course, comprehend marginalized male writers as well as women from all walks of life, and it would be instructive to continue this exploration by examining the interplay between Hardy's neglected novels, such as *A Pair of Blue Eyes* and *Two on a Tower,* and frequently taught classics, such as *Tess of the d'Urbervilles* or *Jude the Obscure.* Hardy, of course, has shared Margaret Oliphant's evaluation: He wrote too much, too fast. In such assessments we can easily trace the connection between aesthetic evaluations of writers' works and the material determinants of their represented lives.

Obviously, such questions of aesthetic assessment invite further thought. But in conclusion I would have us seriously consider how the educational, social, and material capital that ground cultural distinction have gendered inflections and are therefore generally more problematic for a woman writer to achieve. She is forced to demonstrate an educational capital a man is presumed to have, and, if she speaks of money, she is denied the disinterestedness requisite to great art that he is granted. George Eliot brilliantly negotiated the Scylla and Charybdis of cultural distinction for women, and for that achievement she has been awarded the accolade that she thinks "like a man."

Observing even in this cursory way how gendering the biographies of writers is not neutral but rather enters into assessments of aesthetic value prepares us for the final chapter in this study, an analysis of Queen Victoria. She was England's monarch through two-thirds of the nineteenth century, and her influence is everywhere felt in representations of the age, the nation, and the values governing the period.

Nation and Nationality: Queen Victoria in the Developing Narrative of Englishness

Building a national identity depends crucially upon narrative, and in mid-nineteenth-century England, certain prominent figures and significant events in the island's history were being mobilized in the construction of a particular historical imaginary: an idea of Englishness. In contrast to the novelistic narratives I have earlier explored, which play with and disrupt conventional generic expectations to open up the field of meaning, narratives of nations and nationality often move in a different, opposite direction, framing and circumscribing diverse and proliferating discourses of difference and multiplicity into an overarching idea. This also saw this kind of condensation in narratives of space and aesthetic value. In the case of nationality, it has recently allowed prominent politicians, Margaret Thatcher notable among them, to call for the English to return to England's Victorian values, a kind of shortcut for solving complicated national problems. What such appeals mask in their simple reductions are the tensions that inevitably inhere in such a project. These appeals rely for their power on a simplification and codification of nineteenth-century images and narratives that are themselves internally fraught; they strive to ignore, like the national narratives themselves, vexed complexities of the icon, Queen Victoria, and the age, England in the nineteenth century, to which they allude so simply. Indeed, the figure that seems to ground these narratives—Victoria herself—is she who most disturbs ideas of what it means to be both English and Victorian.

This chapter examines how representations of the monarch's position in English life and politics complicate developing narratives of Englishness and Victorianism in the nineteenth century. It explores intricate connections among images and ideas, foregrounding varied prominent strands of what is necessarily a rich and entangled network. Ultimately, then, this narrative of nation and nationality has more in common with novelistic narratives than it might wish. Although it purports to rely on and be based on facts, it remains a fiction. To the extent that it tells a story and marshals diverse figures as actors in that story, it works on connotative and suggestive levels. And it produces similar varied and multiple readings, which threaten to disrupt the very coherence it presumably set out to establish.

Victoria and Englishness

In 1701 Daniel Defoe wrote *The True Born Englishman,* a verse satire defending William of Orange against those who said that the English should not have a Dutch king. Defoe's proposition was that no such thing as a true-born Englishman existed. In his words, "We have been Europe's sink, the jakes where she Voids all her offal outcast progeny." However, ideas of "Englishness" and the "Englishman" could not be eradicated simply through mockery, and they took only a firmer hold throughout the eighteenth and nineteenth centuries, achieving a new clarity and definition through representations of Queen Victoria.

In Victoria, a national idea finds its articulation through gender, race, class, and ethnicity. As woman, mother, wife, and widow, empress of India, and queen of England, Victoria becomes a site for the concept's simultaneous consolidation and contradiction. Certainly, Victoria's father, the Duke of Kent, alive to the significance of nationalistic sentiment, early recognized the importance of birthing and raising his daughter in England, exposing his pregnant wife to danger through insisting that his child would "at whatever cost first open her eyes on English soil." And the Duke's measures—which included eliciting a promise from her mother that, whatever the hardships, Victoria would be raised in England—produced a monarch who was, in her biographer Elizabeth Longford's words, "uncompromisingly English" (263). Stanley Weintraub echoes this assessment in claiming that during her reign Victoria "became England," a conclusion cited recently by John Lucas in support of his argument that "the queen became identified as an embodiment of England during the latter half of the nineteenth century," a process involving "not merely the creation of Victoria as England but of England as Victorian" (1987, 64). I find the latter proposition—"England as Victorian"—more troubling than the former, but we must examine both more carefully for the cultural conflicts these formulations elide. Lucas sets out to argue that Victoria as "a complex female figure is produced as the emblem of England and of what are identified as English values" without acknowledging that to be an emblem of England and to embody the essence of Englishness (which is how I read his phrase "identified as English values") are not the same thing.[1] I contend that the concepts Victorianism and Englishness have a different scope in the nineteenth century and a different investment in Victoria as icon.

Victoria's contradictory inscription as ruler and mother/wife facilitated the process by which women and the domestic sphere they "governed" were amalgamated to England's imperialist mission yet also excluded from it by a positioning of the female body as ground and origin for male achievement. In this development England itself emerges as a feminine Britannia, the fertile soil of her English sons' achievements, and Englishness takes on an increasingly masculine construction. Certainly, by the early twentieth century, the association of England with ground or soil is very well established. In "The Soldier," Rupert Brooke readily amalgamates earth with England and posits his own body as English soil:

> If I should die, think only this of me:
> That there's some corner of a foreign field
> That is forever England. . . . (1941, 23)

Hardy's "Drummer Hodge" proleptically parodies such sentiments:

> Yet portion of that unknown plain
> Will Hodge for ever be;
> His homely Northern breast and brain
> Grow to some Southern tree. . . . (1925, 83)

John Lucas cites an episode in which "Eleanor Farjeon asked Edward Thomas why he had decided to fight in the first World War" and "he explained himself by kneeling down, scooping up some earth, and holding it out to her" (63–64). However, such connections did not wait until the early twentieth century to be articulated. Victoria's father, in fact, anticipates all of these in boasting that he had "fulfilled [his] duties in establishing the *English birth* of my child, and giving it material nutriment on the soil of Old England."[2]

Certainly, English identity was at issue when Victoria assumed the throne and chose as husband the German-speaking Prince Albert of Saxe-Coberg-Gotha. Lytton Strachey's 1921 biography of Queen Victoria captures national fears in its remark that "what was immediately and distressingly striking about Albert's face and figure and whole demeanor was his un-English look" (154). Contemporaneous anxieties about the royal family's national allegiance find expression in the journal *Punch,* which revealed itself to be particularly xenophobic in its satiric depictions of Albert: "Mr. Punch's criticism of Victoria and the court stemmed in part from . . . his 'Anti-Albertianism,' " which originated largely in "Albert's Germanism and his attraction to foreign cultures" (Fredeman 1987, 51). Mr. Punch also suffered some spasms of anxiety on the birth of the Princess Royal, whom he satirically depicted as being instilled with "'an utter contempt for everything English, except those effigies of her illustrious Mother which emanate from the Mint'" (Fredeman 50). However, the subsequent arrival of the Prince of Wales elated him because there were now "'two cradles between the Crown of England and the White Horse of Hanover'" (Fredeman 50). Mr. Punch's antagonism toward Albert abated only after the success of the Great Exhibition in 1851, a celebration that Victoria, like *Punch,* credited at once to Albert and to England, enthusing in her journal: "God bless my dearest Albert, and my dear Country which has shown itself so great today" (*Queen Victoria* 1985, 84).

Victoria's own determined linking of Albert and English interests perhaps facilitated gradual refigurations of the queen and her consort as Anglo-Saxons, "guardians of ancient British liberties" in British paintings of the 1850s and 1860s (Strong 1978, 44). Art historian Roy Strong points out that "The Anglo-Saxons were after all German. No wonder that at the tail end of the cult William Theed should have chosen in 1868 to depict Albert and Victoria" in an "astounding tableau" that "could as easily be relabelled 'Alfred the Great and his Queen', so interchangeable had they become" (118). This representation of Victoria both fueled and fed off of a popular impulse at midcentury to locate the very essence of Englishness in Anglo-Saxon roots. But it is important to note what Strong does not remark—that in the refiguration of the royal couple as Anglo-Saxons, Victoria is consort, Albert the king. Theed reconceives Victoria as clinging wife rather than stalwart monarch, an imagery that resonates with other iconic depictions of the royal family as embodying the "bourgeois ideals of family life" (Strong 44): "Kemble, the Anglo-Saxon historian, described her as 'fearless in the holy circle of her domestic happiness'" (Strong 152). Stanley Weintraub dubs Victoria "queenly yet middle-class at heart" (xii).

Images that depict Victoria as middle-class mother derogate from representations of her as queen regnant. They position her within Victorian culture as the ground for her son's achievements and adventures rather than the stimulus for them. Roy Strong remarks differences between representations of the Elizabethan and Victorian ages, calling attention to the freedom and status that Elizabethan women of the upper classes enjoyed, "a freedom and status unknown to the women of Victorian Britain." He adds, "*Pace* Victoria herself, [Victorian women's] kingdom was the fireside and the nursery" (154). But Strong's exemption of Victoria is somewhat illogical because representations of the queen herself serve as a prominent source of depictions of "Victorian" women. At least we must acknowledge the degree to which representations of England's "maternal monarchy," in Adrienne Munich's coinage, are iconographically complicated (1987, 265).

A significant literary work of this period plays with similar tropes, figuring contemporary England through an Anglo-Saxon past and at the same time establishing a gendered ethos of Englishness that became instrumental in Empire building. I refer to *Tom Brown's Schooldays,* published in 1857. Thomas Hughes's novel is born of the same conception of national character that produced the apocryphal "Wellington *mot,*" as it is called: to wit, that the battle of Waterloo was won on the playing fields of Eton.[3] The year that *Tom Brown's School Days* came out, the *Saturday Review* noted that "It is in these sports that the character of a boy is formed. It is from them that the readiness, pluck, and self-dependence of the British gentleman is principally caught" (quoted in Haley 1978, 161). In *The Healthy Body and Victorian Culture,* Bruce Haley explains that "In 1857 that line of thought was quite new but was catching on everywhere: the function of a public school was to turn out gentlemen; a gentleman was a man of character; character consisted of readiness, pluck, and self-dependence; and these virtues were best learned on the playing field" (161).

If those were initially the attributes only of a gentleman, they quickly became rearticulated and expanded as the elements of a national character. In 1928, when E. M. Forster wrote his essay "Notes on the English Character," he identified the character of the English as "essentially middle-class," embodying traits such as "solidity, caution, integrity, efficiency. Lack of imagination, hypocrisy" (3). That is his "First Note"; his second stipulates that "Just as the heart of England is the middle classes, so the heart of the middle classes is the public-school system. This extraordinary institution is local. It does not even exist all over the British Isles. It is unknown in Ireland, almost unknown in Scotland . . . it remains unique, because it was created by the Anglo-Saxon middle classes, and can flourish only where they flourish" (3–4). In Forster's articulations we notice some significant and by now familiar conjunctions: English character takes its shape from Anglo-Saxon roots, finds its embodiment in the Victorian middle classes, and locates its most distinctive expression in English public schools and imperialism.[4]

What, then, of a queen who has been successfully refigured as Anglo-Saxon and bourgeois? Can she be made to embody an Englishness that is articulated through a public school ethos? Although questions of race, ethnicity, and class could all be reinterpreted, gender, it seems, creates a fault line along which national identity is precariously established.

Tom Brown's Schooldays sets forth several dimensions of a developing narrative of Englishness in the mid-Victorian period. The novel opens with a history of the Browns that positions the family as responsible for the greatness of England: "For centuries, in their quiet, dogged, home-spun way, they have been subduing the earth in most English counties, and leaving their mark in American forests and Australian uplands" (13). At the point the narrative begins, the Browns are "scattered over the whole empire on which the sun never sets," and their general diffusion is "the chief cause of that empire's stability" (15). The tale is set in the Vale of White Horse, a locale dear to the hearts of those who "care for England," a "sacred ground to Englishmen. . . . For this is the actual place where our Alfred won his great battle" (16, 19). The invocation of a heroic Anglo-Saxon past constitutive of England and English virtues recalls the positioning of England's monarch in that same frame. And Hughes's novel further underscores the ways in which women are reduced within that frame (as was Victoria herself) to wives and mothers. Women figure only minimally in Tom Brown's world, as individuals against whose "petticoat government" the boy conducts a "war of independence," so that his mother finally acknowledges his "inaptitude for female guidance" (33). This is a world shaped by old country "veasts" with backswording and wrestling and racing, "something to try the muscles of men's bodies, and the endurance of their hearts," a world of "old English home duties" and the "healthy sound expression of English country holiday-making" (42, 43). A world where "English mothers," as ground and material nutriment (like the soil of old England), fortify their sons with a love "as fair and whole as human love can be" in order that a "young and true heart" can achieve the full realization and expression of English values (57).

Englishness is here articulated differentially through gender. For women it consists of the passive virtues such as perfect self-sacrifice, "love and tenderness and purity" (Hughes 288); Englishmen, in contrast, are invested with all the active virtues that have formed the Empire. Mr. Brown stipulates as specific goals for Tom's education that his son turn out "a brave, helpful, truth-telling Englishman" (66). Of Tom's journey to Rugby, the narrator remarks that his protagonist has "the consciousness of silent endurance, so dear to every Englishman—of standing out against something, and not giving in" (67). And the first Rugby match at school is imaged in terms of battle and heroic tradition: "Meet them like Englishmen, you School-house boys, and charge them home. Now is the time to shew what mettle is in you—and there shall be a warm seat by the hall fire, and honour, and lots of bottled beer to-night, for him who does his duty in the next half-hour" (93). This pattern culminates, perhaps predictably, in a celebration of fighting and Englishness: "After all, what would life be without fighting. I should like to know? From the cradle to the grave, fight, rightly understood, is the business, the real, highest, honestest business of every son of man" (218). Further, "fighting with fists is the natural and English way for English boys to settle their quarrels" (231). And finally, "if you do fight, fight it out; and don't give in while you can stand and see" (232).

At this point, women, as embodiment of the mother country England, have been written out of the script of Englishness; the public-school world exists oblivious to them except as the occasional angelic inspiration; they are mothers, wives, and widows who bear England's sons and then suffer silently and endure patiently.

This representation is not very far from those of Victoria as mother of her nation. Two poems by Barrett Browning on the occasion of Victoria's coronation and a poem and jubilee ode by Tennyson several years later demonstrate a remarkably similar imagery. In "The Young Queen" and "Victoria's Tears," Barrett Browning images the child-queen as mother of her nation—whose "grateful isles/Shall give thee back their smiles/And as thy mother joys in thee, in them shall *thou* rejoice" (2:108)—and as the embodiment of feminine sympathy whose tears influence her nation more effectively than the "tyrant's sceptre" (2:109).

First fourteen and then fifty years later, Tennyson draws on the same tropes when he celebrates Victoria in "To the Queen" (1851) and "An Ode in Honour of the Jubilee of Queen Victoria" (1887). The former poem ostensibly praises Victoria as ruler, entrusted with the "care that yokes with empire," but it concludes by emphasizing her role as static feminine icon ("Mother, Wife, and Queen") while the responsibility for initiating policy devolves on her "statesmen":

> Her court was pure; her life serene;
> God gave her peace; her land reposed;
> A thousand claims to reverence closed
> In her as Mother, Wife, and Queen;
>
> And statesmen at her council met
> Who knew the seasons when to take
> Occasion by the hand, and make
> The bounds of freedom wider yet
>
> By shaping some august decree
> Which kept her throne unshaken still,
> Broad-based upon her people's will,
> And compass'd by the inviolate sea. (1–2)

Victoria is directed by her statesmen who represent "her people's will." The jubilee ode, much parodied in its day for its prosy preachiness, has significance for us in the ease with which it trots out clichés of Victorian womanhood. Tennyson celebrates Victoria for possessing

> Nothing of the lawless, of the despot,
> Nothing of the vulgar, or vainglorious,
> All is gracious, gentle, great and queenly.
> * * *
> Queen, as true to womanhood as Queenhood,
> Glorying in the glories of her people,
> Sorrowing with the sorrows of the lowest! (529)[5]

These poetic images resonate with the portrayals of the queen in portraiture of the early and middle Victorian period. In his article "Portraits of the Queen," Ira Nadel comments that "Victoria's portraits . . . are conscientious efforts to record the certainty and assuredness of the Queen and what she and her family represent: the domestic, bourgeois values of stability, comfort, and security" (1987, 170). Nadel, however, identifies three distinctive phases in the development of Victoria's portraits, "each related to a different period of her life, and emphasizing a different set of iconographic elements" (173). The first phase, princess/queen, "suggests domesticity as well as sentiment" (175). The second, "Queen and Mother," becomes "insistently historic and domestic," emphasizing

Victoria and Albert as Anglo-Saxons guarding ancient British liberties (the icon Roy Strong also identified), an image that "reflected the domestic bliss they projected on to the nation." Curiously, a third phase appears to contravene the previous images. Following the widow's seclusion and withdrawal from public life, portrait painters felt it imperative to respond explicitly "to public criticism over Victoria's neglect of public duties following the Prince's death" and to depict the queen no longer as "idealized regent or mother" but as "the resolute guardian and embodiment of English power" (179). Thus, portraits of Victoria in this last phase seem to contradict what I have been arguing about the way the queen is deployed in a developing narrative of Englishness. And, indeed, Nadel acknowledges that "The image of the stern monarch, renewing her claim on the monarchy, contradicts, of course, the maternal and self-conscious figure in the portraits from her middle period" (182).

Surprisingly, too, the iconography of the late portraits seems to run counter to literary representations, which, as we have already seen in Tennyson's jubilee ode, tended to deploy conventional feminized images. Is there a profitable way to explore these apparent contradictions? In fact, the 1875 von Angeli portrait of the queen, in which Nadel locates the new iconography of regal power, also embodies these same contradictions, a fact Nadel acknowledges but does not investigate. Nadel notes that, "wearing a black dress accentuated by a double strand of pearls, large ruby bracelet, and white handkerchief, Victoria is a portrait in contrasts. At once she is the grieving widow and the Empress exerting her power" (179). Thus, if she is an icon for England, it is still mother England, the Britannia to which John Lucas points in his article "Love of England: The Victorians and Patriotism." Lucas argues that the successive images of Victoria became "merged in other significant images: of Liberty and Britannia" (1987–1988, 64): "Victoria as Liberty may be under threat and so expect chivalric defense; Victoria as Britannia may have a warriorlike invulnerability and so command deferential awe" (65).

Portraits of Victoria as Liberty and Britannia find literary echoes that suggest how even this puissant icon becomes complicit in conventional feminine values when England is articulated separately from Englishness. As we have seen, in this gendered division woman becomes the body that nourishes true Englishmen and that subsequently demands their loyal defense.[6] George Eliot's essay "The Modern Hep! Hep! Hep!"(n.d.) provides a narrative of this process. Purportedly from the hand of Theophrastus Such, this essay sets forth Englishness in terms derived from the "seafaring, invading, self-asserting men [who] were the English of old time" (131) because the "the eminence, nobleness of a people" depends on "this living force of sentiment in common which makes a national consciousness" (n.d. 132). It is, however, the immediately succeeding comment that is most telling here: "Nations so moved will resist conquest with the very breasts of their women" (132). Apparently, nation is so precious that men will sacrifice even their women in its defense. Logically, then, nation is herself that most sacred feminine figure requiring defense, and her men enact their pride of nationality in defending her. This passage and others like it work at a differential gendering of nation and nationality that accords well, I would argue, with the iconography of Queen Victoria. Woman, queen, mother England—Britannia is that which must be defended by stalwart sons animated by a consciousness of their "national life" or Englishness: "The only point in this connection on which Englishmen are agreed is, that England itself shall not be subject to foreign rule. The fiery resolve to resist invasion, though with an improvised array of pitchforks, is felt to be virtuous, and worthy of a historic people. Why? Because there is a national life in our veins. Because there is something specifically English which we feel to be supremely worth striving for, worth dying for, rather than living to renounce it" (144). A woman and a queen, Victoria was gradually shaped into an icon of England in ways that left the narrative of Englishness to be articulated through discourses of masculinity.

Victoria and Victorianism

The first part of my argument has forwarded the proposition that in Victorian England different and gendered sites developed for the cultural investments that inform the concepts of nation and nationality. But what, then, we might inquire, of the age to which she gave her name: the Victorian? How is the concept of Victorianism related to Victoria herself, and how is it differently inflected from the idea of Englishness in the nineteenth century?

Obviously, this question cannot be easily or comprehensively answered, and its very formulation poses the danger—one also present in my discussion of Englishness—of encouraging oversimplification and generalization. Victorianism itself has become a catch-all term for movements, behaviors, and beliefs that extend beyond England's borders. G. M. Young, looking back on the Victorian Age from the perspective of the early twentieth century, admits that "the more carefully one studies the years between the death of William IV and the accession of Edward VII, the more difficult it becomes to find anything to which the word Victorian can be correctly and exclusively applied. Much to which we commonly give the name, turns out on a closer acquaintance to be simply nineteenth century, or simply European" (1962, 158–59). Or he reminds us that "the Victorian Age, as we call it, is the insular phase of a movement common to the whole of Western Europe and its offshoots beyond the seas" (110–11). In fact, the concept has become so broad that its association with the person Victoria may seem purely adventitious—a historical convenience. Although aware of the dangers of generalization, Margaret Homans has recently called attention to a corollary problem, the fact that little, if any, notice has been paid to the figure who gave her name to an age. Indeed, the Victorian period is persistently and commonly discussed without even an allusion to Victoria.[7] Homans argues that, "while Victoria may have been subject to an ideology over which no individual had control, it is impossible not to think that she had some active hand in shaping the ideology that bears her name" (1994 245). Homans's goal, therefore, as well as my own cautious attempt here, is to begin "to put Victoria back into Victorian" (258 n. 11).

I have already indicated that early portraiture of Victoria cast her as mother—of a nation, of a family, of a nation as family. The domestication of the monarch helped produce and was itself produced by an ideology of domesticity that commentators often seize upon when seeking something quintessential to define the last half of the nineteenth century in England. And, certainly, here we may locate one prominent intersection of Englishness and Victorianism. In his essay "Tempus Actum," G. M. Young puzzles over the concept of Victorianism and confesses that "the truth is that much of what we call Victorianism is a picture at second hand, a satirical picture drawn by the Victorians themselves. The word does undoubtedly mean something, but what it means has to be built up by going behind the criticism, the invention, and the caricature, and examining the originals" (1962, 159). What Young calls an "origin" is precisely that generally privileged construction of the concept that we are looking for. Young's search culminates, perhaps predictably, in "the ordinary educated, evangelical household [as] in many ways the pivot of Victorian life" (160), by which he also means the "respectable" family (122).[8] Later he claims of this period that the "family counts for everything" (122). This ideology has been remarkably durable; in his book

Victoria's Year (1987), Richard Stein identified this adulation of domesticity as the heart of Victorianism and its parodies.

Certainly Victoria has lent her name to *this* familial ideology of Victorian life. Indeed, the virginal young queen embodied a dramatic change from her predecessors, and she was readily seized upon as an icon of emergent bourgeois values. Writing in 1937 on the centenary of Victoria's accession to the throne, Young remarked of the period that the "transference of the Crown from an elderly, undignified, and slightly crazy sailor to a girl endowed with remarkable self-possession and much force of character, could hardly be without its picturesque circumstances" (1962, 24). For him it represented a "waft of Arcadia" (25).[9] Associations of conventional propriety and familial devotion accumulated around Victoria despite the fact that, as Dorothy Thompson points out, "if the stereotypical Victorian woman was well-mannered, self-effacing, demure and devoid of passion, Queen Victoria was so far from the stereotype as to be almost its opposite" (1990, 44). Indeed, Victoria is memorable for her distress at being forced repeatedly to bear children; she described herself as "furious" when she learned of her first pregnancy, complained that an "ugly baby is a very nasty object," and always expressed distaste for "that terrible frog-like action" of newborns (*Dearest Child* 1964, 191). Albert, more maternal, was continually admonishing the queen to be more of a mother and less a monarch with her nine children. But the public conferred upon Victoria an image of itself that confirmed both the emergence and importance of middle-class domesticity. That self-portrait was facilitated by the "diffusion of cheap printed words and pictures [that brought] the image of the monarch and her family regularly into the consciousness of her subjects" (Thompson 139). In 1867 Walter Bagehot summarized the effect of familiarizing the populace with a wifely and maternal Victoria: "A *family* on the throne is an interesting idea. It brings down the pride of sovereignty to the level of petty life."[10] Albert's death in 1861 further solidified Victoria's bourgeois image because she "refused ever again to wear the robes of state, appearing in versions of widow's weeds" (Thompson 141).

Thus, as this analysis suggests, the markers of domesticity that helped define Victorianism for both the nineteenth and twentieth centuries also ultimately distinguished it from emerging concepts of Englishness that accumulated around more imperial and masculine representations. To the extent that Victoria embodied wifehood and maternality, she became the imagined essence of Victorianism but therefore not the quintessence of Englishness.

We may examine more fully the way gendered qualities were shaping a split between Victorianism and Englishness by continuing with the writings of Young and Lytton Strachey. These two prominent intellectuals were both born in Victorian England: Strachey in 1880 and Young in 1882. They thus experienced the last two decades of Victoria's rule but also lived through the early modern period during which images of the queen and her age continued to be consolidated along certain gender lines. In his biography of Queen Victoria, Strachey reveals himself to be surprisingly sympathetic to the queen and her consort, especially in view of harsher assessments his peers within the Bloomsbury group were voicing. Strachey writes of Victoria's early life that "it was her misfortune that the mental atmosphere which surrounded her during these years of adolescence was almost entirely feminine. No father, no brother, was there to break in upon the gentle monotony of the daily round with impetuosity, with rudeness, with careless laughter and wafts of freedom from the outside world" (1921, 45). He adds, "henceforward, female duty, female elegance, female enthusiasm, hemmed her completely in" (45). While Strachey focuses on the misfortune of Victoria's personal development, G. M. Young sets out to define what he sees as the great misfortune of the Victorian age: its failure to develop a national secondary school system. He says, "Fundamentally, what failed in the late Victorian age and its flash Edwardian epilogue, was the Victorian public, once so alert, so masculine, and so responsible" (Young 6–7). It is, frankly, hard to know what to make of this statement; it is so confident in its sweeping generalizations. It implies that the Victorian public had become self-absorbed, feminine, and insular—all of which adjectives could easily have described the queen—first by training and then through her reclusive mourning for Albert. Significantly, these two ostensibly different commentaries both play on gender tropes to develop their meanings. Strachey positions Victoria as effectively crippled by her femininity, and then Young depicts the age as crippled by its feminization.

The differentiation between Victorianism and Englishness receives its most interesting and compelling articulation in relation to the Great Exhibition in 1851. Tracing the earliest example and subsequent popularization of the term *Victorian,* Richard Stein notes that "the adjective came into use in 1851, the year of the Crystal Palace and the founding of the Australian colony of Victoria" (1987, 274). Significantly, Strachey's biography locates the consolidation of the Victorian Age and Victorianism in the Great Exhibition. Defining Victoria as having "surrendered her whole soul to her husband," Strachey depicts her as upholding a "standard of moral purity with an inflexibility surpassing, if that were possible, Albert's own" (Strachey 1921, 169, 195). Strachey then launches into peroration, introducing the concept of a Victorian age through what he terms its "living apex," Victoria:

> But she was no longer Lord M.'s pupil: she was Albert's wife. She was more—the embodiment, the living apex of a new era in the generations of mankind. The last vestige of the eighteenth century had disappeared; cynicism and subtlety were shriveled into power; and duty, industry, morality, and domesticity triumphed over them. Even the very chairs and tables had assumed, with a singular responsiveness, the forms of prim solidity. The Victorian Age was in full swing. (195)

This passage then segues into a discussion of the Crystal Palace: "Only one thing more was needed: material expression must be given to the new ideals. . . . It was for Albert to supply this want. He mused, and was inspired: the Great Exhibition came into his head" (Strachey 1921, 195–96).

The opening of the Crystal Palace was, as I noted earlier, a pivotal point in England's embrace of Victoria's German consort, Albert. His achievement brought distinction to England and therefore national gratitude to him. Again, an ironic but not unsympathetic Strachey comments from his perspective in Bloomsbury, England: "In 1851 the Prince's fortunes reached their high-water mark. The success of the Great Exhibition enormously increased his reputation and seemed to assure him henceforward a leading place in the national life" (204). Then the reader is informed that, "before the year was out another triumph, in a very different sphere of action, was also his": During a country visit, he "had ridden to hounds and acquitted himself remarkably well" (204).

Certainly, although subtly parodic, this assessment remarkably conflates events of enormously different magnitudes and therefore provides a pressure point for analyzing concepts of Victorianism and Englishness. Strachey goes on to remark that "This was a serious matter." It seemed to suggest that Albert "was a good fellow after all" (205). But then he failed to follow up his advantage because hunting bored him, and, although it was agreed that he "could keep in his saddle well enough," he was pronounced "no sportsman" (205). Or, in Strachey's rendition of the popular sentiment, "The Prince, in a word, was un-English. What that word pre-

cisely meant it was difficult to say; but the fact was patent to every eye"
(206). Strachey then constructs an archetypal struggle between Albert and
Lord Palmerston, then foreign secretary. Strachey represents Palmerston as
"the very antithesis of the Prince" and "English through and through."
There was "something in him that expressed, with extraordinary vigour,
the fundamental qualities of the English race" and thus, "all the mysterious forces in Albert's soul leapt out to do battle with his adversary, and,
in the long and violent conflict that followed, it almost seemed as if he
was struggling with England herself" (206). This remarkable narrative
creates out of Lord Palmerston a kind of democratic imperialist who had
"an English gentleman's contempt and dislike of foreign potentates deep
in his heart" and enjoyed protecting "the interests of Englishmen abroad"
(219, 210). The phrase that is supposed to capture his Englishness is
"happy valiance," expressed in conduct at once bold and prudent in the
pursuit of national and international affairs (209). Albert, in Strachey's
narrative, remains tied to monarchical interests throughout Europe and
committed to "due order, with careful premeditation" (222). In short,
Albert was Victorian but not English, and he "remained as foreign as
before," although Victoria "had won for him the title of prince consort,"
asserting that " 'the Queen has a right to claim that her husband should
be an Englishmen'" (1857).[11] And the consort's position helped construct
the frame in which the queen would be understood and interpreted:
Victorian to the core, the image of England herself, but not possessed of
"happy valiance," that masculine insouciance that makes one quintessen-
tially English. That trait belonged to her foreign secretary, who would
later rise to the post of prime minister.

Victoria and Elizabeth I

This is, of course, an inflection of Englishness similar to that touted in
Tom Brown's Schooldays and elaborated in the public school mythology
Hughes's novel helped to create. But in touching on the relations of true
Englishness to conflicts with foreign potentates, it introduces the third
context—a subtext of Victorianism—in which I wish to consider
Victoria's place in the narrative of nationality: that is, in the Victorians'
construction of the Elizabethan age. By participating in defining another
age in terms of its queen—the designation "Elizabethan is a nineteenth-
century coinage" (Ormond 1987, 30)—the Victorians forwarded and jus-
tified their own project of nation and empire building under Victoria. Just

as Queen Elizabeth faced down Spain and Parma, so, too, would England, under Victoria, achieve international supremacy.

The comparative project of English queens began immediately with Lord John Russell's expressed hope on Victoria's accession that she would be an Elizabeth without her tyranny, an Anne without her weakness.[12] It is notable, however, that similarities between the sixteenth- and nineteenth-century rulers that may seem apposite "from the vantage point of the late twentieth century," did not readily present themselves to the Victorians, who focused on the differences between the women (Ormond 1987, 30). Lord Macaulay's *History of England from the Accession of James the Second* speaks eloquently about its orientation toward early monarchs, Elizabeth among them, by effectively beginning its narrative with James the Second.[13] The *History*'s first chapter covers the long period "Before the Restoration," and the sense that Macaulay has done justice to England's history in this compacted narrative of its early period suggests Macaulay's assessment of this period's relative lack of importance to England's identity. Indeed, for Macaulay, England takes her identity from the distinctive way in which, after the accession of James the Second, monarchical interests became bound up with the rights of the English people, a process marked by the increasing cooperation rather than struggle between "our sovereigns and their Parliaments" (1899, 1).

This historical and national narrative suggests why periods of Elizabeth's reign were read as abusive; the story of the English people required that reading. For example, when Elizabeth "took upon herself to grant patents of monopoly by scores," we learn that "there was scarce a family in the realm which did not feel itself aggrieved by the oppression and extortion which this abuse naturally caused" (62). Macaulay continues, "The language of the discontented party [the House of Commons] was high and menacing, and was echoed by the voice of the whole nation. The coach of the chief minister of the Crown was surrounded by an indignant populace, who should not be suffered to touch the old liberties of England" (62). This evocation of the "old liberties of England" and "the voice of the whole nation" posits a condition and disposition to Englishness that make it incompatible with monarchal authority/power. England herself, in all her potential, emerges only when monarchy cooperates with, bows to, the "natural" authority of the people. Thus, at this moment of crisis in Elizabeth's reign, when "there seemed for a moment to be some danger that the long and glorious reign of Elizabeth would have a shameful and disastrous end," she "with admirable judgment and temper, declined the contest, put herself at the head of the reforming party, redressed the grievance, thanked the Commons . . . brought back to herself the hearts of the people, and left to her successor a memorable example of the way in which it behooves a ruler to deal with public movements which he has not the means of resisting" (62–63). Elizabeth is positioned therefore as one who had to learn the lesson of sovereign cooperation with the people, a lesson fully inculcated by Victoria's rule.

Although historians and politicians perceived the women themselves to be different and to function differently in the narrative of Englishness, the fact that they were both female monarchs facilitated comparisons between the two ages and the discovery of similarities there. Victoria on the throne encouraged contemporaneous commentators to construct a link between the period of her reign and Elizabethan England and to imagine in the two ages a shared English heroism and sense of English destiny. In " 'The spacious times of great Elizabeth': The Victorian Vision of the Elizabethans," Leonée Ormond points out the extent to which the Victorians self-consciously constructed the Elizabethan age, often ignoring historical accuracy in the interest of certain heroic myths (1987, 34–35). For the Victorians, "the Elizabethan age had two great strengths: One being its writers, the other its seamen" (32). To the Victorians, language and its uses were as central in creating national identity as was bold and heroic action.[14] They brought them together in their choice of Elizabethan worthies: Shakespeare, Spencer, and Sidney on the one hand; Grenville, Raleigh, and Drake on the other. In evolving an English vernacular, the literature and language of the Elizabethans forged the beginnings of a national consciousness; the exploits of their sea heroes created foundations for national supremacy and empire building.

Charles Kingsley's novel *Westward Ho!* and James Anthony Froude's essay "England's Forgotten Worthies," in particular, helped to popularize new versions of England's past, in contradistinction to Macaulay's *History of England,* which opens with the Glorious Revolution of 1688 and the establishment of constitutional monarchy as "the event from which the true development of the English people could be traced" (Ormond 37). In "England's Forgotten Worthies," Froude so effectively contended that Englishmen of the sixteenth century forged an indispensable link in the chain of English national identity that he set in motion a process through which "the Elizabethans were no longer regarded as a barbaric and unfortunate element in England's history, and an increasingly celebratory attitude began to emerge," culminating in an "almost mythic status" for

Elizabeth and her age (Ormond 43, 46). Ormond convincingly traces this process in her essay but stops short of what interests me here: the necessity of the Elizabethan myth to developing Victorian myths of empire. That connection emerges clearly in Froude's and Kingsley's accounts of England's relations to the West Indies.

In *At Last! Christmas in the West Indies,* Kingsley chronicles his own journey from Southampton, England, to the Spanish Main, celebrating that he is "on the track of the old sea-heroes; of Drake and Hawkins, Carlile and Cavindish, Cumberland and Raleigh." As he passes the Azores, he recalls and quotes Richard Grenville's famous words after his 1591 defeat in valiant battle[15] and poses the question, "There were heroes in England in those days. Are we, their descendants, degenerate from them? I, for one, believe not" (1871, 6). This is nation building tied to empire building as Kingsley joyfully prepares to touch ground in the "New World" of England's West Indian colonies.

In *The English in the West Indies,* Froude refers to those same seafaring men, and he closes the first chapter of his book with a warning that for England to allow the West Indies to "drift away" from her power "because they have no immediate marketable value, would be a sign that she had lost the feelings with which great nations always treasure the heroic traditions of their fathers" (1888, 10). He concludes, "When those traditions come to be regarded as something which concerns them no longer, their greatness is already on the wane" (10). Although couched in the language of fathers, the argument is implicitly ad feminam, gesturing for its logic to two queens, who embody Britannia herself.

This connection between a heroic past and a present condition recalls passages in George Eliot's "The Modern Hep! Hep! Hep!" in which Theophrastus Such locates the origins of Englishness in an even earlier tradition of seafaring men, praising the "language and genius" of those "old English seamen, who, beholding a rich country with a most convenient seaboard, came, doubtless with a sense of divine warrant" (130). Mr. Such concludes, "Let us know and acknowledge our common relationship to them, and be thankful that, over and above the affection and duties which spring from our manhood, we have the closer and more consistently guiding duties that belong to us as Englishmen" (131). The presence of Victoria has been all but swallowed up in a narrative of nation, ages, and empire, but that narrative found its initial impetus in the meaningful coincidence of queens on England's throne: two distinctive women, two heroic periods, one great nation.

This chapter only begins what must be a longer project: teasing out Victoria's complex relationship to developing, interwoven narratives of Englishness and Victorianism in nineteenth-century England. The terms necessarily resist simple codification. Even a preliminary study reveals the complex relationship between the figure of Victoria and the articulation of key elements of nation and national identity. Where she seems most tangential—in the Victorian creation of the Elizabethan Age—she is perhaps most central because her very longevity as queen increasingly fed notions of similarities between the ages and helped to nurture a vision of imperial destiny played out over centuries. The Victorian age is thus thoroughly imbued with the figure who gave it her name although that individual has often been effectively erased from accounts of the period.[16] To return her to those stories of national identity, however, is not to stabilize them. It is not simply that they are destabilized to the extent they rely on narrative and representation. Because both nation and national identity are associated with specifically masculine virtues, the monarch's gender further clouds the very concepts she supposedly crystallizes. Thus, the historical figure that seems to ground these narratives—Victoria herself—is she who most disturbs ideas of what it means to be both English and Victorian and thus fully exposes the fictive nature of this particular national story.

This final chapter, then, shares with those that have preceded it an awareness of gender's importance in reading narrative. It is by no means the only term I might have adopted in this study, and, to the extent I have been able without dissipating the focus, I have worked to bring in other terms, particularly class and, in this final essay, nationality. Jointly, these perspectives illuminate the resources and tendencies of narrative in Victorian England, even as, I trust, they cast light into various recesses of the age itself.

Notes

Introduction

1. The work of historian Hayden White has been instrumental in helping us to appreciate the ways that historical documents and lives are "constructed." Recently, Kali Israel has completed a fascinating biography of Victorian Emilia Dilke that argues for her subject as a complex site for narrative representation, both by herself and others. Israel explains that "Emilia Dilke is a point of entry into a range of historical and contemporary issues and an incitement to consider the relations—contradictions and reversals as well as homologies and importations—of diverse political, intellectual, social, and aesthetic histories" (*Names and Stories* 8).

2. Series editor's foreword, in Joseph Boone, *Tradition, Counter Tradition,* p. vii.

3. See D. A Miller, *The Novel and the Police,* and Lennard J. Davis, *Resisting Novels: Ideology and Fiction.*

4. "A Criticism of Our Own," in *Feminisms: An Anthology of Literary Theory and Criticism,* ed. Warhol and Herndl (New Brunswick, N.J.: Rutgers University Press, 1991), p. 184.

5. *Outside in the Teaching Machine,* p. 5.

6. Elizabeth Grosz, *Volatile Bodies,* develops a similar argument. Grosz argues, "It is not adequate to simply dismiss the category of nature outright, to completely retranscribe it without residue into the cultural: this is in itself the monist, or logocentric, gesture par excellence" (21).

7. In *Making a Social Body,* Poovey continues:

As this last point should make clear, I am suggesting that the late twentieth-century feminist debate about whether experience is a more politically acceptable basis than theory for feminist analysis is one legacy of the preservation of an alternative mode of knowing *within* the epistemology of modern abstraction. The preservation of this alternative and its current appeal to so many of us is *not* proof of its superiority, however, or even of its ability to survive outside the context of modern abstraction in which it has come down to us. Instead, the preservation of an alternative mode of knowing is simply one sign that the power distributed through the institutions associated with modern abstraction will never be as total as its early theorists dreamed it could be. (54)

8. The Victorian age has benefited particularly from recent work. In *Victorian Masculinities: Manhood and Masculine Poetics in Early Victorian Literature and Art* (1995), Herbert Sussman argues, for example, that manhood was even more problematic than womanhood because there existed a "masculine plot" as a counterpart to the much-discussed "marriage plot." Sussman illuminates how the domestic ideal—by managing male energies yet also vitiating male creative potency—disciplined men as well as women in Victorian England.

The disciplining of women in Victorian England is, of course, a topic much canvassed by feminist critics. James Eli Adams's *Dandies and Desert Saints: Styles of Victorian Masculinity* takes up gender to demonstrate that " 'Manliness' is exemplary of all gender norms in being always under pressure from the very social dynamics that authorize it." Like Sussman, Adams discovers Victorian men laboring under the "burdens of masculine self-fashioning," and he traces the contradiction within Victorian patriarchy that "the same gender system that underwrote male dominance also called into question the 'manliness' of intellectual labor," a conflict Mary Poovey earlier called to our attention in her discussion of Charles Dickens. See her chapter on Dickens in *Uneven Developments*, pp. 89–125.

9. See, for other examples, Claudia Nelson, *Boys Will Be Girls* and *Invisible Men*. See also Michael Mason, *The Making of Victorian Sexuality*, and Andrew H. Miller and James Eli Adams, eds., *Sexualities in Victorian Britain*.

10. My foci here on space, aesthetic value, and nationality cut a broad swathe through Victorian culture, but much more remains to be done. For example, Patricia Murphy has recently published a book that examines the intricate interplay of gender and time. *Time Is of the Essence: Temporality, Gender, and the New Woman* argues that the gendering of time helped to reinforce the rigid boundaries between masculinity and femininity.

11. Alison Blunt and Gillian Rose, eds., *Writing Women and Space*, p. 2. There has been a spate of important work recently on the gendering of geography. See, especially, Beatriz Colomina, ed., *Sexuality and Space*; Gillian Rose, *Feminism and Geography*; and Doreen Massey, *Space, Place, and Gender*.

12. See, particularly, the significant work on gender and American national identity by Lauren Berlant, *The Queen of America Goes to Washington City*.

13. See, for example, Benedict Anderson's *Imagined Communities*; Homi Bhabha's *Nation and Narration*; Julian Wolfreys's *Being English*; or Simon Gikandi's more recent *Maps of Englishness*. These critics are all highly attuned to the performativity of nationality, considering Englishness or national identity, in Peter Mason's words, as "the product of an economic of structuring discourse which produces in the act of discourse that very object which it purports to describe" (cited in Wolfreys, p. 5).

Chapter 1

1. In the concept of intertextuality with which I engage, readers will recognize the influence of Jacques Derrida. His memorable formulation—"Il n'y a pas de hors-texte" [There is nothing outside the text] (158)—challenges a traditional mimetic understanding of literature as referring both to world and to precursor works, and thus it opens up rich possibilities for our understanding of narrative interrelationships.

2. Andrew and Judith Hook make a fine argument for the thematic unity of *Shirley.* They identify four narrative strands: "The life histories of Caroline Helstone, and Shirley Keeldar and their romantic involvement with the Moore brothers, the women's rights, tutor-governess theme; the regional Yorkshire manners theme; and the unemployed poor, Luddite theme" (20). They define "denial of the world of feeling" as the overarching theme, making these diverse threads into a unified fabric (25). I agree that feeling (also related to imagination and fancy) is an important theme, but I am interested in probing the formal dimension of the work, the contradiction in the novel's definition of reality that I believe is the true source of the repeated claims of disunity, not the simple presence of different stories.

3. Gilbert and Gubar, in their excellent analysis of hunger, have already pointed out that the novel opens with male curates gorging themselves and that Brontë sets that image alongside those of women languishing and starving (373–74). We should note further that, as readers, we are apparently not to be gorged but to partake of a meager, acerbic fare, perhaps all that a woman writer within patriarchy has to offer since that is all that patriarchy has to offer women.

4. Many critics, such as John Maynard and Helene Moglen, take at face value the narrator's protestations that she will confine herself to the "real," and they never question her narrative practice. Maynard comments, "Brontë's half-hearted, somewhat backsliding conversion toward realism and away from passion, stimulus and melodrama provides the aesthetic context for the diffuse form and content of *Shirley*" (151). Making a similar argument for *Shirley's* realism, Robert Keefe sees the conclusion of *Shirley* as "escapist" precisely because the rest of the novel "so convincingly portrays the real world" (147, 148).

5. Brontë's myth of Eve supplants the patriarchal reading of reality, where Eve is Milton's "cook" (315), replacing it with a "woman-Titan": "[V]ast was the heart whence gushed the well-spring of the blood of nations; and grand the undegenerate head where rested the consort crown of creation" (315). The novel further affirms a new feminist reality of "mother Eve undying mighty Being!" (316) by asserting the subjectivity of reading. Brontë's Caroline, a nineteenth-century forerunner of reader-response critics, argues with Joe Scott, who cites Genesis in support of women's inferiority to men: "He may read it [Genesis] in his own fashion" (323). Brontë's new myth of mother Eve reveals the corruptions of our "Great Mother" by patriarchal mythologists such as Milton.

6. Just as patriarchy replaces parity with hierarchy in male/female relationships, so, too, it corrupts female bonds of friendship and kinship. Much could be made of the essential sympathy between Caroline and Shirley, the way in which they complete each other's thoughts and words. Much, too, might be, and has been, made of the ways in which Shirley—as alter ego—can act out what Caroline can only dream of. We need here to acknowledge Brontë's representation of the ways in which patriarchal society, with its masculine privilege mirrored in class prerogatives, tends to fragment female bonds—separating friend from friend, sister from sister, mother from daughter—so that a feminist ideality remains in tension with a patriarchal experiential reality. Caroline may aver to Shirley as part of a dawning feminist consciousness that "I never had a sister—you never had a sister, but it flashes on me at this moment how sisters feel towards each other. Affection twined with their life, which no shocks of feeling can uproot. . . . I am supported and soothed when you—that is you only are near" (265). But her assertion comes on the heels of Shirley's recognition of female competition in patriarchy in her admission that

Robert "keeps intruding between you and me: without him we should be good friends; but that six feet of puppyhood makes a perpetually recurring eclipse to our friendship" (264).

7. The fragmentation of persons mirrored in fragmented relationships gives rise to a female anger that is covertly expressed. It is revealed in Shirley's vision of mermaids described as "temptress-terror! monstrous likeness of ourselves!" (249). Shirley has told Caroline that "Were we men, we should spring at the sign, the cold billow would be dared for the sake of the colder enchantress" (249). Despite Caroline's denial that "she is not like us; we are neither temptresses, nor terrors, nor monsters," the narrator ultimately enacts against Robert on Caroline's behalf precisely that anger that might fuel the temptress's deadly enchantment (250).

8. Charlotte Brontë's own words are illuminating. She reports in a letter to W. S. Williams, 29 August 1849: "The occupation of writing it [Shirley] has been a boon to me. It took me out of a dark and desolate reality into an unreal but happier region" (Correspondence 115). I suggest that Brontë used her awareness of what was real and what was romantic to interrogate each concept.

9. Mr. Yorke is typical: He is "without the organ of Veneration . . . without the organ of Compassion—a deficiency which strips a man of sympathy . . . and he had too little of the Organ of Benevolence and Ideality" (796). The narrator settles upon this last deficiency of ideality or imagination—acknowledging that in men like Yorke imagination is seen as a "rather dangerous, senseless attribute—akin to weakness" (77–78). But the narrator affirms its value to its possessors: "[F]anatics cling to their dream, and would not give it up for gold" (78). Dismissive as the term "dream" may seem, the judgment works against those like Mr. Yorke who possess no imagination, who construct their realities narrowly. Men such as Yorke and his clerical brother Helstone are pragmatic men, priding themselves on their freedom from illusions, particularly as they concern women and marriage. Helstone speaks of his earlier marriage as a form of madness (125) even though he won the coveted Mary Cave, and Yorke, who lost her to Helstone, makes the damning confession to Moore that "if Mary had loved and not scorned me . . . the odds are, I should have left her!" (505).

10. The isolation of Robert begins even before Mrs. Horsfall arrives. The narrator first presents Mrs. Yorke practically gloating because Moore has been "committed to her charge . . . left in her arms, as dependent on her as her youngest-born in the cradle. . . . She chased Jessie and Rose from the upper realm of the house: She forbade the housemaid to set foot in it" (524). Further, "visitors they [Hortense and Mrs. Yorke] both of them agreed in excluding sedulously from the sick-room. They held the young millowner captive, and hardly let the air breathe or the sun shine on him" (525).

11. Martin Yorke is explicitly associated with fairy tales. We see him in the woods with a "contraband volume of fairy tales," reading of "a crowd of foam-women—a band of white, evanescent Nereides," when Caroline Helstone appears (528), recalling Shirley's earlier described murderous mermaids.

12. Terry Eagleton, in his Marxist analysis, has also perceived in Shirley a conflict between a romantic and a realistic view, and he defines the novel's resolution as an alliance of "Romantic conservatism and bourgeois realism" (56). For Eagleton, Shirley "has in the end the best of both worlds . . . a middle ground between the most objectionable extremes of reverence and rebellion, land and trade, gentry and bourgeoisie." Eagleton's "middle

ground" spells reconciliation in a monology; I argue, in contrast, that the oppositions are not—cannot be—ultimately harmonized, and they remain in dialogic tension.

13. *Narratologies.*

Chapter 2

1. To the extent Charlotte responded to her sister in *Shirley*, she appears to heed her sister's critique because she denies her later male protagonist Rochester's massive sensual appeal and returns to the austerity and autocratic probity of her professor, Crimsworth.

2. Only recently has Anne Brontë's *Tenant of Wildfell Hall* begun to receive the attention it deserves. The reasons for the neglect are many. See my *Anne Brontë: The Other One*.

3. George Moore, *Conversations in Ebury Street*, p. 254. On the subject of narrative infelicities in Brontë's *Tenant*, Moore is joined by other, later critics, notably Winifred Gérin, Introduction, *The Tenant of Wildfell Hall*, p. 14. However, some fine recent articles have attempted to do more justice to the narrative structure of the novel, particularly as it revises Emily's *Wuthering Heights*. See Jan Gordon, "Gossip, Diary, Letter, Text: Anne Brontë's Narrative Tenant and the Problematic of the Gothic Sequel" and Naomi Jacobs, "Gender and Layered Narrative in *Wuthering Heights* and *The Tenant of Wildfell Hall.*" More recent essays have addressed the question of the novel's technique in its own right. See Edith A. Kostka, "Narrative Experience as a Means to Maturity in Anne Brontë's Victorian Novel *The Tenant of Wildfell Hall*," who reads the framed narration as a technique for bringing Gilbert Markham to maturity, and Catherine MacGregor, " 'I Cannot Trust Your Oaths and Promises: I Must Have a Written Agreement': Talk and Text in *The Tenant of Wildfell Hall*," who connects Brontë's choice of technique to her experience of her brother's alcoholic addiction. See also Carol Senf, " *The Tenant of Wildfell Hall:* Narrative Silences and Questions of Gender."

Chapter 3

1. In 1895 Hardy wrote about *Jude the Obscure*, "Sue is a type of woman which has always had an attraction for me, but the difficulty of drawing the type has kept me from attempting it till now" (letter to Edmond Gosse, 20 November 1895, in F. E. Hardy, p. 280). Albert J. Guerard, *Thomas Hardy: The Novels and Stories*, p. 113. Irving Howe has characterized that type as the "epicene woman"—the ethereal, spiritualized, undersexed coquette who drives men to distraction. So summarized, Sue Bridehead may seem a monstrously unpleasant person, as unpleasant as most fictional neurotics. But she is, as it happens, "one of Hardy's most appealing heroines" (*Thomas Hardy* 143). See also A. Alvarez, who asserts, "in creating [Sue] Hardy did something extraordinarily original: he created one of the few totally narcissistic women in literature, but he did so at the same time as he made her something rather wonderful" (Thomas Hardy, *Jude the Obscure*, afterword). These contradictory assessments result in part from a failure to account for Jude's perspective on and construction of his cousin.

2. See Langland, "A Perspective of One's Own: Thomas Hardy and the Elusive Sue Bridehead." Michael Millgate locates an ambivalence in Hardy himself: "[T]he book's implied judgment of Sue's character and conduct seems finally uncertain and inconsistent" (*Thomas Hardy: A Biography* 353–54).

3. Hardy's novel *The Well-Beloved*, the writing of which frames *Jude the Obscure*, also deals with a man's idealization of a female figure, but here the idealization is so explicit that critics immediately recognize the women—Avice one, two, and three—as reflections of Jocelyn Pierson's needs. For example, J. Hillis Miller remarks, "The drama of *The Well Beloved* is throughout a more internal one [than that of *Jude*]. It is the story of the single consciousness divided against itself, striving to merge again with itself, seeing in others even of the opposite sex, only its own double" (*Fiction and Repetition* 160). From the perspective of *The Well Beloved*, it is not difficult to see how Sue Bridehead, too, is a narcissistic projection of Jude's ambivalent wishes. We might also argue that Jocelyn's fitful response to the beloved and her shifting incarnations also expresses his desire for—yet fear of—the feminine.

4. One critic who has, surprisingly, approximated some of my insights, although within a very different theoretical framework, is D. H. Lawrence (*Phoenix: The Posthumous Papers of D. H. Lawrence*). That is, where I would not follow Lawrence's essentializing discourse of male and female, I find very insightful his apprehension of the coercive force Jude exerts on Sue to fulfill his needs. Joseph Wiesenfarth points to the Lacanian implications of Jude's and Sue's behavior, noting that "they see the Other to validate their own sense of self. . . . [but ultimately] Jude and Sue repudiated the penis [sexual desire] for the phallus ['an approved male dominated cultural code']." I emphasize instead Hardy's focus on Jude and the social construction of character (*Gothic Manners and the Classic English Novel* 52).

5. Laura Green incorporates a discussion of *Jude the Obscure* within a consideration of the "complexity of the gender and class identifications of the self-made man of letters whose position Hardy exemplifies." Green reads Hardy's novel as challenging "precisely such distinctions between character as socially contingent and character as inherently constituted and, most fundamentally, between masculine and feminine fulfillment" (523, 537). See " 'Strange (In)difference of Sex': Thomas Hardy, the Victorian Man of Letters, and the Temptations of Androgyny."

6. In an illuminating article that employs the insights of Austin and speech theory, William R. Goetz makes a similar observation about the status of the "natural." Goetz notes that "In *Jude the Obscure* the natural law initially seems to be prior to the social law, which must be interpreted as either an "enunciation" or a deformation of it. By the end of the novel, these two laws are threatening to collapse into one." Ultimately, we discover these are "false options . . . between a life in society and a life in nature. There is no authentic possibility of a life outside of the law in *Jude*" ("Felicity and Infelicity of Marriage in *Jude the Obscure*" 212–13).

Chapter 4

1. This connection, which may be otherwise formulated as the connection between country house and madhouse, is early suggested in Mary Wollstonecraft's *Maria or the Wrongs of Woman*, in which the wife is drugged and transferred to a madhouse so her husband can seize her property, and in Charlotte Brontë's *Jane Eyre*, a novel whose gothic influences make it a kind of precursor to sensation fiction. Here the connection emerges in the relationship between Jane Eyre, the would-be mistress of Thornfield, and Bertha Mason, the actual mistress of Thornfield, who is mad and confined to its upper quarters. The relationship between Jane and Bertha was early adumbrated in Elaine Showalter's *A*

Literature of Their Own. The motif of the female carceral in nineteenth-century literature was identified by Sandra Gilbert and Susan Gubar in *The Madwoman in the Attic.*

2. Insofar as Collins's novel explored these relationships between women and madness, that exploration has been nicely adumbrated by D. A. Miller in *The Novel and the Police.* However, Miller's focus on gender issues leads him to ignore significant class issues that also haunt Collins's novel, so that he notices but does not analyze the allusions to Limmeridge as an "asylum." Nonetheless, Miller gives a fine analysis of female confinement in Collins's novel: "Male security in *The Woman in White* seems always to depend on female claustration" (166). Miller also observes that "the suitably feminine wife must have been schooled in a lunatic asylum, where she is half cretinized" (166).

3. See my book *Nobody's Angels* for an analysis of the conclusion of *The Woman in White,* pp. 233–38.

4. Again, D. A. Miller's analyses of the rhetoric of madness lead him to a similar conclusion: "The achievement of blowing this cover belongs to *Lady Audley's Secret* (1862), the novel where, writing under the ambiguous stimulus of *The Woman in White,* Mary Elizabeth Braddon demonstrates that the madwoman's primary 'alienation' lies in the rubric under which she is put down" (169). Miller does not take up the emerging meanings of the country house in the nineteenth century that are producing these connections. His gendered analysis thus leads him to conclude that "Lady Audley is mad, then, only because she must not be criminal. She must not, in other words, be supposed capable of acting on her own diabolical responsibility and hence of publicly spoiling her assigned role as the conduit of power transactions between men" (170–71).

5. The enclosure of common lands had been going on for a couple of centuries by the dawn of the nineteenth century, and critics are beginning to analyze questions of enclosure and sexuality. Specifically, *Enclosure Acts,* edited by Richard Burt and John Michael Archer, emphasizes the "figure of enclosure itself as the uneven ground on which sexuality and politics meet in the cultural study of early modern England" (2). The collection's essays, like mine, "deal variously with bodily enclosure and the enclosure of property" (2).

6. See my *Nobody's Angels,* pp. 1–61, for an extended discussion of the role of the middle-class woman as household manager.

7. Girouard notes the institution of afternoon teas in the 1840s (280). I discuss these etiquette practices in Chapter 2 of *Nobody's Angels.*

Chapter 5

1. Speaking to class issues, Gareth Stedman Jones, in *The Languages of Class,* argues that "separation from the working class" was a "novel product of the Victorian period" (184). Previously, "social distinctions abounded at every level, but there was no great political, cultural or economic divide between the middle class and those beneath them. . . . All classes shared in the passions for gambling, theatre, tea gardens, pugilism and animal sports. All except the richest merchants lived within a short distance of their work, if not at the place of work itself. The pub was a social and economic centre for all and heavy drinking was as common among employers as among the workmen" (185).

Describing the intersections of a gendered geography with class interests, feminist geographers Gillian Rose and Alison Blunt note that "Feminist historians, for example, have described the emergence of the division between public and private spaces from the early

19th century onward in Europe and North America as part of the cultural project of an emerging middle class. The elaboration of the private as a domestic haven of feminine grace and charm, and of the public as the arena of aggressive masculine competition, is increasingly seen as a development that enabled the bourgeoisie to distinguish themselves from other social groups" (3).

2. See, particularly, Patricia Boling, who argues for "a more complex way of thinking about privacy, one that is cognizant of its "both/and" quality (*both* empowering *and* depriving), and that attends to the crucial task of connecting private—especially intimate—life experience to political language, categories, and claims" (xiii). Also, Joan Landes notes that, "Far from being a platform for personal fulfillment, in feminist writings the private sphere first figured as a site of sexual inequality, unremunerated work, and seething discontent" (1). Leonore Davidoff and Catherine Hall, in turn, focus on the gendering of public and private spheres in Victorian England and their close intersections with the institutions of private property and the market (*Family Fortunes*).

3. Feminist analyses of the power relations embedded in such geographies for a long while focused almost exclusively on the distinction between public and private space. See Carole Pateman, p. 118, who claims that the public/private distinction has structured feminist discourse.

4. I have benefited from the work of feminist geographer Doreen Massey, herself influenced by Lefebvre, who argues that "we need to conceptualize space as constructed out of interrelations, as the simultaneous coexistence of social interrelations and interactions at all spatial scales" (264). See also Gillian Rose and Alison Blunt, who note that "More recent anthropological work exploring the relationship between gendered identity and space has suggested that gendered spaces should be understood less as a geography imposed by patriarchal structures, and more as a social process of symbolic encoding and decoding that produces 'a series of homologies between the spatial, symbolic and social orders.' The social construction of gender difference establishes some spaces as women's and others as men's; those meanings then serve to reconstitute the power relations of gendered identity. However, since the outcome of the decoding process can never be guaranteed, contestation and renegotiation of the meaning of spaces is also always possible" (3).

5. In "Shall the CD Act Be Applied to the Civil Population?" *Contagious Diseases Act*.

6. Cited in Wilkinson, epigraph.

7. Cited in Felix Driver, *Power and Pauperism*, 58.

8. Cited in S. Jackman, *Galloping Head* (London: Phoenix House, 1958), p. 63

9. George W. M. Reynolds's 1853 novel *The Seamstress, or The White Slave of England*, concludes with a similarly scathing indictment of workhouses:

Ah! that terrible word—the *Workhouse!* What miseries—what degradations—what sufferings are summed up in that appalling dissyllable! A severance from all the ties of human fellowship—a state of vile prisonage, characterised by the same gray garb that felons wear in gaols and hulks—an awful monotony in the routine of existence—the utter abasement of the mind beneath a sense of consummate humiliation,—all these ideas are condensed in the one word that expresses the lowest and most abject condition of human misery . . . that living tomb which the heartless rich have formed for their worn-out serfs and superannuated slaves! (91)

10. Reprinted from *The Church of England Monthly Review.*

11. Bourdieu defines corporeal or bodily "hexis" as "the political mythology realized, *em-bodied,* turned into a permanent disposition, a durable way of standing, speaking, walking, and thereby of feeling and thinking" (*The Logic of Practice* 69–70).

Chapter 6

1. Bourdieu notes that Woolf "criticizes the novels of Wells, Galsworthy and Bennett because 'they leave one with a strange sense of incompleteness and dissatisfaction' and the feeling that it is 'necessary to do something—to join a society, or, more desperately, to write a cheque', in contrast to works like *Tristram Shandy* or *Pride and Prejudice,* which, being perfectly 'self-contained', 'leave one with no desire to do anything, except indeed to read the book again, and to understand it better'" (35). This is an aesthetic practice that privileges detachment and distance, the very distance and detachment that Woolf notes were largely unavailable to women writers in patriarchal societies. Her female Shakespeare still needs another hundred years to emerge.

2. See John Guillory's *Cultural Capital,* pp. 10–17. Guillory claims that the author returns in critique of canon, not as genius, but as a "representative of a social identity" (10), and he argues that the process of canon formation is too complex to be reduced to determination by a single factor of the social identity of the author (17).

3. Bourdieu notes that "it must never be forgotten that the working-class 'aesthetic' is a dominated 'aesthetic' which is constantly obliged to define itself in terms of the dominant aesthetic" (41).

4. Bourdieu adds, "[the ideology of natural taste] only recognizes as legitimate the relation to culture (or language) which least bears the visible marks of its genesis, which has nothing 'academic', 'scholastic', 'bookish', 'affected' or 'studied' about it, but manifests by its ease and naturalness that true culture is nature—a new mystery of immaculate conception" (68).

5. For a critic who effectively elucidates George Eliot's patriarchal dispositions, see Daniel Cottom, *Social Figures.* Cottom claims that,

> in treating Eliot as a liberal intellectual, I am treating her as a figure of patriarchy. There is a nominal justification for this treatment in the pseudonym she adopted as a novelist, as well as a more important justification in the way intellectual power was generally denominated a male quality in the social practices of nineteenth-century England. Despite the fact that she was often critical of the contemporary condition of women in her novels, letters, and other writings, Eliot was by no means exempt from adopting the stereotypes involved in these social practices, and insofar as she identified herself with a form of thought she considered to be neutral, she identified with a form of thought that systematically demeaned women as well as other groups of people, such as the poor and working classes. (xx–xxi)

6. Lewes, quoted in Langbauer (1990, 204–5).

7. Naomi Schor, who helpfully identifies contempt for the detail with its association with women, also notes the prominence of the detail in the theories of Barthes, Derrida, and Foucault: "Viewed in a historical perspective, the ongoing valorization of the detail

appears to be an essential aspect of that dismantling of Idealist metaphysics which looms so large on the agenda of modernity" (1987, 3–4).

8. See, for example, Ruth apRoberts, who beautifully summarizes this position:

> Not only are we told that Mr. Harding is a good man, and not only do we see him and know him as virtuous—and his virtue can only be as real as it is because he is highly individuated—not only is all this so, but further, we *love* Mr. Harding. We are involved. We know he accepted the sinecure innocently, and he performs his duties with the greatest devotion and success; he is not one to stick by the Letter of the Law—he supplies the old men with extra allowances out of his own income. He glorifies God in the excellent sweetness of his music, and the corresponding excellent sweetness of his life. (140)

9. In an interesting and related note, J. C. Eade (1992) has documented that the monetary figures cited in *The Warden* don't add up, either in what Mr. Harding imagines it will cost him to increase the bedesmen's allowance or in what Hiram's estate is producing. Such carelessness about the economic issues, which Eade attributes to Trollope rather than to Mr. Harding, suggests in both author and character that disdain for material capital that is possible only to those at a sufficient distance from want.

10. *Selections from George Eliot's Letters*, p. 230.

11. Elisabeth Jay's biography of Margaret Oliphant notes that, "As the *only* woman admitted to the great tradition, until recent years, George Eliot then became the paradigm for discussing the woman's experience as writer. This exception really did begin to prove the rule by which other women writers were judged. This has proved damaging because, as it so happened, George Eliot's life and work could very neatly be fitted into another male-centred, nineteenth-century myth: the myth of progress" (246).

12. Bourdieu notes that literary works are often denied cultural distinction if they are believed to proceed from mercenary motives.

Chapter 7

1. Lucas adds of Victoria's cultural construction that "Moreover, this loved body is largely put together by and for male consumption. (Victorian patriotism had little to offer women beyond their being encouraged to develop as images of the queen, in which sign husbands might conquer.) This requires some comment" (65). However, he fails to comment on the explicit contradiction of the maternal monarch, confining his discussion instead to the gradual emergence of Victoria from the 1870s onward as a figure "somehow 'above' politics" (65).

2. Quoted in Strachey, p. 27.

3. Bruce Haley notes that "The Duke of Wellington did not, we now know, claim that the battle of Waterloo was won on the playing fields of Eton. But the authenticity of the 'Wellington mot' . . . was accepted by almost everybody, and the myth inspired a sort of lugubrious pride. It is hard to say when the story got started, but it is at least as old as the Comte de Montalembert's remarks on Eton in 1856" (1978, 170).

4. Bruce Haley notes that the "process begun with *Tom Brown* culminates with 'Vitaï Lampada': the highest values of the schoolboy become the guiding principles of the adult"

(260). Haley explains that the phrase " 'play the game' was immortalized in Henry Newbolt's poem 'Vitaï Lampada.' An ex-schoolboy soldier, his regiment under bloody siege, rallies his comrades with inspiriting words recalled from his days on the cricket field:

> This is the work that year by year,
> While in her place the School is set,
> Every one of her sons must hear,
> And none that hears it dare forget.
> This they all with joyful mind
> Bear through life like a torch a flame,
> And falling fling to the host behind—
> 'Play up! play up! and play the game!' " (260)

5. It is interesting that parodies of Tennyson's *Ode* often debunked the image of Victoria as tender "mother" and guardian to her people, depicting her instead in images of familial partiality, cupidity, and malfeasance:

> Fifty times the rose has flower'd and faded,
> Fifty times it would have bloomed without her—
> smelt as sweet without "the crown, the sceptre."

Or,

> Fifty times the State has fooled and blundered,
> Fifty times the royal pension's risen
> Since the Queen assumed the globe, the sceptre.

The final stanza is revised thus,

> Are there thunders moaning in the distance?—
> 'Tis the German band of near relations;
> Trust the mother Queen to guide her people
> Where they'll live in plenty without labour,
> And her Alberts, Victors, Georges, Henries,
> Families raise for Jubilees for ages. (Cited in Fredeman 20, 21)

6. Again, Lucas automatically conflates the concepts of England and Englishness, as in this claim: "That was why it was so important to promote images of the monarchy as 'above' politics or party interest, and as reconciling opposing points of view in a single, seamless concept of 'Englishness'" (66).

7. It is notable, for example, that Walter Houghton's magisterial *The Victorian Frame of Mind* alludes to Victoria only four times, all passing references: for example, "Frederic Harrison, brought up from the country at the age of seven to see Queen Victoria's coronation . . ." (1957, 308); or, "Levity is what Queen Victoria found 'not amusing'" (357). For Houghton, Victoria is not a relevant figure to discuss in assessing the Victorian frame of mind.

8. Young explains this concept at length:

The great dividing line in 1860 is not rich and poor, but the respectable and the others. You may be rich, but if you are not respectable you will not pass muster in the eyes of society. The Queen will not have you at Court. Mothers will not let their daughters dance with you. On the other hand, you may be poor, but if you are respectable the world will think well of you. And what are the outward and visible signs of respectability? Well, by now I think you know: cleanliness—the children at school—sobriety (a pint of beer may pass, the respectable man never enters a gin shop)—the benefit club—the family walk of a Sunday afternoon—the weekly magazine, like the *Weekly Welcome* or the *British Workman*. You can complete the tale yourselves. (122)

9. It is interesting to note the structural and stylistic similarities between Young's description of this transition and Strachey's from his biography:

What, above all, struck everybody with overwhelming force was the contrast between Queen Victoria and her uncles. The nasty old men, debauched and selfish, pig-headed and ridiculous, with their perpetual burden of debts, confusions, and disreputabilities—they had vanished like the snows of winter, and here at last, crowned and radiant, was the spring. (1921, 72)

We have a glimpse of ideology in the making.
10. Quoted in Thompson, p. 139.
11. Victoria's letter quoted in Strachey, p. 288.
12. Cited in Strachey, p. 72.
13. *The Complete Works of Thomas Babington Macaulay,* vol. I (New York: Sully and Kleinteich, 1899).
14. Macaulay's "Minute on Indian Education" (1835) famously recommends unequivocally that English, instead of Arabic or Sanskrit, be employed in the instruction of Indians. He argues that, "Whether we look at the intrinsic values of our literature, or at the particular situation of this country, we shall see the strongest reason to think that, of all foreign tongues, the English tongue is that which would be the most useful to our native subjects" (723). He adds, "The literature of England is now more valuable than that of classical antiquity" (724). Macaulay's goal is to "form a class [of Indians] who may be interpreters between us and the millions whom we govern; a class of persons, Indian in blood and colour, but English in taste, in opinions, in morals, and in intellect" (729). Language and national identity go hand in hand.

In a similar nationalistic vein, George Eliot's Theophrastus Such argues that "it is a calamity to the English, as to any other great historic people, to undergo a premature fusion with immigrants of alien blood; that its distinctive national characteristics should be in danger of obliteration" (142). He "groans" over the threatened danger manifest every day in the foreigners' corruptions of English:

To one who loves his native language, who would delight to keep our rich and harmonious English undefiled by foreign accent . . . it is an affliction as harassing as the climate, that . . . we must expect to hear our beloved English, with its words clipped, its vowels stretched and twisted, its phrases of acquiescence and politeness, of cordiality, dissidence, or argument, delivered always in the wrong tones, like ill-rendered melodies, marred beyond recognition. (Eliot 142–43)

15. "Here die I, Richard Grenville, with a joyful and quiet mind; for that I have ended my life as a true soldier ought, fighting for his country, queen, religion, and honour" (Kingsley 5).

16. Two new studies of Victoria that consider the importance of the queen to her age are Margaret Homans's *Royal Representations: Queen Victoria and British Culture, 1837–1876* (Chicago: University of Chicago Press, 1998) and Gail Turley Houston's *Royalties: The Queen and Victorian Writers* (Charlottesville: University of Virginia Press, 1999).

Works Cited

Abel, Elizabeth, Marianne Hirsch, and Elizabeth Langland, eds. *The Voyage In: Fictions of Female Development.* Hanover, N.H. : University Press of New England, 1983.

Acton, William. "Shall the CD Act Be Applied to the Civil Population?" *Contagious Diseases Act.* London: John Churchill and Sons, 1870.

Adams, James Eli. *Dandies and Desert Saints: Styles of Victorian Masculinity.* Ithaca: Cornell University Press, 1995.

Alcoff, Linda. "Cultural Feminism versus Post Structuralism: The Identity Crisis in Feminist Theory." *Signs* 13 (Spring 1988): 405–36.

Alvarez, A. Afterword to *Jude the Obscure,* by Thomas Hardy. New York: New American Library, 1961.

Anderson, Benedict. *Imagined Communities: Reflections on the Origin and Spread of Nationalism.* London and New York: Verso, 1983.

apRoberts, Ruth. "The Shaping Principle." In *The Trollope Critics,* ed. N. John Hall, 138–51. Totowa, N.J.: Barnes and Noble Books, 1981.

Argyle, Gisela. "Gender and Generic Mixing in Charlotte Brontë's *Shirley.*" *Studies in English Literature* 35, no. 4 (Autumn 1995): 741–56.

Armstrong, Nancy. *Desire and Domestic Fiction: A Political History of the Novel.* Oxford: Oxford University Press, 1987.

Auerbach, Nina. *Woman and the Demon: The Life of a Victorian Myth.* Cambridge: Harvard University Press, 1982.

Austen, Jane. *Pride and Prejudice.* New York: Norton, 1966.

Bakhtin, M. M. *The Dialogic Imagination: Four Essays,* trans. Caryl Emerson and Michael Holquist. Austin: University of Texas Press, 1981.

———. *Problems of Dostoevsky's Poetics,* ed. Caryl Emerson. Minneapolis: University of Minnesota Press, 1984.

Bal, Mieke. "Sexuality, Semiosis and Binarism: A Narratological Comment of Bergen and Arthus." *Arethusa* 16, no. 1–2 (1983): 117–35.

Barthes, Roland. *S/Z: An Essay,* trans. Richard Miller. New York: Hill and Wang, 1974.

———. *Sade-Fourier-Loyola,* trans. Richard Howard. New York: Hill and Wang, 1976.

———. "The Death of the Author." In *Image-Music-Text,* trans. Stephen Heath, 142–48. New York: Hill and Wang, 1977.

Bauer, Dale. *Feminist Dialogics: A Theory of Failed Community.* Albany: State University of New York Press, 1988.

————. "Gender in Bakhtin's Carnival." In *Feminisms: An Anthology of Literary Theory and Criticism,* ed. Robyn Warhol and Diane Price Herndl, 671–84. New Brunswick, N.J.: Rutgers University Press, 1991.

Beer, Patricia. *Reader, I Married Him: A Study of the Women Characters of Jane Austen, Charlotte Brontë, Elizabeth Gaskell, and George Eliot.* London: Macmillan, 1974.

Berlant, Lauren. *The Queen of America Goes to Washington City: Essays on Sex and Citizenship.* Durham: Duke University Press, 1997.

Bhabha, Homi, ed. *Nation and Narration.* London and New York: Routledge, 1990.

Blunt, Alison, and Gillian Rose, eds. *Writing Women and Space: Colonial and Postcolonial Geographies.* New York and London: The Guilford Press, 1994.

Boling, Patricia. *Privacy and the Politics of Intimate Life.* Ithaca and London: Cornell University Press, 1996.

Boone, Joseph A. *Tradition, Counter Tradition: Love and the Form of Fiction.* Chicago: University of Chicago Press, 1987.

Booth, Wayne. Introduction to *Problems of Dostoevsky's Poetics,* by M. M. Bakhtin. Ed. Caryl Emerson, xiii–xxvii. Minneapolis: University of Minnesota Press, 1984.

Bourdieu, Pierre. *Distinction: A Social Critique of the Judgement of Taste.* Cambridge: Harvard University Press, 1984.

————. *The Logic of Practice,* trans. R. Nice. Cambridge: Polity Press, 1990.

Braddon, Mary Elizabeth. *Lady Audley's Secret.* New York: Dover Publications, 1974.

Brontë, Anne. *The Tenant of Wildfell Hall.* Harmondsworth: Penguin, 1979.

Brontë, Charlotte. *Jane Eyre,* ed. Richard J. Dunn. New York: Norton, 1971.

————. *Shirley,* ed. Andrew and Judith Hook. Harmondworth: Penguin, 1974.

Brooke, Rupert. "The Soldier." In *The Poetical Works of Rupert Brooke,* ed. Geoffrey Keynes. London: Faber and Faber, 1941.

Brooks, Peter. "Freud's Masterplot: Questions of Narrative." *Yale French Studies* 55–56 (1977): 280–300.

Brown, Marshall, ed. *The Uses of Literary History.* Durham: Duke University Press, 1995.

Browning, Elizabeth Barrett. *The Complete Works of Elizabeth Barrett Browning.* 2 vols. New York: Thomas Y. Crowell, 1900. New York: AMS Press, 1973.

Buckley, Jerome. *Season of Youth: The Bildungsroman from Dickens to Golding.* Cambridge, Mass., and London: Harvard University Press, 1974.

Burt, Richard, and John Michael Archer, eds. *Enclosure Acts: Sexuality, Property, and Culture in Early Modern England.* Ithaca and London: Cornell University Press, 1994.

Butler, Judith. *Gender Trouble: Feminism and the Subversion of Identity.* New York: Routledge, 1990.

————. *Bodies That Matter.* New York and London: Routledge, 1993.

Calder, Jenni. *Women and Marriage in Victorian Fiction.* New York: Oxford University Press, 1976.

Case, Alison A. *Plotting Women: Gender and Narration in the Eighteenth- and Nineteenth-Century British Novel.* Charlottesville and London: University of Virginia Press, 1999.

Chitham, Edward, and Tom Winnifrith. *Brontë Facts and Brontë Problems.* London: Macmillan Press, 1983.

Christ, Carol. "Victorian Masculinity and the Angel in the House." In *A Widening Sphere: Changing Roles of Victorian Women,* ed. Martha Vicinus, 146. Bloomington and London: Indiana University Press, 1977.

Church of England Monthly Review. London: Longman, Brown, Green, Longmans, and Roberts, 1858.

Cixous, Hélène. "The Laugh of the Medusa." In *New French Feminisms: An Anthology,* ed. Elaine Marks and Isabelle de Courtivron, 245–64. New York: Schocken, 1981.

Clayton, Jay, and Eric Rothstein, eds. *Influence and Intertextuality in Literary History.* Madison: University of Wisconsin Press, 1991.

Cobb, Frances Power. *Friendless Girls and How to Help Them: Being an Account of the Preventive Mission at Bristol.* London: Emily Faithfull, 1861.

Collins, Wilkie. *The Woman in White.* New York: Oxford University Press, 1973.

———. *Man and Wife,* ed. and introd. Norman Page. Oxford and London: Oxford University Press, 1995.

Colomina, Beatriz, ed. *Sexuality and Space: Princeton Papers on Architecture.* New York: Princeton Architectural Press, 1992.

Cottom, Daniel. *Social Figures: George Eliot, Social History, and Literary Representation.* Minneapolis: University Minnesota Press, 1987.

Crews, Frederick. *E. M. Forster: The Perils of Humanism.* Princeton: Princeton University Press, 1962.

Culler, Jonathan. *On Deconstruction: Theory and Criticism after Structuralism.* Ithaca: Cornell University Press, 1982.

Cullwick, Hannah. *The Diaries of Hannah Cullwick, Victorian Maidservant,* ed. Liz Stanley. New Brunswick, N.J.: Rutgers University Press, 1984.

Davidoff, Leonore, and Catherine Hall. *Family Fortunes: Men and Women of the English Middle Class, 1780–1850.* Chicago: University of Chicago Press, 1987.

Davis, Lennard J. *Resisting Novels: Ideology and Fiction.* New York and London: Methuen, 1987.

Dearest Child, Letters between Queen Victoria and the Princess Royal, 1858–1861, a selection from the Kronberg Archives, ed. Roger Fulford. London: Evans Brothers, 1964.

DeLauretis, Teresa. *Technologies of Gender: Essays on Theory , Film, and Fiction.* Bloomington: Indiana University Press, 1987.

Dellamora, Richard. "Textual Politics/Sexual Politics." In *The Uses of Literary History,* ed. Marshall Brown, 143–57. Durham: Duke University Press, 1995.

Derrida, Jacques. *Of Grammatology,* trans. Gayatri Chakravorty Spivak. Baltimore: Johns Hopkins University Press, 1976.

Dickens, Charles. *Our Mutual Friend.* New York: Modern Library, 1960.

Diengott, Nilli. "Narratology and Feminism." *Style* 22, no. 1 (1988): 42–51.

Dilke, Charles. *Greater Britain.* 2 vols. London: Macmillan, 1868, II, 403.

Dinnerstein, Dorothy. *The Mermaid and the Minotaur: Sexual Arrangements and Human Malaise.* New York: Harper, 1976.

Dreyfus, Hubert, and Paul Rabinow, eds. *Michel Foucault: Beyond Structuralism and Hermeneutics,* 2d rev. ed. Chicago: University of Chicago Press, 1983.

Driver, Felix. *Power and Pauperism: The Workhouse System, 1834–1884.* Cambridge: Cambridge University Press, 1993.

Eade, J. C. " 'That's the Way the Money Goes': Accounting in *The Warden.*" *Notes and Queries* 39 (June 1992): 182–83.

Eagleton, Terry. *Myths of Power: A Marxist Study of the Brontës.* London: Macmillan Press, 1975.

Eliot, George. "Art and Belles Lettres." *Westminster Review* 9 (January/April 1856): 625–50.

———. *The George Eliot Letters,* ed. Gordon S. Haight. 9 vols. New Haven: Yale University Press, 1954–78.

———. *Middlemarch,* ed. Gordon S. Haight. Boston: Houghton, Mifflin, 1956.

———. *The Mill on the Floss.* Boston: Houghton, Mifflin, 1961.

———. *Daniel Deronda,* ed. Barbara Hardy. Harmondsworth: Penguin, 1967.

———. *Adam Bede,* ed. John Paterson. Boston: Houghton, Mifflin, 1968.

———. *Selections from George Eliot's Letters,* ed. Gordon S. Haight. New Haven and London: Yale University Press, 1985.

———. "The Modern Hep! Hep! Hep!" In *The Essays of Theophrastus Such.* New York: William Allis, n.d.

"English Bastille, The." *Social Science Review* 3 (1865): 197.

Fernando, Lloyd. *"New Women" in the Late Victorian Novel.* University Park and London: Penn State University Press, 1977.

Fitzgerald, Penelope. Introduction to *Phoebe Junior,* by Margaret Oliphant. Harmondsworth: Penguin, 1989.

Forster, E. M. "Notes on the English Character." In *Abinger Harvest.* New York: Harcourt, Brace, and Company, 1936.

———. "The Art of Fiction." *Paris Review* 1 (1953).

Foucault, Michel. *The Archaeology of Knowledge and the Discourse on Language,* trans. A. M. Sheridan Smith. New York: Pantheon, 1972.

———. *Discipline and Punish: The Birth of the Prison,* trans. Alan Sheridan. New York: Vintage, 1979.

———. *The History of Sexuality,* vol. 1. Trans. Robert Hurley. New York: Vintage Books, 1980.

———. "The Subject and Power." In *Michel Foucault: Beyond Structuralism and Hermeneutics,* 2d rev. ed. Ed. Hubert Dreyfus and Paul Rabinow, 208–26. Chicago: University of Chicago Press, 1983.

Fredeman, William E. "A Charivari for Queen Butterfly: *Punch* on Queen Victoria." *Victorian Poetry* 25, no. 3–4 (1987): 47–73.

———. "Introduction: England Our Home, Victoria Our Queen." *Victorian Poetry* 25, no. 3–4 (1987): 1–8.

———. "Lord Tennyson's Jubilee Ode from Walter Hamilton's Parodies." *Victorian Poetry* 25, no. 3–4 (1987): 10–27.

Friedman, Susan Stanford. "Weavings: Intertextuality and the (Re)birth of the Author." In *Influence and Intertextuality in Literary History,* ed. Clayton Jay and Eric Rothstein, 146–80. Madison: University of Wisconsin Press, 1991.

Froude, James Anthony. *The English in the West Indies; or The Bow of Ulysses.* New York: C. Scribner's Sons, 1888.

Garrett, Peter. *The Victorian Multiplot Novel: Studies in Dialogical Form.* New Haven: Yale University Press, 1980.

Genette, Gérard, *Narrative Discourse: An Essay in Method,* trans. Jane E. Lewin. Ithaca: Cornell University Press, 1980.

Gérin, Winifred. Introduction to *The Tenant of Wildfell Hall,* by Anne Brontë, 194–211. Harmondsworth: Penguin, 1979.

Gikandi, Simon. *Maps of Englishness: Writing Identity in the Culture of Colonialism*. New York: Columbia University Press, 1996.

Gilbert, Sandra, and Susan Gubar. *The Madwoman in the Attic: The Woman Writer and the Nineteenth-Century Literary Imagination*. New Haven: Yale University Press, 1979.

Gillooly, Eileen. *Smile of Discontent: Humor, Gender, and Nineteenth-Century British Fiction*. Chicago and London: University of Chicago Press, 1999.

Gilmour, Robin. Introduction to *The Warden*, by Anthony Trollope. Harmondsworth: Penguin, 1984.

Girouard, Mark. *Life in the English Country House*. New Haven: Yale University Press, 1978.

Goetz, William R. "Felicity and Infelicity of Marriage in *Jude the Obscure*." *Nineteenth-Century Literature* 38, no. 2 (September 1983): 189–213.

Gordon, Jan. "Gossip, Diary, Letter, Text: Anne Brontë's Narrative Tenant and the Problematic of the Gothic Sequel." *English Literary History* 51, no. 4 (1984): 719–45.

Green, Laura. "Strange (In)difference of Sex: Thomas Hardy, the Victorian Man of Letters, and the Temptations of Androgyny." *Victorian Studies* 38, no. 4 (Summer 1995): 523–49.

Grosz, Elizabeth. *Volatile Bodies: Toward A Corporeal Feminism*. Bloomington: Indiana University Press, 1994.

Guerard, Albert J. *Thomas Hardy: The Novels and Stories*. Cambridge: Harvard University Press, 1949.

Guillory, John. *Cultural Capital: The Problem of Literary Canon Formation*. Chicago: University of Chicago Press, 1993.

Haight, Gordon S. Introduction to *The Mill on the Floss*, by George Eliot. Boston: Houghton, Mifflin, 1961.

———. *George Eliot: A Biography*. New York and London: Oxford University Press, 1968.

Haley, Bruce. *The Healthy Body and Victorian Culture*. Cambridge: Harvard University Press, 1978.

Hall, N. John, ed. *The Trollope Critics*. Totowa, N.J.: Barnes and Noble Books, 1981.

Harding, James M. "The Signification of Arabella's Missile: Feminine Sexuality, Masculine Anxiety and Revision in *Jude the Obscure*." *Journal of Narrative Technique* 26, no. 1 (Winter 1996): 85–111.

Hardy, Barbara. *Particularities: Readings in George Eliot*. London: Peter Owen, 1982.

Hardy, F. E. *The Life of Thomas Hardy, 1840–1928*. London: Macmillian, 1962.

Hardy, Thomas. *The Well-Beloved*. The Wessex Edition. London: Macmillian, 1903.

———. *Jude the Obscure*. The Wessex Edition. London: Macmillian, 1912.

———. "Drummer Hodge." In *Collected Poems of Thomas Hardy*. New York: Macmillan, 1925.

———. *The Collected Letters of Thomas Hardy*. 2 vols. Ed. Richard Little Purdy and Michael Millgate. Oxford: Clarendon Press, 1978–88.

Harvey, W. J. *The Art of George Eliot*. London: Chatto and Windus, 1963.

Haythornthwaite, J. "A Victorian Novelist and Her Publisher: Margaret Oliphant and the House of Blackwood." *The Bibliotheck: A Scottish Journal of Bibliography and Allied Topics* 15, no. 2 (1988): 27–50.

Helsinger, Elizabeth, Robin Lauterbach Sheets, and William Veeder, eds. *The Woman Question: Defining Voices, 1837–1883*. New York and London: Garland, 1983.

Herman, David, ed. *Narratologies: New Perspectives on Narrative Analysis.* Columbus: Ohio State University Press, 1999.

Himmelfarb, Gertrude. *Marriage and Morals among the Victorians.* New York: Alfred A. Knopf, 1986.

Homans, Margaret. *Bearing the Word: Language and Female Experience in Nineteenth-Century Women's Writing.* Chicago and London: University of Chicago Press, 1986.

———. " 'To the Queen's Private Apartments': Royal Family Portraiture and the Construction of Victoria's Sovereign Obedience." *Victorian Studies* 37, no. 1 (Autumn 1993): 1–41.

———. "The Powers of Powerlessness: The Courtships of Elizabeth Barrett Browning and Queen Victoria." In *Feminist Measures: Soundings in Poetry and Theory,* ed. Lynn Keller and Cristanne Miller, 237–59. Ann Arbor: University of Michigan Press, 1994.

———. *Royal Representations: Queen Victoria and British Culture 1837–1876.* Chicago: University of Chicago Press, 1998.

Hook, Andrew, and Judith Hook. Introduction to *Shirley,* by Charlotte Brontë. Harmondworth: Penguin, 1974.

Houghton, Walter. *The Victorian Frame of Mind, 1830–1870.* New Haven and London: Yale University Press, 1957.

Houston, Gail. *Royalties: The Queen and Victorian Writers.* Charlottesville: University of Virginia Press, 1999.

Howe, Irving. *Thomas Hardy.* New York: Macmillan, 1967.

Hughes, Thomas. *Tom Brown's Schooldays.* Harmondsworth: Penguin, 1971.

Irigaray, Luce. *The Sex Which Is Not One,* trans. Catherine Porter. Ithaca: Cornell University Press, 1985.

Israel, Kali. *Names and Stories: Emilia Dilke and Victorian Culture.* New York: Oxford University Press, 1999.

Jackman, Sidney. *Galloping Head.* London: Phoenix House, 1958.

Jacobs, Naomi. "Gender and Layered Narrative in *Wuthering Heights* and *The Tenant of Wildfell Hall.*" *Journal of Narrative Technique* 16, no. 3 (Fall 1986): 204–19.

Jay, Elisabeth. *Mrs. Oliphant: "A Fiction to Herself."* Oxford: Clarendon Press, 1995.

Jones, Gareth Stedman. *Outcast London: A Study in the Relationship between Classes in Victorian Society* (1971). Rpt. Harmondsworth: Penguin, 1976.

———. *The Languages of Class: Studies in English Working-Class History, 1832–1982.* Cambridge and London: Cambridge University Press, 1983.

Keating, Peter. Review of *Victorian Women Poets: An Anthology. Times Literary Supplement,* January 26, 1996, no. 4843, 27.

Keefe, Robert. *Charlotte Brontë's World of Death.* Austin: University of Texas Press, 1979.

Keller, Lynn, and Cristanne Miller, eds. *Feminist Measures: Soundings in Poetry and Theory.* Ann Arbor: University of Michigan Press, 1994.

Kingsley, Charles. *At Last: Christmas in the West Indies.* London: Macmillan, 1871.

Knoepflmacher, U. C. *George Eliot's Early Novels: The Limits of Realism.* Berkeley and Los Angeles: University of California Press, 1968.

Kostka, Edith A. "Narrative Experience as a Means to Maturity in Anne Brontë's Victorian Novel *The Tenant of Wildfell Hall.*" *Connecticut Review* 14, no. 2 (Fall 1992): 41–47.

Kramer, Dale. *Thomas Hardy: The Forms of Tragedy.* Detroit: Wayne State University Press, 1975.

Kristeva, Julia. *Desire in Language: A Semiotic Approach to Literature and Art,* trans. Thomas Gora, Alice Jardine, and Leon S. Roudiez. New York: Columbia University Press, 1980.

Landes, Joan, ed. *Feminism, the Public and the Private.* Oxford and New York: Oxford University Press, 1998.

Langbauer, Laurie. "Women in White, Men in Feminism." *The Yale Journal of Criticism: Interpretation in the Humanities* 2, no. 2 (April 1989): 219–43.

———. *Women and Romance: The Consolations of Gender in the English Novel.* Ithaca: Cornell University Press, 1990.

Langland, Elizabeth. "A Perspective of One's Own: Thomas Hardy and the Elusive Sue Bridehead." *Studies in the Novel* 12, no. 1 (Spring 1980): 12–28.

———. *Anne Brontë: The Other One.* London: Macmillan, 1989.

———. *Nobody's Angels: Middle-Class Women and Domestic Ideology in Victorian Culture.* Ithaca: Cornell University Press, 1995.

Lanser, Susan. "Toward a Feminist Narratology." *Style* 20, no. 3 (Fall 1986): 341–63. Rpt. in *Feminisms: An Anthology of Literary Theory and Criticism,* ed. Robyn Warhol and Diane Price Herndl, 674–93. New Brunswick, N.J.: Rutgers University Press, 1991.

Laqueur, Thomas. *Making Sex: Body and Gender from the Greeks to Freud.* Cambridge: Harvard University Press, 1990.

Lauretis, Teresa de. "Feminist Studies/Critical Studies: Issues, Terms and Contexts." In *Feminist Studies: Critical Studies,* ed. Teresa de Lauretis, 1–19. Bloomington: Indiana University Press, 1986.

———, ed. *Feminist Studies: Critical Studies.* Bloomington: Indiana University Press, 1986.

Lawrence, D. H. *Phoenix: The Posthumous Papers of D. H. Lawrence,* ed. E. D. McDonald. New York: Viking, 1936.

Lawson, Kate. "Imagining Eve: Charlotte Brontë, Kate Millet, Hélène Cixous." *Women's Studies* 24, no. 5 (1995): 411–26.

Leavis, F. R. *The Great Tradition.* London: Chatto and Windus, 1948.

Leavis, Q. D. *Collected Essays: The Novel of Religious Controversy.* Vol. 3 of 3 vols. Cambridge: Cambridge University Press, 1989.

Lefebvre, Henri. *The Production of Space,* trans. Donald Nicholson-Smith. Oxford: Blackwell, 1991.

Lentricchia, Frank, and Thomas McLaughlin, eds. *Critical Terms for Literary Study.* Chicago: University of Chicago Press, 1990.

Levine, George, "Intelligence as Deception: *The Mill on the Floss.*" *PMLA* 80 (September 1965): 402–9.

Litvak, Joseph. *Caught in the Act: Theatricality in the Nineteenth-Century English Novel.* Berkeley, Los Angeles, and Oxford: University of California Press, 1992.

Longford, Elizabeth. *Victoria RI.* London: Wiedenfeld and Nicholson, 1964.

Lucas, John. "Love of England: The Victorians and Patriotism." *Browning Society Notes* 17, no. 1–3 (1987–88): 63–76.

Macaulay, Thomas Babington. *The Complete Works of Thomas Babington Macaulay,* vol. 1. New York: Houghton, Mifflin, 1899.

————. "The Minute on Indian Education." In *Prose and Poetry,* by Thomas Babington Macaulay. Cambridge: Harvard University Press, 1952.

MacGregor, Catherine. " 'I Cannot Trust Your Oaths and Promises: I Must Have a Written Agreement': Talk and Text in *The Tenant of Wildfell Hall.*" *Dionysos* 4, no. 2 (Fall 1992): 31–39.

Marks, Elaine, and Isabelle de Courtivron, eds. *New French Feminisms: An Anthology.* New York: Schocken, 1981.

Mason, Michael. *The Making of Victorian Sexuality.* Oxford and New York: Oxford University Press, 1994.

Massey, Doreen. *Space, Place, and Gender.* Cambridge: Polity Press, 1994.

Matus, Jill. *Unstable Bodies: Victorian Representations of Sexuality and Maternity.* New York and Manchester: Manchester University Press, 1995.

Mayhew, Henry. *London Labour and the London Poor, 1849–1862.* Selected and introd. Victor Neuburg. Harmondsworth: Penguin, 1985.

Maynard, John. *Charlotte Brontë and Sexuality.* Cambridge: Cambridge University Press, 1984.

Meyer, Susan. *Imperialism at Home.* Ithaca: Cornell University Press, 1996.

Mezei, Kathy, ed. *Ambiguous Discourse: Feminist Narratology and British Women Writers.* Chapel Hill: University of North Carolina Press, 1996.

Michie, Helena. *The Flesh Made Word: Female Figure and Women's Bodies.* Oxford and New York: Oxford University Press, 1987.

Mill, John Stuart, and Harriet Taylor Mill. "The Subjection of Women." In *Essays on Sexuality,* ed. Alice S. Rossi, 123–242. Chicago and London: University of Chicago Press, 1970.

Miller, Andrew H., and James Eli Adams, eds. *Sexualities in Victorian Britain.* Bloomington and Indianapolis: Indiana University Press, 1996.

Miller, D. A. *The Novel and the Police.* Berkeley, Los Angeles, and London: University of California Press, 1988.

Miller, J. Hillis. "Theory and Practice: Response to Vincent Leitch." *Critical Inquiry* 6, no. 4 (Summer 1980): 609–14.

————. *Fiction and Repetition: Seven English Novels.* Cambridge: Harvard University Press, 1982.

Miller, Nancy K. "Emphasis Added: Plots and Plausibilities in Women's Fiction." *PMLA* 96, no. 1 (January 1981): 36–48. Rpt. in *The New Feminist Criticism: Essays on Women, Literature, and Theory,* ed. Elaine Showalter. New York: Pantheon, 1985.

————. *Subject to Change: Reading Feminist Writing.* New York: Columbia University Press, 1988.

Millgate, Michael. *Thomas Hardy: A Biography.* Oxford: Oxford University Press, 1982.

Modleski, Tania. *Feminism without Women: Culture and Criticism in a "Postfeminist" Age.* New York: Routledge, 1991.

Moers, Ellen. *Literary Women.* Garden City, N.Y.: Doubleday, 1976.

Moglen, Helene. *Charlotte Brontë: The Self Conceived.* New York: Norton, 1976.

Moore, George. *Conversations in Ebury Street.* New York: Boni and Liveright, 1924.

Munich, Adrienne Auslander. "Queen Victoria, Empire, and Excess." *Tulsa Studies in Women's Literature* 6, no. 2 (1987): 265–81.

Murphy, Patricia. *Time Is of the Essence: Temporality, Gender, and the New Woman.* Ithaca: State University of New York Press, 2001.

Nadel, Ira B. "Portraits of the Queen." *Victorian Poetry* 25, no. 3–4 (1987): 169–91.

Nelson, Claudia. *Boys Will Be Girls: The Feminine Ethic and British Children's Fiction, 1857–1917.* New Brunswick, N.J.: Rutgers University Press, 1991.

———. *Invisible Men: Fatherhood in Victorian Periodicals, 1850–1910.* Athens: University of Georgia Press, 1995.

Oliphant, Margaret. *The Autobiography of Mrs. Oliphant,* ed. Mrs. Harry Coghill. Chicago: University of Chicago Press, 1988.

———. *Miss Marjoribanks.* Harmondsworth: Penguin, 1989.

———. *Phoebe Junior.* Harmondsworth: Penguin, 1989.

O'Mealy, Joseph H. "Scenes of Professional Life: Mrs. Oliphant and the New Victorian Clergyman." *Studies in the Novel* 23, no. 2 (Summer 1991): 245–61.

———. "Mrs. Oliphant, *Miss Marjoribanks,* and the Victorian Canon." *The Victorian Newsletter* 82 (Fall 1992): 44–49.

Ormond, Leonée. " 'In the Spacious Times of Great Elizabeth': The Victorian Vision of the Elizabethans." *Victorian Poetry* 25, no. 3–4 (1987): 29–46.

Pateman, Carole. *The Disorder of Women: Democracy, Feminism and Political Theory.* Cambridge: Polity Press, 1989.

Peters, Margot. *Unquiet Soul: A Biography of Charlotte Brontë.* Garden City, N.Y.: Doubleday, 1975.

Phelan, James, ed. *Narrative Poetics: Innovations, Limits, Challenges.* Columbus: Ohio State University Press, 1997.

Pinion, F. B. *A Brontë Companion: Literary Assessment. Background and Reference.* London: Macmillan Press, 1975.

Poovey, Mary. *Uneven Developments: The Ideological Work of Gender in Mid-Victorian England.* Chicago: University of Chicago Press, 1988.

———. *Making a Social Body: British Cultural Formation, 1830–1846.* Chicago and London: University of Chicago Press, 1995.

Qualls, Barry V. *The Secular Pilgrims of Victorian Fiction: The Novel as Book of Life.* Cambridge and New York: Cambridge University Press, 1982.

Queen Victoria in Her Letters and Journals: A Selection, ed. Christopher Hibbert. New York: Viking, 1985.

Renza, Louis A. "Influence." In *Critical Terms for Literary Study,* ed. Frank Lentricchia and Thomas McLaughlin, 186–202. Chicago: University of Chicago Press, 1990.

Reynolds, George W. M. *The Seamstress or, The White Slave of England.* London: John Dicks, 1853.

Rivkin, Julie. "Resisting Readers and Reading Effects: Some Speculations on Reading and Gender." In *Narrative Poetics: Innovations, Limits, Challenges,* ed. James Phelan, 11–22. Columbus: Ohio State University Press, 1997.

Roby, Kinley. "Irony and Narrative Voice in *Howard's End." Journal of Narrative Technique* 2 (May 1972): 116–24.

Rogers, Katharine. "Women in Thomas Hardy." *Centennial Review* 19, no. 2 (1975): 249–58.

Rose, Gillian. *Feminism and Geography: The Limits of Geographical Knowledge.* Cambridge: Polity Press, 1993.

Schor, Naomi. *Reading in Detail: Aesthetics and the Feminine.* New York: Methuen, 1987.

Sedgwick, Eve Kosofsky. *Between Men: English Literature and Male Homosocial Desire.* New York: Columbia University Press, 1985.

Senf, Carol. "*The Tenant of Wildfell Hall:* Narrative Silences and Questions of Gender." *College English* 52, no. 4 (April 1990): 446–56.

Showalter, Elaine. *A Literature of Their Own: British Women Novelists from Brontë to Lessing.* Princeton: Princeton University Press, 1977.

———, ed. *The New Feminist Criticism: Essays on Women, Literature, and Theory.* New York: Pantheon, 1985.

———. "A Criticism of Our Own: Autonomy and Assimilation in Afro-American and Feminist Literary Theory." In Ralph Cohen, ed. *The Future of a Literary Theory.* New York: Routledge, 1989. Rpt. in *Feminisms: An Anthology of Literary Theory and Criticism,* ed. Robyn Warhol and Diane Price Herndl, 168–188. New Brunswick, N.J.: Rutgers University Press, 1991.

Smith, Barbara Herrnstein. *Contingencies of Value: Alternative Perspectives for Critical Theory.* Cambridge: Harvard University Press, 1988.

Smith, Emma (pseudonym). *A Cornish Waif's Story: An Autobiography.* Foreword by A. L. Rowse. London: Odhams Press, 1954.

Spivak, Gayatri. *Outside in the Teaching Machine.* New York: Routledge, 1993.

Stein, Richard. *Victoria's Year: English Literature and Culture, 1837–1838.* New York: Oxford University Press, 1987.

Stimpson, Catharine. Foreward to *Tradition Counter Tradition.* Chicago: University of Chicago Press, 1989, vii–ix.

Stone, Donald D. *The Romantic Impulse in Victorian Fiction.* Cambridge: Harvard University Press, 1980.

Strachey, Lytton. *Queen Victoria.* New York: Harcourt, Brace, 1921.

Strong, Roy. *Recreating the Past: British History and the Victorian Painter.* New York: Thames and Hudson, 1978.

Sussman, Herbert. *Victorian Masculinities: Manhood and Masculine Poetics in Early Victorian Literature and Art.* Cambridge: Cambridge University Press, 1995.

Tennyson, Alfred, Lord. *The Complete Poetic Works of Tennyson.* Boston: Houghton-Mifflin, 1898.

Thackeray, William Makepeace. *Vanity Fair, A Novel without a Hero.* Boston: Houghton, Mifflin, 1963.

Thompson, Dorothy. *Queen Victoria: Gender and Power.* London: Virago, 1990.

Trela, D. J. "Jane Welsh Carlyle and Margaret Oliphant: An Unsung Friendship." *The Carlyle Annual* 11 (1990): 31–40.

Trollope, Anthony. *The Warden.* Harmondsworth: Penguin, 1984.

Vicinus, Martha, ed. *A Widening Sphere: Changing Roles of Victorian Women.* Bloomington and London: Indiana University Press, 1977.

Warhol, Robyn. "Narrating the Unnarratable: Gender and Metonymy in the Victorian Novel." *Style* 28, no. 1 (Spring 1994): 74–94.

———. " 'Reader, Can You Imagine? No, You Cannot': The Narratee as Other in Harriet Jacobs's Text." *Narrative* 3, no. 1 (January 1995): 57–72.

———. "Guilty Cravings: What Feminist Narratology Can Do for Cultural Studies." In *Narratologies: New Perspectives on Narrative Analysis,* ed. David Herman, 340–355. Columbus: Ohio State University Press, 1999.

Warhol, Robyn, and Diane Price Herndl, eds. *Feminisms: An Anthology of Literary Theory and Criticism.* New Brunswick, N.J.: Rutgers University Press, 1991.

Weintraub, Stanley. *Victoria: An Intimate Biography.* New York: E. P. Dutton, 1987.

Wiesenfarth, Joseph. *Gothic Manners and the Classic English Novel.* Madison: University of Wisconsin Press, 1988.

Wigley, Mark. "Untitled: The Housing of Gender." In *Sexuality and Space: Princeton Papers on Architecture,* ed. Beatriz Colomina, 327–89. New York: Princeton Architectural Press, 1992.

Wilkinson, John James Garth. *The Forcible Introspection of Women for the Army and Navy by the Oligarchy, Considered Physically.* London: F. Pitman, 1870.

Williams, Merryn. *Margaret Oliphant: A Critical Biography.* Basingstoke: Macmillan, 1986.

Williams, Raymond. *The Country and the City.* New York: Oxford University Press, 1973.

Winnett, Susan. "Coming Unstrung: Women, Men, Narrative and Principles of Pleasure." *PMLA* 105 (May 1990): 505–18.

Wise, T. J., and J. A. Symington, eds. *The Brontës: Their Lives, Friendships, and Correspondence in Four Volumes.* 4 vols. Oxford: Shakespeare Head Press, 1932.

———. *The Miscellaneous Unpublished Writings of Charlotte and Patrick Branwell Brontë.* 2 vols. Oxford: Shakespeare Head Press, 1936–38.

Wolfreys, Julian. *Being English: Narratives, Idioms, and Performances of National Identity from Coleridge to Trollope.* Albany: State University of New York Press, 1994.

Wollstonecraft, Mary. *Maria or the Wrongs of Woman.* New York: Norton, 1975.

Woodward, Katherine. *Jipping Street: A Childhood in the London Slums.* New York and London: Harper & Brothers, 1928.

Woolf, Virginia. *A Room of One's Own.* New York: Harcourt Brace, 1929.

———. *Three Guineas.* New York: Harcourt, Brace, 1938.

———. *To the Lighthouse.* New York: Harcourt, Brace, 1955.

Young, G. M. *Victorian Essays.* London: Oxford University Press, 1962.

Index

Acton, William, 79
Adam Bede (Eliot), 107–8
Adams, James Eli, 132n. 8
advice to graduate students, 92–93
aesthetics. *See* value; canon
Alberti, Leon Battista, 68
Alcoff, Linda, 48
Alvarez, A., 135n. 1
Anderson, Benedict, 132n. 13
Angel in the House, xxiii, 5, 16, 26, 84, 101
Anglo-Saxonism. *See* Englishness
Anne, queen of England, 126
apRoberts, Ruth, 140n. 8
arachnology, 2
Archer, John Michael, 137n. 5
architecture, 17; relationship to gender 68, 72–73. *See also* country house
"Art and Belles Letters" (Eliot), 100
asylum, 70; as refuge/confinement in *Woman in White*, 66; 136n. 1, 137n. 2
Austen, Jane, 68, 136n. 6
authoritative discourse, 48–49, 50, 54, 59, 62
Autobiography (Oliphant), 108

Bagehot, Walter, 122
Bakhtin, M. M., xiv, xviii, xx, 2–3, 16, 48

Balzac, Honoré de, 34
Barthes, Roland, xviii, xix, 2, 3, 21, 33–35, 139n. 7
Bennett, Arnold, 139n. 1
Bentham, Jeremy, 20
Berlant, Lauren, 132n. 12
Bhabha, Homi, 132n. 13
Bible, The, 56, 57–58
"A Biographical Notice of Ellis and Acton Bell" (Brontë, C.), 30–31
Blunt, Alison, xviii, 132n. 11, 137n. 1, 138n. 4
Boling, Patricia, 138n. 2
Boone, Joseph, 131n. 2
Bourdieu, Pierre, xix, 83, 91, 95, 96, 97–98, 100, 101, 106, 108, 110, 139n. 11, n. 1, n. 3, n. 4, 140n. 12
Braddon, Mary Elizabeth, ix, xxi, xxii, 63, 92, 98
Brontë, Anne, vii–ix, xvii, xvii, xxii, 29, 30–46, 92, 98, 135n 2, n. 3
Brontë, Charlotte, ix, xii, xiii, xviii, xxii, 1–29, 30, 40, 46, 64–65, 92, 98, 99, 100, 133–35, 136n. 1
Brontë, Emily, viii, 30, 34, 99, 135n. 3
Brooke, Rupert, 113
Broughton, Rhoda, 92
Browning, Elizabeth Barrett, 21, 117

Burt, Richard, 137n. 5
Butler, Judith, xv, xvi, 25

canon, x–xi, xiii, xiv, xxii, 92, 98, 108,
139n. 2; arguments for more diversity
in, 93–94; Brontës and Eliot in, 99;
challenged by Oliphant's aesthetics,
101, 104–105; counter-, 96–97; and
cultural capital, 106; disadvantages of
women writers in, xi, 93–94; economic
necessity a factor in excluding women
writers from, 109–110; Eliot's aesthetics
and, 100–101; Oliphant's life excludes
from, 109; relationship to class, 97–98;
relationship to educational capital, 97;
relativism and universality in, 94–95;
valuation of autonomy in, 96. See also
value
capitalism, 26
Case, Alison, xviii
childishness, 73–74; in Lady Audley's
Secret, 65, 73; and sexuality, 73; in
Woman in White, 73; and madness, 74
Christmas Carol, A (Dickens), 81
Chronicles of Carlingford (Oliphant), 99
class, xi, xxi–xxii 44, 62; aesthetic value
judgment and, 91–92, 107; chivalric
code as marker of in Jude the Obscure,
51–52; Englishness as middle-,
115–116; as formative of identity, 50;
gender relationship to, 11, 44, 137n.
1; integrity as determined by, 102–6;
relations challenged by Oliphant, 100;
relations reinscribed in women's literature, 99–101;and sexuality in Lady
Audley's Secret, 73; and surveillance in
Lady Audley's Secret, 69–70, 75; and
taste in The Warden, 103–4.
Cobb, Frances Power, 82–83
Collins, Wilkie, ix, xxi, xxii, 63, 64, 73,
79, 88, 98, 137n. 2
Colomina, Beatriz, 132n. 11
Conrad, Joseph, 34
Contagious Diseases Act, 79–81
Contingencies of Value (Herrnstein Smith),
93

Conversations in Ebury Street (Moore),
135n. 3
Cornish Waif's Story, A (Smith, E.), 79, 82,
83
Cottom, Daniel, 139 n5
Country and the City, The (Williams), 67
country house, 136n. 1, 137n. 4; as asylum, 65–67, 75–76; as enclosure,
67–68; and surveillance, 75. See also
architecture
Cullwick, Hannah, 79, 88
Cultural Capital (Guillory), 95
cultural capital, xxii, 91, 95–96; gender
and, 92, 98; relationship to value,
91–92; reliance on economic power,
97; women's disadvantage in, 106–7
cultural studies, xiii, 92
culture: and form, ix, x; role of literature
in xiv; subsumed by patriarchy, 37–38;
text-in-, 28; text-of-, 21–23

Dafoe, Daniel, 112
Davidoff, Leonore, 138n. 2
Davis, Lennard J., xiv, 131n. 3
Dearest Child (Queen Victoria), 122
deconstruction, 13, 16
DeLauretis, Teresa, 48–49
Derrida, Jacques, 3, 132n. 1, 139n. 7
dialogism, xiv, xix, 2–3, 6, 9; intertextuality and, 2–3, 31–33
dialogue, xx, 5, 28, 31–33
Diaries (Cullwick), 79
Dickens, Charles, 14, 79, 81, 85, 109,
132n. 8
Dilke, Emilia, 131n. 1
Dilke, Sir Charles, xxiii
Dinnerstein, Dorothy, 23–24
discipline, 16, 17, 20–21; calling as form
of, 20; norm, 17, 20–21; sewing as
form of, 18–19; tea as form of, 20–21;
work as form of, 18–19. See also surveillance; punishment
discourse, 3, 5, 16–21, 28; double voiced,
2–3; and power, 3–4. See also authoritative discourse; internally persuasive
discourse

disguise, 23. *See also* theft
domestic comedy. *See* marriage plot
domestic ideology, 17, 21, 121–22
domestic novel, 47, 64
Dostka, Edith A., 135 n3
Driver, Felix, 81, 138 n7
"The Drummer" (Hardy), 113
Duke of Kent, 112, 113
Duke of Wellington, 140n. 3

Eade, J. C., 140n. 8
Eagleton, Terry, 134–35n. 12
educational capital, 96, 97, 105, 108,
    110. *See also* cultural capital
Edward, Duke of Kent, xxii, xxiii
Egerton, George, 92
Eliot, George, x, xvi, xxii, 40, 98–101,
    106, 107–108, 110, 119–20, 128, 139
    n5, 140 n11, 142–43n. 14
Elizabeth I, queen of England, 125–28
Enclosure Acts, 64, 67
"England's Forgotten Worthies" (Froude),
    127, 128
"The English Bastille," 81
English in the West Indies, The (Froude),
    128
Englishness, xi, xii, xxii, xxiii, 111, 141n.
    6, 142–43n. 14; and Anglo-Saxonism
    113–16, 119; as defined in *Tom
    Brown's School Days* 115–16; defined as
    middle class 115–16; exclusion of
    women by definition of 117; and gen-
    der differences 116–17; related to
    Victorianism through domestic ideolo-
    gy 121–22; and Queen Victoria
    111–20; and sport 115
etiquette books, 20
Eve, 10, 12, 133n. 5

fairy tale, 11, 14–15, 134n. 11
fallen women, 42
Faucher, Léon, 18–19
feminine desire, xix, 33–34, 36, 38,
    40–46; and narrative structure,
    33–34; and nested narrative, 34–36
femininity, 46; masculinity defined in

opposition to, 55–56. *See also* gender;
    tears
feminist criticism, xv–xviii, xxi, 2, 92–95,
    96
feminist reality, 10–15
Fielding, Henry, 9
Fitzgerald, Penelope, 104
focalization, 7, 39–40; and narrative
    exchange 39–40, 42, 45
Forster, E. M., 95, 115–16
Foucault, Michel, xviii, 2, 3–4, 16–17,
    19, 21, 28, 73, 139n, 7
fragmentation. *See* theft
Frankenstein (Shelley), 34, 39
Fredeman, William E., 114
Friedman, Susan Stanford, 2
Froude, James Anthony, 127, 128

Galsworthy, John, 139n. 1
gender, ix, xvi, xviii, 29, 48, 54–57; and
    architecture, 17; and authority, 3, 5; as
    category of analysis, xv, xvii, xx; as cat-
    egory of experience, 11; and construc-
    tion of Englishness, 113, 115–20;
    122–25, 129; and counter-canon,
    96–97; gendered poetic, xix; and iden-
    tity, x, xiv, xvii, 1, 2; identity in *Jude
    the Obscure*, 49, 54–57; and narrative
    voice, 6–8; and privacy, 78–81, 88;
    and pseudonyms, 106–107; relation-
    ship to nationalism, xi, xxiii, 132n. 12;
    and time, 132n. 10; and work in
    Phoebe Junior, 105. *See also* femininity;
    masculinity
Genette, Gérard, 7
Gérin, Winifred, 135n. 3
Gikandi, Simon, 132n. 13
Gilbert, Sandra, xviii, 7, 8, 26, 133n. 3
Gillooly, Eileen, xviii
Gilmour, Robin, 102
Girouard, Mark, 20, 68, 75, 137n. 6
Goetz, William R., 136n. 6
Gordon, Jan, 135n. 3
Grand, Sarah, 92
Great Exhibition, The, 114, 123–24
Green, Laura, 136n. 5

Gross, Elizabeth, 131n. 6
Gubar, Susan, xviii, 7, 8, 26, 133n. 3
Guerard, Albert J., 135n. 1
Guillory, 95–97, 139n. 2

Haley, Bruce, 115, 140 n3, 140–41n. 4
Hall, Catherine, 138n. 2
Hardy, F. E., 135–36n. 1
Hardy, Thomas, x, xvi, xix, 46, 47–63,
    113, 135n. 1; compared to Oliphant
    109–110
Healthy Body and Victorian Culture, The
    (Haley), 115
Heart of Darkness (Conrad), 34, 39
hegemony, 98–99
Herman, David, 135n. 13
Herrnstein Smith, Barbara, 93–94, 95
Hexis, 83, 85, 139n. 11
History of England from the Accession of
    James the Second (Macaulay), 126–27
Homans, Margaret, 121, 143n. 16
homosocial desire, xix
Hook, Andrew and Judith, 133n. 2
Houghton, Walter, 141n. 7
Houston, Gail Turley, 143n. 16
Howards End (Forster), 95
Howe, Irving, 135n. 1
Hughes, Thomas, 115, 125

imperialism, 116, 122, 125, 127, 128,
    142–43n. 14
incarceration, 20, 90
influence. *See* intertextuality
internally persuasive discourse, 48–50, 52
intertextuality, ix, xviii–xix, xxi, xxii, 1–29,
    132n. 1; between *Lady Audley's Secret*
    and *Woman in White*, 64–66, 73–76;
    between *Phoebe Junior* and *The Warden*,
    101–06; between *Shirley* and *Vanity*
    Fair, 1–29; between texts by Anne and
    Charlotte Brontë, 98; and dialogue,
    2–3; political, 2; strategic, 5, 28
Irigaray, Luce, xviii, 2, 4–5, 24
irony, 13, 14, 22
isolation, 17–19, 88. *See also* privacy
Israel, Kali, 131n. 1

Jackman, Sidney, 138n. 8
Jacobs, Naomi, 135n. 3
Jane Eyre (Brontë, C.), xix, 30, 40, 46, 99,
    100, 136n. 1
Jay, Elisabeth, 140n. 11
Jipping Street (Woodward), 79, 83–88
Jones, Gareth Stedman, 137n. 1
Jude the Obscure (Hardy), ix, xix, 46,
    47–64, 110, 135n. 1, 135–6n. 2, 136n.
    3, 136n. 4, 136n. 5, 136n. 6; alienation
    in, 53, 55; chivalric code in, 51–52, 57;
    construction of gender in, 48, 54–57;
    manual labor valued in, 52–53; middle-
    class identity in, 52–53, 60; seduction
    in, 51–52, 60; social codes in, 50, 53;
    space in, 63; subjectivity in, 48, 53, 57,
    62

Keating, Peter, 95
Keefe, Robert, 133n. 4
Kingsley, Charles, 127, 128, 143n. 15
Kristeva, Julia, xviii, 2, 3

Lacan, Jacques, 3, 136n. 4
Lady Audley's Secret (Braddon), ix, 64–76,
    92, 137n. 4; childishness in 65, 73;
    class in 73; country house in 64, 67–68;
    intertextuality between *Woman in White*
    and 64–66, 73–76; madness in 74–75;
    penetration and exclusion in 70–73;
    relationship to Enclosure Acts 67; sexu-
    ality in 73; surveillance in 68–72, 75
Langland, Elizabeth, 91, 98, 135n. 2,
    136n. 4, 137n. 3, 137n. 5, 137n. 6
Lansar, Susan, xvii
Lawrence, D. H., 136n. 4
Leavis, Q. D., 98
Lefebvre, Henri, xxi, 78, 138n. 4
Lewes, G. H., 100–101, 139n. 6
Life in the English Country House
    (Girouard), 68
Longford, Elizabeth, 112
Lord Palmerston, 125
Lucas, John, 112–13, 119, 140n. 1, 141n. 6

Macaulay, Lord Thomas, 126–27, 142n. 14
MacGregor, Catherine, 135n. 3
madness: in *Lady Audley's Secret*, 74–75; in *Woman in White*, 65, 73. *See also* asylum
Man and Wife (Collins), 79, 88–90
Maria of the Wrongs of Woman, (Wollstonecraft), 136n. 1
marriage plot, 25, 27–28, 132n. 8; subversion of in *The Tenant of Wildfell Hall*, 37, 43–44
masculinity, xix–xx, 46, 132n. 8; as class construct in *Jude the Obscure*, 47, 62; construction of, defined in opposition to femininity, 55–56, 61–62; education as formative of, 50; and evasion of manhood in *Jude the Obscure*, 49–50, 58; and feminist criticism, xxi; role of authoritative discourse in formation of, 54; in *The Tenant of Wildfell Hall*, 31–33; tied to social status, 54. *See also* gender
Mason, Michael, 132n. 9
Mason, Peter, 132n. 13
Massey, Doreen, 132n. 11, 138n. 4
Maynard, John, 133n. 4
mermaid, 23–25
Middlemarch (Eliot), 40, 98, 99–100, 101, 107, 108
Miller, Andrew, 132n. 9
Miller, D. A., xiv, 75, 131n. 3, 137n. 2, 137n. 4
Miller, J. Hillis, 136n. 3
Miller, Nancy, xviii, 2, 5, 92
Millgate, Michael, 135n. 2
Milton, John, 133n. 5
mimicry, 1, 5, 23–28. *See also* parody
"Minute on Indian Education" (Macaulay), 142n. 14
Miss Marjoribanks (Oliphant), 98
"The Modern Hep, Hep, Hep" (Eliot), 119–20, 128
Modleski, Tania, xv–xvi
Moglen, Helene, 133n. 4
monologism, 9, 15–16

Montalembert, Comte de, 140n. 3
Moore, George, 35–36, 135n. 3
mosaic, 3, 5–16, 28
Murphy, Patricia, 132n. 10

Nadel, Ira, 118–19
narration, xiii, xviii, 1, 2, 6–8, 14, 23, 27; and discipline, xv; power of, xi; structure and, 33, 41; and subversion, xv. *See also* narrative exchange
narrative exchange, 33–40, 42–43, 45; and feminine desire in *The Tenant of Wildfell Hall*, 38–39
nation, xi, xiii, xxii–xxiii, 120, 127; and nationalism, 132n. 13; relationship to class, xi; relationship to gender, xi, xxiii; reliance on narrative, 111, 128. *See also* Englishness
Nelson, Claudia, 132n. 9
nested narration, 33, 35
Newbolt, Henry, 141n. 4
Newby (publishers), 30
Nobody's Angels (Langland), 91, 98, 137 n3, 137n. 6
"Notes on the English Character" (Forster), 115–16
Novel and the Police, The (Miller), 75; 137n. 2
novel, xi; relationship to material reality xii; as subversive form, xvii–xviii
"An Ode in Honour of the Jubilee of Queen Victoria" (Tennyson), 117–18, 119, 141n. 5

Oliphant, Margaret, ix, x, xvi, xxii, 92, 98, 99–107, 108–110, 140n. 11; compared to George Eliot, 99–101; compared to Hardy, 109–110
Oliver Twist (Dickens), 81
On the Art of Building in Ten Books, (Alberti), 68
Ormond, Leonée, 125, 127–28
Our Mutual Friend (Dickens), 79, 85–86

Pair of Blue Eyes, A (Hardy), 110
paradoxisms, xix, 34, 44–45

parody, 1, 5, 25–26, 28. *See also* mimicry
Pateman, Carole, 138n. 3
patriarchal culture, 50, 58; as structures
    subjectivity, 47
patriarchal reality, 10–14
patriarchy, 9–15, 25, 26, 133n. 6; con-
    tempt for feminine desire by, 40; and
    realism, 9–13; in *The Tenant of Wildfell
    Hall,* 33–34, 37–38
Phoebe Junior (Oliphant), ix, 101–6
Poor Laws, 81
Poovey, Mary, xvii, 131–32n. 7, 132n. 8
postmodernism, xvii
Pride and Prejudice (Austen), 68, 139n. 1
Prince Albert, 113–14, 119, 123–25
privacy: Contagious Disease Act as inva-
    sion of women's, 79–81; feminism's
    attempts to reclaim, 78; ideological
    effects on working-class women,
    78–79; as isolation for middle-class
    women, 88; lack of for working-class
    women, 88; as maintaining class and
    gender status quo, 90. *See also* isola-
    tion; private sphere
private sphere, 77–78, 137–38n. 1
Production of Space, The (Lefebvre), 78
public schools, 115–16
public sphere, 77–78, 137–38n. 1
Punch, 114
punishment, 5. *See also* discipline

realism, 9–15, 133n. 4
relativism, 94–95
Reynolds, George W. M., 138n. 9
romance, 9–15, 25, 27, 28, 30, 31,
    32–33, 46, 60
Room of One's Own, A (Woolf), 7, 96
Rose, Gillian, xxi, 132n. 11, 137n. 1,
    138n. 4
Ruskin, John, 100

"Sarrasine" (Balzac), 34, 39
Saturday Review, 115
Schor, Naomi, 139–40n. 7
Seamstress, The (Reynolds), 138n. 9
Sedgewick, Eve Kosofsky, xix

Senf, Carol, 135n. 3
sensation fiction, 64
sexuality, 17, 50–51, 53, 54–57, 60, 73;
    and childishness in *Lady Audley's Secret*
    and *Woman in White,* 73; and enclo-
    sure, 137n. 5. *See also* feminine desire
Shelley, Mary, 34
Shirley (Brontë, C.), ix, xiii, xviii, 1–29,
    92, 132n. 2, 132n. 3, 132n. 4, 132n.
    5, 132n. 6, 134n. 7, 134n. 8, 134n. 9,
    134n. 10, 134n. 11, 134–35n. 12,
    135n. 1; and *Vanity Fair,* 1–29, 64–65
Showalter, Elaine, xv, 131n. 4, 136n. 1
Smith and Elder (publishers), 30–31
Smith, Emma, 79, 82, 83
social capital, 91, 96, 97, 105
social codes, 50, 53
"The Soldier" (Brooke), 113
space, x, xi, xiii, 132n. 11; constructed by
    gender and class, 63, 68, 72–73;
    domestic, 17; feminine, 16, 20; and
    gender, xxi–xxii, 138n. 3, 138n. 4; pri-
    vate, xxi; social production of, 78; and
    surveillance in *Lady Audley's Secret,*
    68–70; workhouse as regulatory-,
    81–87; working class social-, 86–87.
    See also workhouse
"'The spacious times of great Elizabeth':
    The Victorian Vision of the
    Elizabethans" (Ormond), 127
spiritual reform, 40–41
Spivak, Gayatri, xv–xvii, 131n. 5
Stein, Richard, 122–23
Sterne, Laurence, 139 n1
Stimpson, Catherine, xiv
Strathcey, Lytton, 113, 123–25, 142n. 9
Strong, Roy, 114–15, 119
surveillance, 17, 20, 75; in *Lady Audley's
    Secret,* 68–72, 75
Sussman, Herbert, 132n. 8
symbolic code, 34, 40, 41–43
sympathy, 6, 22

tears, 4, 5, 21–23; as sign of enfeeblement
    22; as sign of femininity, 4, 21–23; as
    women's work 22

Technologies of Gender (DeLauretis), 48–49

"Tempus Actum" (Young), 121–22

Tenant of Wildfell Hall, The (Brontë, A), xiii, xix, 30–46, 92, 135n. 2, 135n. 3; antithesis in, 34, 36, 39, 41–45; and *Jane Eyre*, 30; and *Wuthering Heights*, 30; narrative structure in, 33, 41; and nested narratives, 33–34; relationship between class and gender in, 44; relationship between dialogue and intertextuality in, 31–33; spiritual reform in, 40–41; subversion of marriage plot in, 37, 43–44; transgression and narrative exchange in, 33–46

Tennyson, Alfred, Lord, 117–18, 119, 141n. 5

Tess of the D'Urbervilles (Hardy), 110

Thackeray, William Makepeace, xi, xviii, xxii, 1–10, 16–17, 22–26, 28, 64–65, 98, 103

Thatcher, Margaret, 111

Theed, William, 114

theft, 1, 4, 5, 28, 212–13. *See also* disguise; intertextuality

Thompson, Dorothy, 122

Three Guineas (Woolf), 109

"To the Queen" (Tennyson), 117–18

Tom Brown's School Days (Hughes), 115–17, 125, 140–41n. 4

Tom Jones (Fielding), 9

torture, 6–7, 16, 27. *See also* discipline; punishment

Tristram Shandy (Sterne), 139n. 1

Trollope, Anthony, ix, xxii, 98; compared to Oliphant, 101–6

True Born Englishman, The (Dafoe), 112

Two on a Tower (Hardy), 110

value: canon and, 93–94; feminist challenges to, 94; institutionally located, 95; natural taste, 97–98, 101, 139n. 4; relation to class, 107; relativism and, 94–95. *See also* canon

Vanity Fair (Thackeray), xviii, 1, 2, 5, 22–23, 25, 26, 28, 103; compared to

Shirley, 1–29, 64–65

victimization, xix, 12

Victoria, queen of England, x, xvii, xxii–xxiii, 21, 108; developments in portraits of, 114, 118–19; and Englishness, 111–20; relationship to Elizabeth I, 125–28; representations of as mother figure, 113, 114–15, 117, 119, 121–22; and Victorianism, 120–25

"Victoria's Tears" (Browning), 117

Victoria's Year (Stein), 122

Victorian Women Poets, 95

Victorianism, 111; and domestic ideology 121–22; and Englishness 112–13, 120–25; and women's status 115

Von Angeli, Moriz, 119

Warden, The (Trollope), ix, 101–5, 140n. 8

Warhol, Robyn, xvii, 29

Weintraub, Stanley, 112, 114

Well-Beloved, The (Hardy), 136n. 3

Wells, H. G., 139n. 1

Westward Ho! (Kingsley), 127, 128

White, Hayden, 131n. 1

Wigley, Mark, 68, 72

Wilkinson, Garth, 80

William of Orange, 112

Williams, Merryn, 104

Williams, Raymond, 67, 71

Williams, W. S., 31

Wolfreys, Julian, 132n. 13

Wollstonecraft, Mary, 136n. 1

Woman in White (Collins), ix, 64–66, 137n. 2, 137n. 3, 137n. 4; and childishness, 73; country house in, 64–66; and *Lady Audley's Secret*, 64–66, 73–76; madness in, 65, 73

woman question, xix

women writers, ix; excluded from canon for economic reasons, 109–10; recent critical interest in 92–95; and women's signature, ix, 4, 5, 28

women's work: compared in Oliphant and Eliot, 99; portrayed as undervalued in

Phoebe Junior, 105; tears as, 22; and
    workhouses, 82; and working-women's
    narrative, 82–88; and writing for
    income, 109
Woodward, Kathleen, 79, 83–88
Woolf, Virginia, 7, 96–97, 100, 109,
    139n. 1
workhouses, 81–88, 138n. 9; and hexis,
    83, 85; and women's work, 82; and
    working-women's narrative, 82–88
working-class women, x
Wuthering Heights (Brontë, E.), 30, 34,
    39, 135n. 3

Young, G. M., 120–22, 123, 142n. 8, n.
    9
"The Young Queen" (Browning), 117

The Theory and Interpretation of Narrative Series
James Phelan and Peter J. Rabinowitz, Editors

Because the series editors believe that the most significant work in narrative studies today contributes both to our knowledge of specific narratives and to our understanding of narrative in general, studies in the series typically offer interpretations of individual narratives and address significant theoretical issues underlying those interpretations. The series does not privilege any one critical perspective but is open to work from any strong theoretical position.

Misreading Jane Eyre: A Postformalist Paradigm
Jerome Beaty

Invisible Author: Last Essays
Christine Brooke-Rose

Narratologies: New Perspectives on Narrative Analysis
Edited by David Herman

Matters of Fact: Reading Nonfiction over the Edge
Daniel W. Lehman

Breaking the Frame: Metalepsis and the Construction of the Subject
Debra N. Malina

Framing Anna Karenina: Tolstoy, the Woman Question, and the Victorian Novel
Amy Mandelker

Narrative as Rhetoric: Technique, Audiences, Ethics, Ideology
James Phelan

Understanding Narrative
Edited by James Phelan and Peter J. Rabinowitz
Before Reading: Narrative Conventions and the Politics of Interpretation
Peter J. Rabinowitz

Narrative Dynamics: Essays on Time, Plot, Closure, and Frames
Edited by Brian E. Richardson

The Progress of Romance: Literary Historiography and the Gothic Novel
David H. Richter

A Glance beyond Doubt: Narration, Representation, Subjectivity
Shlomith Rimmon-Kenan

Psychological Politics of the American Dream: The Commodification of Subjectivity in Twentieth-Century American Literature
Lois Tyson

Ordinary Pleasures: Couples, Conversation, and Comedy
Kay Young

Telling Tales:
Gender and Narrative Form in
Victorian Literature and Culture

Elizabeth Langland

The Ohio State University Press
Columbus

Library of Congress Cataloging-in-Publication Data
Langland, Elizabeth.
Telling tales : gender and narrative form in Victorian literature and
culture / Elizabeth Langland.
p. cm.—(The theory and interpretation of narrative series)
Includes bibliographical references and index.
ISBN 0-8142-0905-X (hardcover : alk. paper)
1. English fiction—19th century—History and criticism. 2. Sex role
in literature. 3. Women and literature—Great Britain— History—19th
century. 4. Working class women in literature. 5. Narration
(Rhetoric) I. Title. II. Series.
PR878.S49 L36 2002
823'.809353—dc21
2002005531

Cover design by Dan O'Dair
Printed by Thomson-Shore Inc.

9 8 7 6 5 4 3 2 1